GOING OUT OF OUR MINDS: THE METAPHYSICS OF LIBERATION

SONIA JOHNSON

THE CROSSING PRESS
FREEDOM, CALIFORNIA 95019

About the Author

Sonia Johnson is a radical feminist speaker and writer. Her first book, *From Housewife to Heretic*, about her excommunication from the Mormon church for "uppityness" (in a word), was published by Doubleday in 1981. Since the excommunication in 1979, she has been speaking professionally at colleges and universities and for a wide variety of organizations and groups. Those wishing to book her for speaking engagements should contact Susan Horwitz, 3318 2nd Street South, Arlington, Virginia 22204, (703) 553-9113.

Cover art and design: Diana Souza

Printed in the U.S.A.

Library of Congress Cataloging-in-Publication Data

Johnson, Sonia.
    Going out of our minds.
    (The Crossing Press feminist series)
    Bibliography: p.
    1. Johnson, Sonia. 2. Feminists--United States--Biography. 3. Women's rights--United States.
4. Feminists--United States--Psychology. I. Title.
II. Series
HQ1236.5.U6J64 1987   305.4'2   87-8991
ISBN 0-89594-239-9
ISBN 0-89594-240-2 (pbk.)

Contents

This book is for Susan
with all my heart

I Want to Affirm

Susan Horwitz, who was with me through it all; the bravest, brightest, truest aerialist that ever leapt from tall buildings;

Mary Ann Beall, another conspirator, whose laser-like mind helped me cut through the father's fog;

Linda Barufaldi, who commented cogently on the manuscript; as a friend and firebrand she has my passionate endorsement;

Carole Presser and Ann Taylor who also read and wisely suggested, and to Adele Gorelick, Pat McDaniel, and Kathryn Larson who read it all for errors; their generosity humbles and inspires me;

Sharon Lebell, than whom no writer ever had a more creative and diligent agent;

Kate Dunn, my editor, whose clear thinking illuminated the way to this final version;

Diana Souza, cover artist, who translated so magically to paper how women's liberation, world consciousness, and transcendence can feel;

Elaine Gill and John Gill of The Crossing Press; their courage in publishing this book fills me with hope;

To all of them — and to the many whose affection and support I have not mentioned: my warmest gratitude. May our collaboration be a blessing to us all.

Preface

Long ago, when I was a graduate student in English at the University of Minnesota, I had a professor whose arrogance thoroughly intimidated me. His disdain extended to practically everything ever written. I remember the day he warned us, in falsetto, against the fatuous horrors of the "suddenly she realized . . . !" genre of literature. Deeply into male worship then, a condition that tends to afflict even the strongest women at universities, I was ashamed that any woman had ever stooped to writing in such a concrete and personal, such a silly, mode. I vowed that, though I was but a young worm, I would forever eschew both the reading and the writing of it.

In the intervening years, I rejected that professor's critical yardstick along with his entire world view. *Of course* he despised — and feared — the "suddenly she realized . . . " genre. Every sudden realization is a step out of the old habit of thought, bringing women closer to the forbidden truth and to freedom from male tyranny. *Of course* he wanted women scholars to follow the "objective" model; it would bind us securely to the male-centered universe. He wanted us to stay comfortably and tamely in our old minds.

i

Sonia Johnson

An irredeemable feminist, I recognize now, as he unconsciously recognized then, the revolutionary power of each woman's telling her own story, taking herself seriously enough, trusting her own experience enough, to detail for the rest of us the consequences of the many large and small moments of connection in her life. I know now that if just enough women were to describe the moments when feeling and thought came together in a new way and for just a moment we were free, we would begin at last, and not a moment too soon, to "remember" the path out of the old doomed phallocentric world. To recover that long-lost, deeply hidden path and to walk it steadfastly together is to grasp our destiny.

Feminist analysis, more than any other analysis of the human situation, has its origins in direct experience. All feminist theorists first observe and draw conclusions from their own lives; all feminist theory results from the transformation of that experience and observation into principle. But not all feminist theory reveals its underlying process, the specific experience and the analysis of it that led to the generalization.

I have thought for some time that more of us need to include the substructure of our analysis in our writing. Feminism is concerned principally with process, not—as patriarchy—with product. Feminists affirm that all women are leaders in the women's movement, which to me means that we are all able to examine deliberately our own process of breaking free. I believe we are not only able but obligated to do so, that it is necessary for the success of our movement for all of us to spin theory out of the strands of our lives.

Since philosophy has been so mystified by the men, however, most women genuinely and profoundly doubt that they are capable of creating it. But if many of us who write feminist philosophy of one sort or another were to trace our ideas back to their generation in our lives, we would clarify for other women how theory comes into being. That in itself would instantly demystify the process, make creating it appear as the distinct and satisfying possibility it is for all women. In making our process conscious and visible, we would also provide a

ii

model for other women for understanding the significance of their own personal experience, feelings, and ideas, and for depending for guidance on the inner voice. If the women's movement is to transform global society—and this is its purpose— women who do not think of themselves as theorists, or their thinking as critical to the movement, must begin to take themselves—their feelings, thoughts, observations, conclusions, their women's lives—very, very seriously indeed. We must each believe, because it is true, that the women's movement cannot survive without constant infusions of our thought, infusions of those feminist principles we have distilled from our own lives.

There may be well-known spokeswomen in our movement, but there are no hierarchical leaders. The presidents and officers of women's organizations are not leaders in the women's movement; they are leaders in those organizations only. We may think that the reason there are no leaders in our movement is because we have made a conscious decision against patriarchal-style leadership. But its absence is not a decision we have made: the very nature of feminism prohibits it. When women behave like "leaders" in the male sense, they are at that moment not in the women's movement. Not because we say so, but because non-hierarchy is in the very nature of feminism. We exclude *ourselves* when we act like men in the women's movement.

Because there are no "leaders," only spokeswomen, either we all take responsibility for this movement—for defining it, for clarifying and expanding our own and others' understanding of it—or there will cease to be a movement. Our feelings, our experiences, our examination of them and the conclusions we draw *are* the movement. And the women's movement is the hope of the world. If there ceases to be a women's movement, there will cease to be life on this planet.

Going Out of Our Minds is the documentation of my feminist process over the last five years. I am proud with this account to add the light of my experience to the growing illumination by which we are groping our way toward freedom and life, proud to contribute to the only genuinely revolutionary literary genre on earth, from women's experience to cosmic theory: the "suddenly she realized . . ." genre.

For some time I have been aware that all my sudden realizations have been propelling me around and up a spiraling path, always and inexorably farther out from the center of conventional political thought and toward one conclusion. But at first I resisted mightily. Every time I came closer to understanding, I backed off in confusion and fear. But since in the end I always found myself back in the same place, I finally decided to stop trying to breathe life into dead—and deadly—principles and beliefs. I decided to stop running away. I stood quietly and confronted my new awarenesses, among them the knowledge that the old methods of working for social change were never more than illusory accesses to power encouraged by the men in power to take up our time, to confuse and distract us. I saw that whatever purposes these methods may once have been thought by activists to serve, their true nature was in fact always deeply collaborative and therefore not able to stem but only to add to the avalanche of violence that is crashing down upon us.

Then one day I realized that all these methods are wrong because they attempt to answer the wrong questions, questions that we have been carefully and assiduously trained to believe are the only relevant questions: how can we get our national leaders to change their behavior? What can we do about the state of the world? I concluded that there is really only one question that can direct us in changing the world, and that it is neither of these.

To reach a place in our thinking where this question occurs to us of itself, and we understand its centrality to the survival of life on earth, we must abandon the present global mind that has failed us all utterly. Since truth is reversed in patriarchy, to go out of our minds is to become most truly sane. Then, each remembering our own divinity, relearning the powers that preceded the split atom, the powers that raised the stones at Stonehenge, we can leave behind us the terror and despair

iv

of the old world. We can re-member and act — in time — on the metaphysical equivalent of $E = mc^2$.

I offer this account of my own ideological/political/spiritual journey — deliberately and passionately full of "suddenly I realized . . . !" — as a map for exploring women's part in healing the sick, despairing mind of the world, in bringing it to deepest sanity. My journey has brought me repeatedly up against the limits of my own outer, reactive powers and directed me steadfastly inward. In chronicling it, I celebrate my womanliness, my trust in my own heart, my growing ability to hear my own voice and to obey it. I celebrate all who "dare reject the little that is sure/for the hazardous cliff-face and the promised land";[1] all life, all hope, all that still shines and sings in the gathering storm.

I celebrate with my story the shattering of the father stars and the rising of the race.

1
Suddenly She Realized

One night in April 1977, in a Mormon church meeting in Sterling, Virginia, my mind finally burst the chains that shackled it to the known world and leapt spiraling upward and outward in quest of a new world, the journey for which I was born.

The knowledge — deep and pervasive, locked in the genes and chromosomes of every living woman — that men have built all they have built out of the bones and blood and entrails of women, exploded into my consciousness that night, wounding me in a thousand places, and smashing my bridges to the past.

Yet even at that moment, when on one hand I was angry and wretchedly miserable, on the other I was ecstatic: despite everything, women were rising. We were rising at last — mothers, sisters, daughters, at last! — in every race, every class, every country of the world, rising everywhere to save our own lives, and in saving our lives, to save the planet and all life on it. The classic feminist awakening: twin births of fury and ecstasy.

I went out from that epiphany utterly transformed.[1] Lightheaded with hope, shaking with rage, every cell shouting for joy, full of passion to be part of that vision. I focused like a laser beam on ratification of the Equal Rights Amendment because that was what I could see to do. I didn't look to the right or left. And I didn't lose heart, not even for a moment, not even when I watched the ERA fail in state after state. I never doubted that we would ultimately succeed in the work it was our destiny to do.

The vision of women creating a new heaven and a new earth eclipsed all other suns in my heavens, made all other goals, all other endeavors insipid and banal. It stirred me in the deepest recesses, awakened longings for freedom so intense and poignant I would moan aloud — and surprise other shoppers standing in line at the supermarket. I was giddy with relief at having seen it at last. Like coming home after being half dead with loneliness, like finding again someone I had loved and lost and for whom I had been sick with longing. To bring the dream into reality was worth anything, everything. Nothing was too much to ask of me in its service. It enraptured me, and I lavished upon it a passion of which I hadn't dreamed myself capable.

But passion is not allowed in the service of women. For millennia men have taught us in terribly clear ways that our best and strongest and most courageous and deepest is for them. Women have not been permitted — without paying incredibly severe penalties — to give all our thought and energy, all our courage, all our willingness to try anything, to make mistakes and to try again, to work and to love unfailingly to the end, all the greatest of our great gifts to or for ourselves or other women. To do so is unthinkable. Monstrous.

It is unthinkable and monstrous in patriarchy for women to demonstrate that we care as much about justice and dignity, as much about freedom for ourselves and our sisters — to the laying down of our lives, if necessary — as men and women have always cared about justice and freedom for men. It is the ultimate anti-patriarchal act. It is heresy. It is revolution.

And so the stand-ins for God, the god-men of the Mormon church, excommunicated me.

In doing so, they unwittingly gave me a platform from which to expose the hatred of women fundamental to Mormonism, as to most religions. And even better, a platform from which to make women's oppression visible—the oldest, most widespread, most taboo, and therefore the most invisible of all oppressions. I traveled all over the country exposing patriarchy.

By the time I began to speak for a living and to support my children this way, it was 1980. To use the word "patriarchy" in a formal speech had become declassé in the mainstream women's movement. Just saying it made (and still makes) many people bristle, and even some feminists squirm. Women's lives have depended on keeping an ancient and unspoken agreement not to name the foundation of present planetary violence. To do so is taboo. I broke the taboo.

After that April night in the church, it was easy for me. Growing up Mormon gave me distinct advantage over those feminists who grew up in "liberal" churches—Methodist, Episcopalian, Presbyterian, Unitarian, Quaker.[2] For them, patriarchy as a habit of mind, a system of values, a method of operating in the world, has been camouflaged, rendered murky and ambiguous, hard to pin down. It has been more hidden and padded and veiled and softened for public viewing in those churches than it had been for me. Mormonism is patriarchy at its most arrogant and blatant. I had studied it for 43 years in all its stark nakedness. When I became a feminist I realized that I knew patriarchy inside out, thoroughly, intimately. I knew how it functioned from its bones through to its muscles and flesh, out to its skin and clothing—its odor, its aura, its ambience. I could recognize it with my eyes and ears shut, could sense it immediately, knew the reaction of my skin to it, how it prickled in the roots of my hair. The Mormon elders had trained me to be one of the world's experts on patriarchal ontology, and I could never be deceived again. Neither could I be manipulated by fear not to name it and name it and name it again: the rule of the fathers, the worship of the male, the rule

3

of men over women — patriarchy, the destroyer of joy and hope and life.

Everywhere I went I unveiled it to my audiences. "Everybody born on planet earth since about 2500 B.C.," I told them, "has believed, whether they were religious or not, whether they were conscious of it or not, that God and men are in an Old Boys' Club together . . . with God as President. And because they are all guys, they have a special understanding. They speak the same language. They're in the locker rooms together a lot, and the board rooms, and God only has to take one look at them to see that men are superior in every way to the rest of us, because they look like him. So he loves them very much, and trusts them. He intends them to be the presidents, and prime ministers, the kings of the world. He wants them to be the popes and prophets and priests. He wants them to own all the property and businesses and make all the decisions and all the money and boss everybody else around — meaning women.

"And there we are, outside with our faces pressed up against the window, trying to see what's going on. Pretty soon one of the men comes out of the clubhouse. Because we're hungry and lonely and scared, we run up to him and beg, 'Please, oh please, tell us what God's saying in there!'

"At first he looks surprised, but then a sly, calculating look comes over his face. He leans up against the pulpit and says, in a deep, stirring voice: 'God told me to tell you that he wants you to be sweet and gentle and have a soft voice and never raise it. He wants you to understand that the purpose of *your* life is to make *my* life comfy and cozy, healthy, and happy.' And, warming to his task, 'God told me to tell you that he wants you to send me off to work every morning feeling just terrific about myself, to be just a-wavin' your pom poms for me all the time! Yeah! That's it! That's what God told me to tell you!' Then in a stern voice, he adds, 'And God wants me to warn you that if you don't do this, I have His permission, in fact His command, to punish you, to kill you if necessary.'

"So we have known for a very long time that in order to

propitiate God, who is the President of the Club, we have to placate his cronies, the men.

"And that, in a thimble, is patriarchy. Mary Daly puts it more elegantly and succinctly: 'As long as God is male,' she says, 'the male is God.'[3] Which is why changing our view of God has everything to do with changing the world."

My spiritual release from Mormonism took place shortly after my official physical release. As I looked about myself with new eyes, I lost all illusions about organized religion as a means to moral ends. I saw that *all* churches were the Mormon church—more or less spiritually squalid since they were made by men for men at the enormous expense of women. As Marlene Mountain puts it, "organized religion you bet/organized against women."[4] I saw clearly that religion was the central pillar of patriarchy, the means through which male supremacy became and remains dogma, by which maleness is deified, and by which all that is female is subverted to the purposes of men.

Because its social and political and economic function is to justify and perpetuate the slavery of women, the religion of the churches is not only incompatible with genuine spirituality; religion and spirituality are downright contradictory. Religion as we know it is antithetical to justice, love, mercy, decency, kindness—to all that is good.

But patriarchal religion, the center pillar of patriarchy, is dying. Fifty years from now, if we can keep our small planet spinning coolly in space, we won't recognize the churches. They won't be around in their present forms, except perhaps, like the Amish, as oddities here and there. They are dying because they do not have room in them for women's magnificent, awakening, expanding spirits. Men's mean, narrow, sunless churches can no longer hold us. The fire in our hearts is boundless.

I gave religion up without a backward glance, and I gave it up forever. That doesn't mean that I ceased to believe in a beneficent universe, a universe that wishes all life well. As far back as I can remember, I was always aware of a reality that could be neither seen nor heard, but only most overwhelmingly felt. When I gave up religion, I gave up the nonsense I was taught that this experience of transcendence was named God, that it was male, that it was *other*, outside me, independent of me, and much superior to me in every way, superior beyond description or imagination. I gave up the idea of "worship" altogether. It made me feel small and weak and I knew by then that the true expression of my spirit made me feel invincible.

While I was still in the Church, however, belief in Mother in Heaven provided a transition for me from Father-god to god-within, and I was learning that before there was God, there was the Goddess. But I had no desire to go back to ancient Goddess religion. I rapidly rejected the notion of putting a skirt on God, calling him "the Goddess," and worshipping essentially the same sort of being, enwrapped in dogma and hierarchical trappings. God in drag is still God.

Yet I speak of the Goddess often, lovingly, and carry the image of her in my mind, an image that helps me counter the image of male deity which still insinuates itself in a dozen ways into my psychic landscape. I know that Goddess ritual, insofar as it generates reverence for and celebrates that which is female, which is *us*, is fiercely empowering, and that her image in our minds—images of ourselves as deity—is necessary as a blueprint for a more authoritative mode of being in the world. The Goddess is a metaphor for our own and all women's creative, healing, transformative powers, a representation of our inner selves; "something tangible, a concrete image [that] captures [our] full attention and draws [us] into the metaphoric process. . . ."[5] But she must remain consciously metaphorical and only metaphorical or we risk externalizing and losing our power again, we risk relinquishing responsibility for our lives again. Even with the Goddess established securely in our minds *only* as metaphor, we must be careful to avoid participation in any Goddess rituals or events that stress our helplessness, our need to be rescued or to be dependent on strong spiritual leaders, rituals which encourage self-indulgent emotionalism or involve us in thought-less theatrics. Genuine spirituality for women will always have its foundation in a radical feminist analysis. Feminism *is* spirituality. But it is not "religion." It is about the rising of the spirit of half the human race. It is the foundation of the women's movement which is the greatest spiritual revolution in world history, producing globally the most profoundly transformative human change ever wrought.

I came to view that impetus for growth and for good in the universe with which I felt in greater harmony every passing day not as outside me, but within me, not as separate from me, but part of me as I was part of it, not as infinitely wiser and better than I but as my peer. Together, shoulder to shoulder, we were the creators of heaven and earth and all that lives in them.

So my abandoning all the senile, barbaric religious notions of God did not mean that I ceased to be a spiritual person. On the contrary. Only when I finally wrested responsibility for my own metaphysical life away from the elders and assumed my rightful authority, did my spirit — which had strained against the spurious authority of the god-men all my life — begin to expand as if to fill all available space. Sprung by the patriarchs themselves from the dark, airless little box called patriarchy, my possibilities were suddenly as limitless as the sunshine and the wind. I recognized myself finally as a prophet, all women as prophets, and knew that at this time of the world *only* women are or can be prophets.

One night, several months after my excommunication, I had an unusually vivid dream. I dreamed I was floating high above the earth, looking down upon it as the astronauts do, seeing it spinning below me all blue and white and radiant. I was in my nightgown and my feet were bare, but the air was warm and soft. I dipped and soared and turned somersaults and danced, sometimes in elegant slow motion, sometimes swift and breathtaking, all with a feeling of power and freedom and confidence which, in my waking life, was quite alien to me. It was a wonderful dream, and I smiled every time I thought of it the next day.

Several nights later, I dreamed this dream again—me spiraling upward in the same great arc of unhampered movement, out over the boundaries of time and space. The same warmth, the same sureness and certainty at the center, the same exhilaration of moving effortlessly, with infinite grace and perfect control.

And then, some time during the next week, I dreamed it again. "Sonia," I said to myself when I wakened from it the third time, "I think you're trying to tell me something. I think you're trying to tell me that I'm finally free, and anything is possible!" I remember how I whooped aloud as I sprang out of bed and jigged to the bathroom: "This here ain't called the Women's Liberation Movement for nothin', honey!"

Though years have passed, I haven't forgotten the promise of that dream. I still believe it. In fact, it won't be long now. I've been feeling it coming on. One of these days, soon, I'm going to fly.

One day, shortly after I recognized all churches as the Mormon church in various guises, I was surveying the national and international scenes through my new wide-angled lens when suddenly everything clicked into place. Of course! I should have known! The whole *world* is the Mormon church! I realized that, far from being politically naive, as I'd thought, I was surprisingly and uncommonly savvy; having perceived that global social, political, and economic theory and practice are based on the same principles as the Mormon church, I understood immediately and viscerally the mind that rules every country. I knew the values, the assumptions, the needs, and the motives of those in power everywhere in the world. Having studied these habits of thinking and acting for so long and so thoroughly in the microcosm of the Mormon church, I found their extrapolation to the macrocosm a simple matter.

I also knew a thing or two about fear at the end of my two-and-a-half-year confrontation with the church. I knew that the greatest fear of all accompanies the breaking of taboos, and that since the most powerful taboo in the world for women is the one against disobeying men, those of us who break this one must be prepared to battle intense and apparently irrational terror. We are not afraid because we are fools; we are afraid because the message, "If you go against the men, you will surely die!" is italicized and underlined in blood by the millions of hideous deaths that have been suffered at men's hands by women who have been perceived as "uppity."

At the beginning of my public struggle with the church, I spent a week nearly incapacitated by fear at the prospect of testifying as a Mormon woman before a Senate subcommittee for extension of time to ratify the ERA. But I did it, and I didn't die. I didn't even languish. Quite the contrary — I flourished.

And with every fresh act of daring against the taboo, I blossomed more. Instead of hiding all scrunched up in my fearful skin, clinging to it, I began to slough it off and stand up straight, clear, and clean, my strong new skin gleaming in the sunlight. It felt wonderful! Why hadn't I done it sooner?

But as I looked around me, I saw that many feminists, perhaps because they had not had the great good fortune of being kicked out of the Mormon church (or the equivalent) after a rousing set-to, were still scrunched up in their fearful skins. I wanted them to feel as free of fear as I did now. I wanted all of us ultimately to divest ourselves of fear completely. I knew that didn't mean we would run amok. Those who believe that one must have fear to have good judgment are wrong. Fear undermines good judgment. It prevents us from thinking clearly and from recognizing and exploring alternatives. Fear is the supereminent weapon of the patriarchy to keep women in our place.

I also knew that, though I had never cared much what others thought of me and what I did, I would care even less in the future. And I realized that for the women's movement to succeed, many women had to be similarly free, not just from the terror of breaking taboos, but from the garden-variety fear of social disapproval as well.

9

I had no idea how other women could liberate themselves from it, or how the few who had succeeded had done it. I only knew that it was immensely important to figure out how it could be done on a large scale. I longed for a mass sloughing off of old dry nervous cautious skin—in a mountaintop ritual maybe, somewhere among the sunbaked rocks.

So I put it in the back of my mind where I put problems that need work, and assumed that one day, as is my wont, I would suddenly discover that I had unconsciously accumulated evidence and done research and had some idea how to begin.

2
Aerobic Politics

In the meantime, there was work to do—the usual speaking and writing and lobbying, the mothering. The usual, that is, until at their 1980 convention, the Republican Party officially cast the ERA out of its platform and prompted me to take the first overt step out of the mainstream politics of the national women's organizations.

Twelve of us, dressed in white, with heavy chains draped around our waists, leapt out of the back of a pick-up truck one morning, raced across the lawn, and chained ourselves across the main entrance to the Republican National Headquarters in Washington, D. C. It was August 26, 1980—Women's Equality Day—a fitting day to demonstrate our outrage at the blatant anti-woman, anti-human rights stance of the party that came to power crying for the abolition of slavery. The irony was not lost on us; neither did we misread what lay ahead if a Republican were elected to the White House.

When we rushed the door, two large men began pushing against it from inside, flailing at us and kicking one woman sharply, trying to keep us from bolting the door shut. The pain and confusion at the door caused our first line to fall back in disarray for a split second—long enough for the men to smell victory and to let down their guard a little. Just as they did, two women sprang forward again. With incredible presence of mind, they surveyed the scene, saw the lock they had planned to use hanging useless where in the melee they had accidentally locked it to only one side of the double door, got my lock from me, and manipulated it and the heavy chain successfully—all in the time it took the men inside to do a double take.[1]

As smoothly and calmly as if we'd been doing it together all our lives, the twelve of us chained ourselves to one another, those on the ends chained ourselves to the railings, and in about two minutes from the time we jumped from the back of the truck, we had locked the Republicans up tight in their headquarters. Out on the front porch, we sang at the top of our lungs: "Like Susan B. Anthony, we shall not be moved, just like the suffragists who went before us, we shall not be moved."

The police duly arrived, but when they discovered that their cutters weren't big enough to cut our chains, they decided to wait us out instead of arresting us. So we stood on the porch in the blazing sun all day long, singing, chanting, reading our statement, and burning the Republican platform, while the cops lounged and chatted together in the shade of the trees, and a hundred protestors carrying placards, banners, and signs marched back and forth on the sidewalk.

Others joined us, and after we had together blocked all the doors to the building, we were told that people were climbing in and out of the building through the back windows. So we sang for them: "Go in and out the windows, go in and out the windows, go in and out the windows, we want the ERA!"

It was a well-planned, well-executed action, and it took courage. I was proud of it then and I'm proud of it still.

So far as I know, we were the first group to organize and carry out a civilly disobedient action on behalf of the ERA. At the time, it seemed a giant step, no doubt because the commonly held opinion among heads of women's organizations was that women would make the most headway by appearing politically cool and savvy, by exciting the admiration of men for how well we could play their game, by being sophisticated, dignified, politically mature, blah, blah, blah. Civil disobedience on behalf of women was regarded as undignified and immature; it would turn people off, it would hurt the movement. But mostly, it wasn't respectable, and more than anything else, the leaders of the women's organizations craved respect from the men in power, wanted to appear objective and rational, longed to be seated among them making public policy. They knew that people who respond with appropriate passion do not end up—for the most part—in Congress.

In the years since I became associated with the National Organization for Women, its national leaders have never, to my knowledge, participated in an arrestable action on behalf of women. Even when the ERA was seriously endangered, they frowned upon civil disobedience. So when I read in *The Washington Post* in February 1985 that the president of NOW had been arrested in front of the South African embassy for protesting apartheid, I felt as if I'd been kicked in the stomach.

I deplore apartheid. And I'm glad that it's now become politically and socially acceptable—even sophisticated—to protest racism, even if it's only racism abroad. Senators, congresspersons, movie stars—the cream of society is doing it. Protesters gain in stature and risk nothing.

Racism as an issue has prestige because it involves the freedom of men. Almost everyone understands the necessity—at least in theory, at least rhetorically—for men to be free.

But women? Let's not be ridiculous. I am willing to bet that if apartheid applied only to Black women in South Africa, no one "important"—and I mean *no one*—would be paying the slightest public attention to it, to say nothing of being arrested over it—least of all the National Organization for Women. Women's freedom as an issue has no prestige.*

If apartheid applied only to *women*, even some feminists might argue that apartheid is a purely cultural matter—like the wearing of the chador in the Middle East, or genital mutilation in Africa, or compulsory motherhood in Nicaragua. It strikes me as odd that physical and psychological restraint and damage done to men, violations of men's human rights, are *never* viewed as "cultural" phenomena in this way.

Because the repressive atmosphere in the organized women's movement surrounding civil disobedience encouraged us to care more about "turning people off" than about fulfilling the many powerful purposes of civil disobedience, we tried to involve as many overtly religious women as possible in the Republican Headquarters action. This, we thought, would lend us an aura of seriousness and dignity. Everyone would understand that women still respectful of patriarchal religion are not dangerous at all, not "kooks," not free and independent and wild, not scary as hell. So our caution demanded that we look as respectable in society's terms as possible under our chains and locks. I detested society's terms, but because I loved the ERA, I hid my wobbly integrity from myself and appeared as one of the handmaidens of the Lord.

My decision to move into civil disobedience sprang out of impatience with the cautious, toadying model of behavior be-

---

*Leaders of NOW do not even use the word sexism anymore. They list the ERA, reproductive rights, racism, and discrimination based on sexual preference as their issues. I once found reprehensible their lack of courage in saying the word patriarchy, but now that they have lost the nerve even to say sexism, perhaps I should refer to them as the National Organization *of* Women, not *for* women.

Nonetheless, NOW has its positive aspects. In many communities, because it is the only visible evidence that there is a women's movement, it provides a place for women who are searching for ways to work for women. And it can attract women with a variety of views, so that those with more radical feminist potential, who invariably and quickly become discontented with the organization, can meet and encourage one another and find alternatives to NOW's narrow partisan politics. It gives such women something to measure themselves against. In my own case, knowing that I most definitely was *not* a NOW loyalist enabled me to define more sharply what I was.

ing held up for women by the women's organizations. I remembered Alice Paul (1885-1977) and her similar frustration with the suffrage movement on her return from England and her work with the rambunctious — and successful — Pankhursts. I loved the quotation from Susan B. Anthony:

> Cautious, careful people always casting about to preserve their reputation or social standards never can bring about reform. Those who are really in earnest are willing to be anything or nothing in the world's estimation, and publicly and privately, in season and out, avow their sympathies with despised ideas and their advocates, and bear the consequences.[2]

In a letter to my mother describing our action, I wrote somewhat acrimoniously, "Perhaps NOW and the Caucus and the League held press conferences about the Republican debacle. If so, it was a feeble, inappropriate response. Press conferences don't demonstrate sufficient seriousness. More important, they don't demand courage of the few participants and don't inspire courage in the spectators. Press conferences, lawful marches, protests, demonstrations — none teaches women to step over the line and discover in ourselves undreamed reservoirs of love and daring. Civil disobedience does."

In November 1980, 21 of us were arrested up in Bellevue, Washington for chaining ourselves to the gate of the new Mormon temple that was scheduled to open that day. Throughout the preceding weekend, two young women had remained chained to the gate, protesting the Mormons' nationwide political campaign against the ERA. On Sunday evening when several of us Mormons for ERA spoke at a NOW convention in Seattle, I praised the women who had persevered in that action despite NOW's strong disapproval, and said something such as, "Tomorrow the Temple will open, and I'll be there. Anybody who wants to help me chain the gate shut to demonstrate that Mormons are keeping the gates of justice

15

bolted against all women, meet with me after this meeting and we'll get ourselves organized."

The next morning dawned cold, and the damp wound itself around a body's bones. I bundled up until I could scarcely move. At about 8:30, we advanced upon the gate arm in arm, singing. The Mormon security guards began to attack us at once, throwing at least one woman to the ground, kicking and generally manhandling others. Despite them, we managed somehow to chain up. The Bellevue police arrested us for "failure to quit," carried us to their cars, zipped us to the station and stowed us in holding tanks. (The Bellevue Chief of Police, whose wife was an ardent ERA supporter, later sent us roses, and, later still, Christmas cards.)

We called ourselves "The Bellevue 21," and felt pleased with our action and ourselves. We thought we were the first group in the country to succeed in being arrested for the ERA. We hoped we were pioneers, and that women everywhere would begin to make discrimination increasingly more difficult, time-consuming, and unpleasant for the men in power.

I began to feel downright evangelical about civil disobedience after this. I was desperate to move out of the static posture of supplication and appeasement interspersed with temper tantrums that characterized the behavior of the organized women's movement; desperate to move into an independent, fearless space of women's own definition.

In February I wrote an article for *Common Cause* that I entitled "In Defense of Immoderation" (which they timidly changed to "In Defense of Equal Rights"):

> We are afraid of appropriate feeling and appropriate action because the only appropriate feeling for women in the United States today is fury and the only appropriate action is immoderate. . . .
>
> If women don't soon begin to think we're worthy of the many and immense personal sacrifices it's going to take to get our civil rights, if we don't value

16

ourselves and other women enough to make these
sacrifices and expect and ask and accept them from
others, we are quite simply not going to get justice.
We must learn from the men that to gain *anything* we
must be willing to risk *everything*. Men have always
understood that they had to fight and die for their human rights. They have always understood that justice
is never bestowed, that it is always wrested by the
most incredible courage and daring out of the hands
of fate . . .

Women must demand — now, and if necessary at
the peril of our lives — that we be granted our civil
rights in the same way rich white men in this country
were granted theirs: by constitutional decree. . . .

Women's time has come, but it can pass us by if
we sink into despair, into another "season of silence."
It can pass us by if we are afraid of doing what all
other fighters for human rights have had to do to win
them.

I certainly didn't want to die. I loved life, and was having
the time of mine. I didn't want other women to die either. But
I sensed that we had to stop worrying about the possibility of
dying ("death" meaning also social death, political death) if we
wanted to move on to another place. We had to stop being
afraid of losing credibility, respect, social standing, elections,
our lives. We had, simply, to stop being afraid.

Though I was frantic to escape the deadening conventional political modes, I was still struggling in the masculist
mire of atonement: an eye for an eye, a tooth for a tooth,
Jesus's life for your sins. I wrote in my journal, "I always think
of this as balancing the scales. When you want something
weighty and significant, such as justice, you put it on one side
of the scales and see what it's going to take to make it balance.
On the other side of the scales you can put all the lobbying,
letter writing, fundraising, caring, all the demonstrations, all

17

that, and it still won't balance. It's just not enough. Justice is too expensive. We don't get something for nothing. We pay an exact price. If we want something precious, we pay with something precious. That's how I understand it."

By spring of 1981, Mary Ann Beall, whom I had met in Copenhagen and had immediately seen eye-to-eye with on civil disobedience, was back in Virginia and together we organized a group to do civil disobedience around women's issues in the Washington, D.C. area. In coordination with several women in New York City, we called ourselves the Congressional Union, taking the name and philosophy from the women's suffrage group created in 1914 by Alice Paul and Lucy Burns that later became the National Woman's Party and gave us the Equal Rights Amendment.

In the winter of 1981, beginning with the inauguration of Ronald Reagan, the Congressional Union held a vigil in front of the White House every Wednesday from ll a.m. to 2 p.m.[3] But the first major action was planned for July 4, 1981.

Looking back, I can hardly believe that civil disobedience aroused such fervor in my soul. I can hardly believe it, that is, until I remember how few options seemed open to us, how up against the walls of possibility we had been driven, and how fervently I sought for an opening.

I knew there was one . . . somewhere. Though I never believed that civil disobedience itself would somehow miraculously change the system, I did believe (but believe no longer) that before we can move into the psychological and philosophical place where we can "see" the next step, we must do all we can see to do in the present, inadequate as it may appear and be.

And there seemed to be much to be said for civil disobedience. Through it, I received an invaluable education, one that propelled me still farther up the spiral of my odyssey and further out of my disabling habits of mind.

During the July 4 Congressional Union celebration, for instance, I collected some important data on the problem of fear, which I still had simmering in the back of my mind. I had already seen how civil disobedience made women feel powerful, good about ourselves, even exultant. But somehow this wasn't registering as an *idea*. The events of July 4 brought the loose, disconnected threads of information together. In one small flash of illumination, a coherent theory appeared.

The rain began the night of the 3rd. We couldn't believe it. How could nature betray us like this! We had ordered a grand piano for Margie Adam to be set up in Lafayette Park and a complicated sound system for her and the speakers. We were calling the action "Relighting Feminist Fires" (a tacit acknowledgement that they had gone out), and planned to burn misogynist sayings of famous men. We had expected thousands of women.

When the rain didn't stop by noon, we gathered together in front of the White House, the three hundred or so soggy bodies which had braved the weather, and tried to hear the speeches. After a while, looking over the bedraggled, woebegone assemblage, I couldn't bear it a moment longer. Taking the megaphone, I stood up on the ledge by the fence and shouted, "I'm going out into Pennsylvania Avenue, and I'm going to kneel there and pray for passage of the ERA, and for women. I want the ERA ratified. I want women in the Constitution. Anybody who'd like to join me in the street is very welcome."

Handing the megaphone to someone, I stepped down off the ledge and started through the crowd. "Will you come with me?" I asked the women on either side of me as they fell back to make an aisle. They all shook their heads and looked down. "Well, you've done it now," I chided myself. "You're going to feel mighty foolish out there by yourself in the middle of the street!" But I kept walking — what else could I do? — and just as I reached the curb, someone grabbed my hand. "Thank goodness!" I thought with relief. "At least there'll be two of us!" But when I got into the street and turned to kneel down, I saw that a long line of women had clasped hands and followed us into the street.

19

Sonia Johnson

Sixty women knelt in Pennsylvania Avenue, stopping traffic for over an hour that day. It seemed to us that every policeperson in the District rushed to the scene in police cars, on motorcycles, on horses. Two vans of barking dogs arrived — part of the intimidation program — and a couple of officers handed out billy clubs to all the rest. Finally, the police lined up in formation in front of us, feet apart, arms in front with the billy clubs conspicuously at center, faces set and staring straight ahead.

During all this exercise in bullying, even more women joined us, until we had two rows of bodies across the street, all kneeling and holding hands. By this time the sun was shining. Crowds gathered on both sides of the street and joined us in singing and chanting. The officer in charge gave us the standard warning: "If you don't leave the street in five minutes, you will be arrested." In ten minutes, he warned us again. Fifteen minutes later, he barked at us: "This is absolutely your last warning; if you're not out of the street in five minutes, we'll have to arrest you." Ten minutes later, he shouted, "Now, ladies, this is positively, absolutely your last warning!" Obviously, they did not want to arrest us.

While we were receiving multiple "last" warnings, those of us who had planned the festival were putting our heads together. As far as we knew, none of the women kneeling in the street had received nonviolence training, or knew what to expect if they were arrested. This was a worrisome situation. So we decided to wait as long as we dared and then, just as the arrests were *really* about to begin, direct everyone up and out of the street. Which, much to the relief of the police, is what we did.

Safely back on the sidewalk, many of the women who had been in the street wanted some kind of closure on the experience. They didn't want just to wander off home without any acknowledgment or discussion of what we'd just done, so we formed a circle and began to take turns telling how we had been affected by what had happened.

20

Every woman was euphoric, high with admiration for herself. I remember one woman particularly. "Do you know who I am?" she demanded, as she stepped into the circle. "I'm just a housewife from Maryland. But I knelt in that street for over an hour. I could have been arrested. I *would* have been arrested. And I did it for women! I didn't know I had the courage to do anything like that!" She paused, then turned to me and asked, "When are we going to do it again?"

Many women expressed similar excitement at discovering how much they cared about themselves and other women, how deep their longings for justice and dignity went. They all felt bigger and nobler, capable of so much more than they had thought. Each had caught a glimpse of her true stature and was ready to grow into it as fast as possible. It was all very heady stuff.

I had been through this psychic upheaval while doing religious disobedience in the Mormon church. I knew I was observing a significant phenomenon. Standing there, I tried to put it together.

I knew that women have been deeply socialized to obey the law. Obeying the law is a large part of obeying men generally, and the male god has ordained that obeying men is the fundamental law governing women's lives. Matters of life and death hinge upon obedience to it. So when we prepare to break the law, our spirits bark their shins sharply against the killer taboo. Unconsciously, we make the lethal connection and are overwhelmed with fear for our lives.

But when we stand fast despite our fear and do indeed break the law (leave our battering husbands, or our battering churches, or stop cleaning up after our husbands and kids, or love another woman), preparing on some deep level to die, the miracle happens: We live! Though the taboo tells us we can't disobey the men and live, we are nevertheless alive! In fact, we've never *been* so alive! How can we account for feeling more alive by the second? Has it all been a lie, then? Just a plot to keep us terrified and trapped in our subordinate caste?

21

No, it's not a lie; it's a paradox. The truth is that to displease men, to disobey them, is still deadly for women. But the truth also is that only when we stop obeying men do we truly begin to live.

Daring to ignore the first half of the paradox and to live out fully the second half opens our eyes to the meaning and implications of the unwritten laws we obey. For instance, though the taboo tells us that we can only live if we obey men, our experience teaches us that that is a lie. We see that we live more genuinely and richly when we stop obeying them and start obeying ourselves. But more than this, we realize that men kill us no matter what we do, whether we obey or disobey. It is true that violence against women increases as we as a group show signs of rebellion, as the mere *threat* of violence ceases to keep us in line. Nonetheless, our blood has been fresh on men's hands for millennia.

Civil disobedience can teach women the truth: we do not need to be afraid that in the breach we will not have sufficient courage to do whatever it is we must do. CD can teach us that the inadequacies we fear are mostly imaginary.

As women we have borne our oppression because we have been afraid that the alternative was to die. But when we learn that we die in the same numbers anyway, and that a life lived in fear is also a death, that a life without fear is the only life worthy to be called "life," then we prepare for freedom. When we understand that the *penalties* are the same whether we disobey a little or disobey completely, but that the *rewards* come only when we disobey completely, then we are ready to be free.* And when we are finally ready to be free, the avenues to liberty will open before us, and for the first time in fifty centuries we will see the road signs clearly.

My mind shifted gears as I watched and understood what I was watching. Any capacity that civil disobedience has to

---

*Insight from correspondence with my friend, Linda Barufaldi, November 1985.

change the system, I thought, must come from its ability to profoundly change women's concepts of ourselves and to alter our ways of being in the world. It not only tells others that we know our own worth, but, by providing a stage upon which we can act out our larger selves, it testifies to us, too, that we are worthy. In telling others that we are serious, we realize — often to our own surprise — how very deeply serious we are. And after this, we find it easier to take ourselves and one another seriously, an incredible feat for any woman.

More worthy and more serious, more everything good and strong than we dream we can be, we see how much we have to gain and how little we have to lose, and we slough off our fearful skins.

From that Independence Day on, to guide as many women as possible into and through that process of extinguishing fear and illuminating potential was my principal motive for participating in civil disobedience. Between July 4, 1981, and our leaving to fast for the ERA in Illinois in May 1982, we did at least 13 more actions. These included burning Ronald Reagan and Idaho Federal Judge Marion Callister (the Mormon Federal Court judge who ruled the ERA extension unconstitutional) in effigy — holding hands, as was only fitting, since they are both as homophobic as they are misogynist — to celebrate Alice Paul's birthday, and going over the White House fence to take a message to our otherwise totally inaccessible president on February 15, the birthday of Susan B. Anthony.[4]

After we had returned from the fast, our group held a ritual mourning on the steps of the Archives the night we put the ERA down for a long nap, June 30, 1982, and the next day, July 1, a dozen of us were arrested for pouring blood on the pillars and steps of that building in protest against our exclusion from our country's most sacred document, the Constitution, which is housed there.

I was still too weak from the fast to do civil disobedience that day, but I wasn't too weak to give a speech. (I'm never too weak to give a speech!) In it, I quoted Susan B. Anthony:

23

Overthrow this government! Commit its blood-
stained Constitution to the flames; blot out every ves-
tige of that guilty bargain of the Fathers; break every
fetter, and let the oppressed go free![5]

Several weeks later, when I announced my candidacy for
the presidency of NOW, a woman in the national NOW office
sent out a letter to all members in her home state of Michigan.
The gist of the letter was that I had shouted "Overthrow this
government!" on the steps of the Archives and had urged
women to burn the Constitution—which she revered, as all
good United States citizens should. Such shocking intemper-
ance clearly made me unfit to be president of the National Organization for Women.

Michigan NOW offered to pay postage for a rebuttal, and
I had a wonderful time composing it, especially the closing
line. After I had given proper credit to Susan for her perspica-
cious remarks about the Constitution, I pointed out that apparently Susan B. Anthony was too radical to be elected president
of NOW.[6]

Of course. We are much more conservative and timid
than the women who went before us. They would probably af-
fright and offend us at every turn. Some of the women who do
research into the lives of our foremothers gloss quickly over evidence that perhaps these women were not "politically mature"
—i.e., polite and deferential. While I was writing this book
and trying to find the exact source of the "overthrow this government" quote, I was directed to a woman who is supposed to
be an expert on Anthony. She told me she had never read the
lines I quoted to her, and moreover, she was sure Anthony had
never said them. "It doesn't sound like her at all!" she huffed.
Actually, it sounds very much like her indeed. That we have
lost sight of her radicalism in less than a century (or, more
exactly, of Elizabeth Cady Stanton's, since it was probably she
who wrote Anthony's speech), is astonishing and ominous.

At the end of my year of civil disobedience, I could still

see the functions it — and other mass protests — served. But to me only one of these justified its use at all in the women's movement, and that was as a way for women to get a taste of their own tangy courage — that sharp and addictive surprise. I knew that such experiences could teach us that we have immense sources of untapped strength and bravery and daring. At their best they could put us psychically in places where we could hear far-off echoes of bygone greatness and have visions of greatness in the afternoon of this very day. They could help us believe we are capable of anything, and that's the truth as well as the necessity. Best of all, they could help us begin not to be so afraid — of our own burgeoning powers; of not being polite and nice, and of the censure that will inevitably bring upon us; of not following the eminently "reasonable" leaders of organizations; of physical harm; of hurting the feelings of the men in our lives and of the god-men everywhere; of speaking the truth more boldly. As we become less afraid, we become more dangerous. Patriarchy can exist only so long as women are afraid.

Despite all this, I was troubled by it, troubled enough that by the time I left for Illinois and the fast, I was shedding my zeal for it like yet another skin. To be supportive of friends, I have participated in it several times since but never again with either zeal or conviction.

For one thing, by the end of the ERA decade, I understood more clearly our place on this country's protest timeline. The second wave of feminism in the United States, which had been breaking across and disrupting the old social order for more than a decade before I was struck by it, had arisen at a time in the nation's history when all protest — including civil disobedience — had become passé, or perhaps its inherent futility had only become more evident. By the time women came on the scene the second time, at least four waves of civilly disobedient protest had preceded us in this century: militant suffragism, unionism, the Black civil rights movement, and the anti-war movement. From nearly a century of experience in dealing with this brand of protest, the system had either

25

learned to accommodate it without batting an eye, had ceased to fear it—had, in fact, learned to pirate its energy—or had only learned to do it better.

Protests of all sorts had become so yawningly common that in order to be noticed, larger and ever larger numbers of protesters were needed. Then even numbers lost significance. When a half million people gather in New York City to protest nuclear weapons (as they did in June 1982) and the powers that be pay as little attention as they did then, we must face and accept that these methods have come to the end of their usefulness even as a way of attracting notice, to say nothing of changing things—if indeed they ever fundamentally changed anything.

When I thought civil disobedience was the best way to proceed, I shut my mind to other possibilities, and when I was using my time and vitality to plan and do civilly disobedient actions, I hadn't much left for doing anything else, even if I had been thinking of alternatives. I understood gradually that action of this kind, like electoral politics, deceives us into thinking that we are getting somewhere, achieving something. At least, we think, we are doing all that can be done. There's a grim and deadening complacency in that.

In addition, the very nature of civil disobedience forces us to deal with issues superficially. It can't address the complexities of oppression—certainly not the most subtle, and insidious, and therefore most intractable, of its aspects. These are difficult enough for feminists—people who are *for* women—to keep in mind, and often we don't. (Which explains the many "women's rights" feminists in the movement and the few radical feminists.)[7]

But my strongest objection was to living constantly in reaction; I had begun to feel like a prodded amoeba, an unpleasant sensation that caused me to rethink the whole process. What I learned was that when we identify ourselves in *opposition* to something we become its unwitting accomplices. By bestowing the energy of our belief upon it, by acquiescing to it,

we reinforce it as reality. The very difficult truth is that
WHAT WE RESIST PERSISTS.

Since civil disobedience is based on the same old violent
value system — being the down side of the war model: attack/
resist — we reinforce the very world view that is destroying
women and the planet when we participate in it. I was troubled
about keeping the patriarchs' sadomasochistic power game going, when that was the very game, those the very rules and assumptions, I longed to sweep off the board.

I had a very strong hunch as well — and I was rapidly
learning to trust my hunches — that in protests we give away
our own power, paradoxically give it up to the very group we
are trying to take power from. Which means that in the very
act of trying to wrest power from patriarchy, we strengthen it
instead. Though I hadn't understood the dynamics of this
power giveaway throughout our year-long civil disobedience
campaign for the ERA, I had increasingly felt their operation.

Several years later, in my study of ki-aikido (a method of
coordinating mind and body) I caught at least a glimpse of the
mechanisms of the transfer of power, a glimpse that finally
turned into a steady, wide-angled view just recently. According
to the theory of aikido — and my own and others' experience of
it — if a person grabs me, let's say, by the wrist, and I focus my
attention upon his hold and how I'm going to get out of it, I
direct my energy (my ki, or life force) into his grip and aug-
ment his strength with my own. Now we are both holding me.
I am collaborating in his attack upon me, colluding in my own
defeat.

But if, instead of focusing on his hand on my wrist, I direct my ki — my intent and energy — toward my own goal, if I
think of where I want to go instead of how I'm going to get
away, I have a far better chance of breaking free. If my physical strength is anywhere near that of my attacker, I can surely
break out of his grip. If I am physically much weaker, which
would more likely be the case, I still have a much better chance
if I concentrate on my own goal. And when I don't struggle in

27

the way he expects, he thinks he has won. Momentarily, automatically, and almost imperceptibly, he loosens his grip. In that moment, I extend my ki toward my own goal and escape.

That this really works was made abundantly and amazingly clear even in the first session of the aikido class. My partner grabbed my wrist. Using strength, I wasn't able to get away, and couldn't have done so without a real tussle. But when she grabbed my wrist and instead of concentrating upon her grip I thought instead of how I had to scratch my head, my hand flew out of her grasp to my head almost without effort on my part, though she was expending the same amount of strength to hold me as she had the first time.

My partner's next exercise was to bend my arm by placing one hand on my upper arm, the other on my forearm, and forcing them together so that my elbow bent. At first, I resisted with strength, and she bent my arm easily. But when I focused in my mind on my "one point" (the center of ki, a point about two inches below my navel), held out my relaxed arm and imagined energy pouring through it as water through a fire hose and out through the tips of my fingers into the wall across the room, she could not make my arm bend at all.

I was convinced. But there was yet another test. Our teacher, a very strong woman, positioned herself on one side of the room facing me, in karate stance with her arm extended. Her arm was the barrier I had to get through, first trying strength, and then extending ki. Making myself as strong as I could, I marched resolutely into her arm, and nearly fell over backwards. It was like walking into the side of a barn. I then backed up, centered myself, and focused on the wall on the far side of the room. Thinking about how I wanted to reach that wall, *feeling as if I had already reached it*, and envisioning myself there, I relaxed into my power and walked straight through the barrier.

This principle underlies the story of the old grandmother who, when her grandchild was pinned beneath the wheels of a car, dropped her cane and lifted the car off the child.

There is something very important for the women's movement to be learned from this. But then, in 1982, I was not as clear about just what it was. My intuition was working overtime, but my brain wasn't getting the message. Even when the ERA failed, I was operating on two levels at the same time. For instance, for a speech I intended to give on the steps of the Archives on the night of June 30 at the ritual mourning ceremony, I wrote:

> The men have taught us that we cannot win by working within their system, but that we must come at the problem from where we are—outside their power grid, outside their game. This, however, is our strength. We have our own game out here, one in which they cannot see our cards (for a change), cannot control us or scare us or intimidate us.

So far so good. But then,

> We have learned that we must confront and obstruct the system and make life so miserable and so impossible for those in power that they will be forced to negotiate with us, and to do it seriously. Why not 50,000 women refusing to pay taxes? Why not one million, two million? Why not every self-respecting woman in the nation? The founders of this country fought a revolution for being taxed without representation.
>
> If that should ever happen, we could be in the Constitution in ten weeks instead of working within the system for ten years and getting nowhere.

Well, at least I was struggling toward something, even if I kept lapsing into the wrong-headed notion that confronting the system was working *outside* it, when in truth all reaction places us squarely in the center of its power. Ultimately I would realize that civilly disobedient actions and all confrontation, though they may be exciting aerobic warm-up exer-

29

cises — rousing the heart in preparation for the game — they are only that: warm-up exercises. And only for someone else. They are neither women's game nor appropriate or affordable warm-up exercises.

But for this to become clear, I needed more experience, and I was on my way to getting it.

3

Women Against Women

Along the way, our Congressional Union group in D.C. broke with the New York group and began calling ourselves A Group of Women, a name that signified our desire to be non-hierarchical. From the beginning, we made all decisions by consensus, which was excruciating and only partially success-ful. But we knew the art of functioning consensually was in its infancy, and we wanted to keep trying to live as democratically in all areas of our lives as we could. So despite our unconscious determination to reproduce hierarchy, our inability to disagree at the appropriate times or in appropriate ways and our subse-quent feelings of resentment and uncooperativeness, our lack of process to deter the one or two women who kept members stirred up against one another and who constantly disrupted meetings, the fear (of police, arrest, fines, jail, loss of jobs, loss of child custody, loss of "credibility") out of which we projected anger and blame upon one another, and, dooming all our at-tempts at harmony, our profoundly conditioned lack of respect for women — despite all this we persevered.

As a group we were committed to doing one civilly disobedient action every month. That meant a lot of work and a lot of commitment. It meant a lot of stress on frayed nerves and on a wobbly process. Looking back, I'm amazed that we actually exceeded our goal and did 13 actions in 11 months, especially when one considers the serious fractures that were appearing within the group and threatening to split us apart. As A Group of Women faltered behind the scenes, I thought to myself, "Imagine what we could do if we were *united!*" Imagine our power if we refused to follow the pattern men have cut out for women's groups, patterns of mistrusting and hurting one another so much that some have to leave the group or that the group has to disband altogether. Imagine if those of us who are trying the new feminist pattern of exercising power-with and power-to rather than power-over could somehow avoid the traps of powerlessness that patriarchy has so carefully coached us to fall into, the traps of jealousy and competition among ourselves, of backbiting, trashing, factionalism, and suspicion.

While we were still working together smoothly, however, we staged the most impressive and beautiful spectacle of all. On August 26, 1981, exactly one year from the Republican National Headquarters chaining, 20 of us, dressed in white with purple sashes pinned diagonally across our chests on which were emblazoned names of unratified states, chained ourselves to the White House fence. Our magnificent banner announced that WITHOUT THE ERA ALL WOMEN ARE IN CHAINS.

I can't begin to describe the detailed, painstaking work that went into that action, but it showed. We had to leap from vehicles that year too — this time a rented moving van — but at just the right place in front of the fence, and just so many seconds after the women doing the diversionary action started to cross the street from Lafayette Park, their arms around one another, singing and waving brave banners, titillatingly clanking chains and drawing all attention away from the van that moved slowly in front of the White House and finally stopped directly opposite the fountain.

In fact, the diversionary action was almost too successful. Some of the women in the supporting crowd had to point, while shouting at the top of their lungs (so the police and media folks could hear), "Look! Something's happening over *there!*" By this time, we were all chained securely to the fence and had our hands above our heads in the International Women's Symbol (the shape of a womb), singing.

The police let us stand locked to the fence for an hour. Finally, we realized that they'd let us stand there forever, or at least until the press got tired and left. The Administration had no desire to arrest a group of women imitating the great women of our country's history while network cameras looked on. So we unchained ourselves from the fence, locked ourselves together, and walked singing with our hands over our heads to the driveway, where we sat down in a circle on the hot tarmac. There we read our statement again, sang, chanted, gave impromptu speeches, and were wonderful — until we saw that the police were equally prepared to let us sit *there* until the press left. After we consulted, I unchained myself from the woman on my right, rose from the driveway pulling the others up after me, and headed into the street. When all else fails, there is always stopping traffic.

An enormous policeman met me before I got quite halfway across the street. I walked right into his massive stomach, and as he began pushing me back with it, I wondered wildly if a person could suffocate like that. Someone shouted, "Sit down! Sit down!" Immediately we all recognized the good sense of lowering our centers of gravity so we couldn't be pushed back any farther, and sat down in the street. Freed from the belly of the beast, I breathed again.

Safely down and singing in the steaming August sun, our next problem was how to hide the keys to our locks. One of the objectives of civil disobedience is to inconvenience and slow down and disrupt the system. We wanted to remain chained to one another in order to force the police to figure out how to lift all 20 of us as one into some vehicle and get us to the station —

or to a locksmith. Some of us tried to slip our keys surreptitiously into our shoes or our bras; some threw theirs into the crowd. I watched a little girl—about eight or nine years old—pick up a tossed key and, right in front of the policeman who was searching for it, slip it quietly into her pocket. For weeks afterward that made me grin every time I thought of it. It makes me grin right now. Somewhere there's a girl who's not going to forget that women were arrested one hot August day for trying to get her into the Constitution.

They found most of the keys, unlocked and arrested us, and that's where it turned into another boring, tedious day at the precinct station (because, of course, while we are slowing down and inconveniencing and disrupting the system, we are also slowing down, disrupting, and inconveniencing ourselves). But not before a couple of women had performed acts of courage, or before we had cheered and sung each new arrestee into the police van and celebrated ourselves and our performance.

And it had indeed turned out to be a performance, much more of one than we had intended or anticipated. But that was okay. Just because it was spectacular didn't mean it wasn't also very serious. We congratulated ourselves on the rare presence of mind and sensitivity to one another that had enabled us to play the whole complicated production by ear so remarkably well. (By this time some of us had been involved in so many chainings that we began to refer to ourselves as "The Chain Gang.")

That was our August action. On September 7, 1981, we staged a Labor Day demonstration. Though we blocked the gates of the Mormon temple in Kensington, Maryland, on October 3, as the Mormons' nationally-organized anti-ERA efforts were so effectively blocking ERA, our *big* October action was planned for the following weekend, the weekend of the national NOW conference in Washington, D.C.

As I had traveled around the country speaking, I had been approached by members of NOW time and time again, requesting that our group do an action while they were in Washington for the NOW conference so that they could watch, or better still, could join in if they wished. There was serious and widespread interest in bringing about social change through approaches other than those NOW was advocating. Many members were thinking about expanding their repertoires. So, being NOW members ourselves, we were glad to plan a simple, dramatic, reasonably safe, do-it-yourself breaking of the law for them. We settled for a time on Sunday evening when NOW's formal agenda was finished.

In the meantime, Mary Ann Beall and Maureen Fiedler, another member of our group, had been given official permission to do a civil disobedience workshop at the conference, and had reserved a room at the hotel that would hold about 30 people. But when the time came for the workshop, hundreds of women tried to get into it. When I arrived a little late, they were lined up down the hall and down a half dozen flights of stairs.

We began a frantic search for a large enough space to hold us all, and ended up in the parking garage under the building. Somewhere between four and five hundred women found their way down there and, since there was no place to sit, stood the entire time. Mary Ann and Maureen gamely went forward with the workshop, standing on chairs and shouting to be seen and heard.

Upstairs in the large plenary room, an ERA speakout was taking place—or at least was supposed to be taking place. Hardly anyone was there; they were all down in the garage. Thinking of power in the patriarchal scarcity mode, the NOW leaders' conclusion was: "Sonia's trying to take over the conference!" Despite the obvious question of why I should wish to do that, or what I would do with it if I should suddenly find I had taken it over, the rumor spread. The truth was that I was not only *not* planning to seize control of NOW, but I hadn't even been scheduled to participate in the workshop. I was there simply to lend support and to give whatever assistance they might ask of me.

Close associates of the NOW leadership soon began to turn up in the garage in a frenzy, despite our assurances that the crowd had come because of their interest in civil disobedience, not to form a contingent, with me at its head, to wrest power from them. But when a group acts out of a particular mindset, sees a situation in terms of power politics, they create their own reality. Rather than interpreting the interest in civil disobedience as genuine and intelligent and worthy of their attention, rather even than harnessing and directing all that energy for their own purposes by co-opting the idea, they persisted in competitive win/lose thinking, persisted in viewing it through their own power lens.

The NOW leadership soon made apparent to the women in the garage that they felt their power challenged. One of them climbed on the chair and shouted an impassioned defense of NOW's policies, the implication being that any suggestion of another way of looking at things or another tool for the ratification toolbox impugned NOW and condemned all its work. The total effect was to suggest that grossest treason was afoot there in the garage.

This speech effectively set up the "either-NOW-or-Sonia" dichotomy, and achieved the inevitable result of polarizing the group on the spot. Naturally the woman who had spoken was unaware that her behavior had anything to do with the sudden chanting that interrupted her harangue: "We want Sonia! We want Sonia!"

I was dismayed. "Come on," I pled with them in my mind, "don't buy into this. Don't let her manipulate you and pit us all against one another like this." But she had established the paradigm of hierarchical power—the competitive one-up/one-down format—which everything in society reinforces, and though I had my turn later and did my best, I hadn't a chance in the world of turning it around then.

The civil disobedience workshop group agreed to go upstairs and participate in the speakout, only now the speakout was to be about civil disobedience as a strategy for NOW.

What really happened, however, was something else altogether.

As one woman after another came to the microphone in
the middle of the room and passionately defended the leadership while roundly condemning the upstarts, I began to have
déjà vu on a vast scale. So I arose on the stand where for obvious reasons I had been seated, and said something like, "I
haven't been in a meeting like this since I was in the Mormon
church." (In the Mormon church, members arise in the audience periodically and reaffirm their orthodoxy. They bear testimony to the truth of their belief and—particularly these
days—to the infallibility of their leaders.)

When the hisses and boos died down a little, I went on to
explain that the passionate conformity, the incredible peer
pressure to follow the leaders blindly and to condemn any who
deviated, and to regard any ideas the leaders disapproved—
any diversity of opinion—as insubordination, even treachery:
these were blatant hallmarks of cult membership. More hisses
and boos.

Then the president arose in fury and fumed that she had
never been so insulted in her life; imagine comparing her to
those old woman-hating men at the head of the Mormon
church! I wasn't the only one in the room who noticed the telling change in emphasis from what I had actually said to what
she thought she had heard me say.

Nearly a dozen Mormon women that I know of besides
me were in the audience that night. At least half of them later
told me that, long before I arose and compared the speakout
to a Mormon testimony meeting, they had had the same very
strong impression. I guess it takes an old cult member to recognize cult mentality when she's standing in the middle of it. You
can't fool us ex-Mormons!

As I sat there on the stand watching the unbelievable performance of presumably strong, independent women almost
unanimously condemning civil disobedience and our little
group, I asked myself, "How is it that an hour ago there were

500 women in the garage interested in learning about and doing civil disobedience, cheering and applauding, and now that they're here in this room, suddenly there are only one or two?" I knew the answer. What I was watching was patriarchal power politics — the same shrewd reliance on women's fear of censure, the same reinforcement of their lack of faith in their own judgment, and of their powerlessness, the same insistence on their need to depend on the greater wisdom of a few superior leaders. I felt bleak, as we do when our illusions are strained and weakening, and one or two are shriveling right up and falling by the way.

During this rather disorderly meeting, a friend from Washington state beckoned me off the stand and out into the hall. She was crying, shaking with emotion. "Please," she begged me, "please don't split this organization! Please don't defeat the ERA by disuniting us now!" She went on to bear testimony to the truthfulness of the gospel according to the NOW leadership and the necessity of following them in all things.

As I listened and tried to reassure and calm her, I found myself awash in more déjà vu. I knew this scene, almost word for word, from beginning to end. I had been through it innumerable times with Mormons — in person, on the phone, by letter, even by telegraph — during my early Mormons for ERA days and through the trial. It's known as "cutting off the head of the messenger who brings the bad news." NOW was using the same methods of intimidation and fear to control their group that I had watched the Elders use all my life in the Church. And having, alas, the same enormous success — the room was full of thoroughly cowed women.

The irony is that though the NOW women had considered me courageous, even heroic, to expose these machinations in the Mormon church, pointing them out in NOW was quite another matter — impudent, captious, destructive. I steadfastly refused to make that distinction. Mind control is mind control no matter where it rears its vicious head, and feminists are pledged to freedom of body and mind. The moment we agree that women's organizations shall be exempt from honest appraisal, that they need not be accountable in the same ways we demand of other institutions, when we feel that they are somehow sacrosanct, we're back in our jail cells again. And nothing—I mean *nothing*—is ever going to get me back in there. Especially not now that I am just learning to fly.

Though they had easily won this round, the leaders of the organization were still very worried about the civil disobedience action and determined to stop it. We had put up flyers everywhere announcing it, even in toilet stalls. They were torn down promptly, but the tearers-down couldn't tear down as fast as our putters-up could put up. Our incendiary symbol of red and orange flames could be seen everywhere leaping around our slogan: ON FIRE FOR THE ERA.

We were planning to set a dozen fires—in washtubs—along Pennsylvania Avenue in front of the White House, to burn the rubbishy verbal effluvia of the President of the United States. We saw it vividly in our mind's eye: flames leaping in the night, lighting our huge and splendid banners, women in white electrifying the crowd with speeches, singing, chanting, dancing, committing to the cleansing fire one squalid document after another.

We'd designed it to be safe, and were prepared for any eventuality. But getting all the equipment to the site without alerting the police to our intentions had presented an almost insurmountable barrier; it had been the focus of discussion for several meetings. But finally we worked it all out in our usual creative and nifty way, and were feeling confident about everything—even a little smug.

Up on the stand, after the "NOW-as-the-only-true-church" episode, the president asked me to come up to her room later to talk privately about the action. By this time it was nearly 11 p.m. I told her I'd speak to the group about it and be up around midnight.

I suppose now I should be of two minds about having agreed to that meeting. Perhaps I should wonder if I was wise to have gone. But I don't. If I had been invested in winning male power games, going up there would definitely have been a losing move. But since I wasn't, I went—and learned more about the psychology of the oppressed than I could have learned in an entire graduate sociology program.

Several times during the experience, however, I wished I *had* had a background in sociology or anthropology so I could name what I was seeing. But even though I still don't have the official terminology for it, I understand the dynamics. I saw them vividly portrayed before my eyes that night.

Maureen went with me, and we walked into a suite in which not just the president and one or two close associates sat, as we'd expected, but at least a dozen of the most influential women in NOW, plus the president's husband, sat in a circle ready for the ritual. (I later learned that I was correct in my sense that what happened to me was very well rehearsed. At least a dozen other women whose power had threatened them had been through it before me.)

The president began by assuring me that I did not know my history or I wouldn't be involved in civil disobedience. I was confused. "But history is precisely why I am doing it!" I explained. "Perhaps I'm interpreting it differently, but . . ." At this point, one of the president's most fervent disciples planted herself in front of me, and, shaking her finger in my face, yelled: "Don't you dare speak to the president like that!" "Oh ho," I said to myself. "So it's that way up *here*, too!"

As others joined the fray around the circle, I saw that the point of all comments was to make me question myself. The effort seemed to be to create an image of me that, because they were all forcefully affirming it, I would accept as true, an image that would crush all "uppityness" out of me. The Sonia they urged upon me was simple-minded (how could a woman who'd been a Mormon until she was middle-aged have any brains?), naive, power-hungry, famished for fame, politically bumbling and ignorant, conceited, and weak. "Why are they so afraid of me, then?" I thought wryly as the attacks continued

40

and reality twisted into more and more surreal shapes. I knew I was witnessing a sort of exorcism ritual, in which I was seen as the one possessed of the spirit that could destroy the organization. I realized that it was not meant to be rational, that it was meant to flatten and deaden my creativity, to maim my spirit.

The overt object, the conscious level, of it all was to get me to reveal the specifics of the CD action. I believe that, if one were to ask them today, they would say that this is what they were about. They said they did not want anything to "hurt the movement," especially just now when there was less than a year to go with the ERA. I told them we ran our CD group by consensus and that I didn't have permission to tell them anything; that we'd been exceptionally cautious with this one because otherwise it might be impossible to carry it out—police have many large, keen ears.

One of the powers behind the throne rose to her feet and shouted at me, "We've stayed awake all night, night after night, all of us, many times, trying to think of some CD action that would be ethical as well as effective, and we haven't been able to think of a single thing. That means that whatever you're going to do *has* to be morally reprehensible!"

That one took my breath away. "What an amazing conclusion to have leapt to," I gasped to myself. (When I heard later through the grapevine that they had thought I was going to immolate myself, I understood the "morally reprehensible" part a little better.) It told me a great deal about their political theory, part of which was that they confused working long hours, hardly sleeping night after night, and driving themselves and others mercilessly, with creativity and political acumen. I suspect from having observed these women for many years that, instead, there's a definite inverse correlation.

The president offered to take me off into an adjoining room by myself so I could tell her the CD plans privately. "You're all missing the point," I sighed. "I haven't the authority to tell any of you anything. I'm not 'the boss' in our group; nobody is. We decide together."

41

Well, to cut an old and very sad story short, after a couple of hours we left and went to bed. The next day, I told the others about my experience the night before, that my instinct was to go ahead with the action, but that I was going home to check on my children and to finish the banners and would go along with whatever decision they made in my absence. Soon after I left, the president came down to the group, overwhelmed them with the aura and aroma of power, and persuaded them to change their plans. Despite two or three members of the group holding out firmly against the crumbling confidence of the others, in the face of "authority" our consensus broke down altogether. And though we lit the fires the next month and all went well, several hundred women missed the lessons in courage and self-confidence that civil disobedience teaches.

The extraordinary/ordinary experience in the president's suite gave me pause for several days. "No wonder we're so ineffective," I thought. "We attend to the wrong things. Why on earth try to stop women from *doing* something, doing *anything*?" One of women's serious acculturated disabilities is fear of acting. We're so afraid of making mistakes, of looking foolish, so afraid of public opinion and censure that we hardly dare to move. Thinking of the leaders of a national women's organization working so hard to quell the energy and stop the initiative of women made me wild with frustration. "No wonder we're still slaves," I ranted to myself. "We have slave mentalities. We think small. We cling to caution, concentrate on constraints. We're afraid of freedom. We don't trust ourselves or one another with it. Oh, if only women would do something risky, if only they'd do almost anything unconventional! How much hope that would give me."

Feminism as I understood it included the empowerment of all women, not within the fundamentally unjust system that now prevails on planet earth, but within a new system of our own design and making. I wondered sadly how long this concept was going to be consigned to the fringes of the women's movement. I wondered if in fact it was doomed to be disregarded forever and even ridiculed by many feminists. I began thinking of those feminists whose vision extended no further than women's having equal access to the present corrupt scheme of things, as "women's rights-ists."

That was the frustrating part. The painful part was having to acknowledge finally that NOW was functioning in the very mode the women's movement had come into the world to replace. It was painful because NOW was where I went when feminism burst my life open. It was where there *was* to go. I was grateful for its existence, trusted it as a safe harbor while I learned new strong, scary ways of being a woman. I felt loyal to it. But I was also wary, having so recently experienced the consequences of blind loyalty in both my church and my marriage.

I had been slow to accept what was plain to be seen, but now I could not ignore it. So this was what NOW had become — had always been, perhaps? Well, regardless of when it happened, it was what NOW was at present. On reflection, I wasn't too surprised. I knew that oppressed people always internalize the power mode and the assumptions of their oppressors more strongly than the oppressors do themselves. They think they must do so to survive.

Slaves and prisoners, for example, are always far harder on one another than they are on their keepers and guards. Far less kind and tolerant, for obvious reasons. They also earn the favor of their keepers by betraying one another daily in large and small ways.

How many women have said to me something like, "My supervisor on this job is a woman, but she's lots harder for me to work with than any of my male supervisors," or "I hate to admit this, but I'm almost getting so that I'd rather work for a man than for a woman."

Mary Wollstonecraft said long ago, "Considering the length of time that women have been dependent, is it surprising that some of them hug their chains and fawn like the spaniel?"[1] And since we learn what we live, and women have lived as colonized people longer than any group in history, it is surprising neither that we know more about how to oppress than we do about being free, nor that we collaborate so readily and fundamentally in our own oppression. As slaves, we have so completely identified with those in power, so sided with them against ourselves, so thoroughly internalized their values, that we have come to fear our freedom as our masters fear it. This dynamic functions unconsciously long after we have consciously understood and rejected our oppressed status. Therefore, it is not surprising that even feminists have so bitterly betrayed ourselves and one another for so long.

Once we understand that patriarchy is totally dependent upon our mistrusting and thwarting and hurting one another, and that for this reason we have been deliberately, thoroughly, and fiercely indoctrinated from birth to hate and to hurt women, surely we can forgive one another and learn to resist this most central and deadly of all patriarchal mandates.

Our internalized oppression has at its core the almost unshakable, almost entirely unconscious conviction that we deserve our condition because we are inferior in every way; we cannot rule our own lives, we must depend on men for everything,* and must therefore please them, because we have no personal power and are incompetent, unattractive, stupid. Name something positive and we're not it.

But men are. Every positive attribute finds its home in maleness. So we compete for the recognition and love of these demigods, their affirmation the only affirmation we value. We

---

*We even depend on men to decide which woman among us should represent us, should receive our homage and loyalty, as, for instance, when the men in the Democratic Party presented us with Geraldine Ferraro. Ultimately, regardless of whether or not we would have chosen her if the choice had been ours, and regardless of how fine she may have been, we did *not* choose her; we thought we *couldn't* choose—except to play our traditional role of trying to influence the *men's* choice, and in playing that old game all we did was reinforce our powerlessness. A woman on the Democratic National Committee told me privately many months after the election: "We had to take who we could get." Somehow it's difficult for me to see this as a victory for women.

try to win their acceptance and respect by repudiating that about ourselves — about women — which is different from them, emulating them, becoming more like them, always doing obeisance to their power structures, constantly reassuring them in hundreds of ways, large and small, that they needn't worry; we have no knowledge of the vast power within ourselves and no intention of finding out about it and using it.

I once sat on an airplane in front of two men and a woman, the woman sitting between the men. I gathered that all three of them worked for the same company. They appeared to be hierarchical peers, but the woman kept her status lower by laughing constantly, during and after nearly everything she said, as if to say, "Don't worry, guys. I'm really just a dumb, silly, insignificant woman. I'm not threatening at all. So you can let me be here. And stay here." Through all her laughter, the men didn't laugh once. I wanted to turn around and shout at her: "*Stop laughing!* Stop belittling yourself — and all the rest of us!" But of course I didn't. She — and they — would have thought I'd quite lost grip. So I spent two of the most wretched hours I've spent on a plane in a long time, listening to that self-effacing, self-hating, woman-hating laugh.

As I sat there in pain, I thought that if I could stand on the brow of the world, extend my arms over it all, and pronounce it the way I want it to be, it would be women loving ourselves, feeling deeply and genuinely worthy of and entitled to the earth and all that's in it, entitled to it as home, a safe place, a place of our own.

For that to happen we are going to have to rid ourselves of our internalized oppression. Because if we began truly to love ourselves as women, the world would be home to us. Again and again, I think of Frederick Douglass and his conviction that the limits of the oppressor are set by how much the oppressed will bear.

Much of what we bear that perpetuates patriarchy are patriarchal definitions of and attitudes about ourselves as women, all of which translate into self-hatred. When we cease to bear these, when we cease to be willing to hate ourselves and other women and all things female, when we cease to try to be like the men, cease to pretend that their structures are our structures, their values our values, begin to love and be ourselves, the patriarchal age will be over. That's why the women's movement is the greatest cause for hope on earth.

Back in the days when I spoke about the ERA, I was often asked about Phyllis Schlafly, one its most vociferous opponents. I told my audiences that reporters were always asking me about her, partly because, perhaps unconsciously, they wanted to portray women as our own worst enemies again (which gets everyone's attention off the men behind the scenes), to show us tearing one another apart, clawing away at one anothers' throats — "cat fighting." I refused, always, to give them this satisfaction. I always answered the reporters and audiences — including radio and television audiences: "Mrs. Schlafly is my sister. She and I probably don't agree on a single public (or private) policy, but we have far more in common with one another than either of us has with men of our own political persuasion. We are both women in a global system based on the hatred of women. She is as oppressed in her sphere as any woman in the world."

Consider that she did as much as any one person to get Ronald Reagan elected in 1980. Consider that she is as brilliant on the subject of defense (as perceived by the Reagan administration) as Caspar Weinberger — very likely more brilliant (which wouldn't be hard). Consider that she *wanted* to be Secretary of Defense. And then consider that as far as we know, she was not only never even considered for that position, but that she was not offered *any* cabinet position. Why? Because she is a woman.

That's oppression. *She* may not be angry, but I am. I'm angry on her behalf. Discrimination against her because she is a woman is discrimination against me. It is not acceptable.

I don't find saying — and feeling — this about Mrs. Schlafly difficult at all. I don't have to work with her every day, so I can be dispassionate, admirably fair. I expect her to be what she is — a profoundly patriarchal, male-identified woman, and psychically maimed — so I am never taken by surprise.

But matters are very different when a woman is *us*. Forgetting that all of us, without exception, are maimed in our femaleness, are warped more or less out of healthy shape by internalized oppression, we are apt to find ourselves bleak with disillusionment — or appalled — when a woman falls back into anachronistic male behavior. When we work intimately with other women, sharing the same goals, working toward them on the same feminist principles, it is much more difficult to understand clearly the ways in which we are all susceptible to colluding with the system, the extent to which we are all still accomplices, albeit unwitting, and on a conscious level certainly unwilling. Even though we understand intellectually that we are all in the process of freeing ourselves from our destructive patriarchal mindset, we balk at forgiving one another for such lapses, and have trouble dealing with them in a positive way. But if we want the world to change, we must learn. Awareness of internalized oppression is a beginning.

I had a dream one night toward the end of my campaign for President of the United States. I dreamed I was in Manhattan (where I had in fact been just a few days before), walking down a narrow sidestreet. Large old buildings loomed on either side of me, shutting out the sun, darkening the street. Gradually, I became aware that my feet were slightly off the pavement. So I began to swim upward with my arms, trying to lift even farther off the ground. Sure enough — but slowly, laboriously — I began to rise, swimming upwards past the windows of the buildings until I was level with their fourth floors and out of the shadows in the sunlight. But then, no matter how hard I tried, I couldn't go any higher.

Suddenly I realized that the reason I had been having such difficulty rising, and now could rise no farther, was that a woman was hanging onto my legs, her arms wrapped around my knees. I wasn't angry at her as I hung there treading air with my arms. I didn't even feel impatient or frustrated. There was no room in me for such emotions. My whole soul was flooded with elation that I could fly *at all*. "I'm off the ground! I'm flying!" I thought to myself. I knew the rest would come, that it was just a matter of time. Someday that woman wouldn't be holding me down. Someday I'd soar.

My joy woke me, and just at the moment of waking, still caught in mid-air over a Manhattan street, I recognized the woman hanging onto my legs. Her name was Sonia Johnson.

I didn't have to be a shaman to interpret a dream message as transparent as that! I guess I'd known all along that we keep ourselves from soaring. I'd watched us do it, individually and in groups, more times than I cared to remember. And as I'd watched with increasing awareness and pain, I'd been reminded again and again of what someone once told me about catching lobsters. You don't have to have a lid for the bucket or basket you've thrown lobsters into after you've caught them, because as one lobster tries to climb out, the others pull it right back in again. They never allow one of their number to climb to freedom.

To change the metaphor, we — all women — are in a jail cell. With the door standing wide open. It's always been wide open. But any time any woman gets near the door, we all panic. We have believed for too long what the fathers have told us — that we will die if we go through that door, and, even worse, that if any one of us goes through that door, they will kill us all.

So of course we're afraid. We understand bullies only too well, having dealt with bully brutality on all levels of our lives for at least 50 centuries. We know that bullies always punish the group for any infraction by an individual. The biblical story of Eve is a perfect example. Because she ate the apple, *all* women, according to the religionists, must suffer for that "sin" by bringing forth children in pain, and by being subjugated to their husbands.

That's why we don't want anybody going out that open cell

door, and any woman who gets close gets ganged up on by the rest of us and prevented from escaping. We are our own and one another's jailers.

At breakfast one morning several years ago with some friends, I mentioned my theory of the open prison door. "You're wrong," one of them said flatly. "There's no freedom beyond that door for many women. If you can't get a decent job, if there's no child care, if you're subject to battering, rape, incest, if you're Black or Hispanic, old or poor, there's no freedom. And you make women feel guilty that they're not succeeding when you say it's so easy if we'd just choose it. You make it sound as if it's all our fault that life is so difficult for us."

What I tried to make clear to her that morning is that that door doesn't open *into patriarchy*. The doors to power in the dominant system *are* tightly closed against us (for which we ought to be profoundly and forever grateful, or we'd be truly caught in the most deadly trap). The door that is open is a door to *somewhere else*, to a different world, a different place. It opens to our own power. This is the door we're afraid to go through.

True, we're hardly aware of its existence, hardly aware that there is a door other than that which opens to the known world. Even when we have a yeasty inkling of it, we can hardly figure out how to go through it, let alone what lies on the other side. Our inner voices are urging us to take some incredible risk, but even if we were entirely willing, we couldn't tell precisely what this risk entails.

But something *is* beckoning us, something real and urgent. Another way, another path, another door. A door patriarchy says isn't there; *insists* isn't there, which is evidence of its existence. That which doesn't exist doesn't have to be denied.

Yet they leave the door unguarded. They're not even looking anymore. They think we've forgotten or can't perceive the door. They have almost ceased to believe it is there themselves. It has been such a long time since women used our great personal powers. It's been thousands of years since we raised the stones at Stonehenge.

Being human, we fear the unknown, though we're not generally conscious of our fear. Even those of us who see that the known is deadly and is about to kill us all in the most hideous possible way are afraid to leave behind the electoral politics, the lobbying, the faith in the dead and deadly system of the fathers. Better the old ugly, vicious society than the one we must build ourselves on an entirely different and unknown model. Better what we see before us than a new, barely perceptible "reality" that we ourselves must now call into clarity and power, a place where we have no firm foothold yet, where we must grope every millimeter of the way, where we are infants in our understanding. Where we are very much afraid. The risks of growing up and taking responsibility for the universe daunt us. We search frantically for historical models, but there are none. We must create the model as we go, and we are numb with terror at the challenge. Nothing in our culture tells us this is even possible, to say nothing of giving us a hint about how to do it. So we make no move toward the open door.

C.S. Lewis describes this phenomenon in Book 7 of the Chronicles of Narnia, *The Last Battle*, which my son, Noel, and I read together the winter he was eleven. Lewis intends the story to be a Christian parable, but it illustrates well the emotional bondage of all oppressed people. In the last great battle of good against evil, a group of dwarfs refuses to join sides. When everyone in the book has died, most find themselves in a beautiful open space. But the dwarfs, though sitting there among the others on the sunny lawn, believe they are locked in a dark, stinking stable. Nothing can dissuade them:

"You must have darn good eyes if you can see in here," said the dwarf named Diggle.

"In where?" asked Edmund.

"Why, you bone-head, in *here* of course," said Diggle. "In this pitch-black, poky, smelly little hole of a stable."

"Are you blind?" said Tirian.

"Ain't we all blind in the dark?" said Diggle.

"But it isn't dark, you poor stupid Dwarfs," said Lucy. "Can't you see? Look up! Look around! Can't you see the sky and the trees and the flowers? Can't you see *me*?"

"How in the name of all Humbug can I see what ain't there? And how can I see you any more than you can see me in this pitch darkness?"[2]

They didn't need locks on the door, or guards. They had successfully internalized their own imprisonment, their own small expectations, their own oppressive reality. They had become their own jailers. They didn't want to be free. Aslan, the great golden lion, Lewis' christ figure, tries to free them, but they will have none of it. "You see," said Aslan. "They will not let us help them. Their prison is only in their own minds, yet they are in that prison."[3]

Horizontal violence among conquered people is buttressed by our belief in the lie our conquerors tell us about power. They assure us there is a scarcity of it, and that what little there is is already parceled out.

Historically, power has been defined as a finite thing. As if there were only so much of it and if you wanted some you could get it if you could get enough signatures on a petition or convinced enough legislators, or had enough money to buy an opinion, or enough influence. . . . And if you got power it was surely at the expense of someone else. Well, this theory of power obviously works very well for those who are in power and also works very well to insure that those of us who want more power understand exactly what we have to do to get some and how long we will have to wait for our share. Because if there is only a little bit of power, then clearly those who have the most must have proved themselves most worthy of it.[4]

The men show us this pie of power, all neatly cut up in slices—this slice for this group and that slice for that group. And this little teensy sliver here? This is for women. "This is all there is, girls," they tell us solemnly. Then, shutting the door behind us, they chortle gleefully, "Now go fight over it!"

We believe their pie story, of course; we accept their definition of power as genuine, and agree that it is desirable. They should know. They're white men, the all-time experts on power. (Look at the size of *their* wedge!) We believe we must compete for molecules of this itty bitty sliver of power. And when one of us gets some, the rest of us become very anxious because we think that leaves less for us. Brainwashed by this lie, we tear down and try to destroy other women whom we suspect of trying to sneak a piece. Power is agonizingly scarce, we believe. It must be hoarded and guarded, jealously protected, every atom of it, all the time. In this way the Brotherhood cleverly tricks us into resenting and fearing and disliking, and often attacking, any woman who grabs an atom or two.

The truth is—and everything in society is geared to keep us from recognizing this—*there is plenty of power*, all the power any of us needs or can possibly use. Not the patriarchs' brutal counterfeit, but the authentic power of the spirit. And when any one of us finds within herself and exerts even the teeniest bit of this kind of power, all of us are empowered. We all win. The more genuine power, non-patriarchal, womanly power she finds and uses, the more there is for the rest of us. And the more of us who behave powerfully, the greater and fuller the communal reservoir of power for all women to draw from. Like love, we generate our own power from within. The more power each of us produces, and the more we pass it around, the more of it there is. It multiplies.

My experience with NOW's leaders taught me that though they called themselves feminists their minds were still caught fast in the patriarchal power paradigm. One by one, as strong women arose within the organization and would not toe the official line, they were subjected to exorcism through one

52

ritual or another. Which is all too bad and very heavy, because it is exactly how the men in power want us to behave, have trained us to behave toward one another. As long as we keep it up, we will never be able to change anything, and they know it.

Because I understood this, my feelings weren't hurt by my exorcism. I knew it wasn't about me personally. It was about the misogynist world, and how women are taught to treat other women in that world; it was about one of the most potent mechanisms society has devised for keeping women enslaved.

I began to learn the outline of the psychology of the oppressed that night in the NOW president's hotel room: the horizontal violence, or inappropriate striking out against powerless peers as a substitute for facing the fearsome anger inside and the fearsome and powerful masters; imitation of the oppressors' paradigm, organizational loyalty—instilled through systematic humiliation by peers—as the highest value; confessionalism and group ritual as primary means of maintaining conformity; the absolute belief in the scarcity of power.

In the weeks that followed, when I had time to reflect on the implications of what had happened in that room that night and what was happening to us in A Group of Women, I concluded that woman-hating among women is the most serious problem in the world. That sounded extreme, even to me, but I kept arriving at it in eminently sane and logical ways. If it is true, as I believe it is, that women's destiny is to save the planet by rising out of our own oppression, this compulsion to compete with and destroy other women is our deadliest enemy, absolutely ensuring failure. If we fail—if the women's movement fails—all is lost, and not only for women, but for everyone.

But what could be done about it? This behavior seems to be almost part of our autonomic nervous system. We not only can't seem to control it, but most of the time we can't even see it in ourselves. It is part of the invisibility of our oppression. We have perfectly reasonable explanations for all that we do that hurts another woman. We perform impeccably the art of keeping ourselves and other women powerless and remaining oblivious to the dynamics. But I knew that we must learn to see them and then to transcend them, because either all of us together must have power or none of us will have it — or even survive to lament its absence. But how?

With my awareness of the problem at the NOW conference had come an urgent feeling of responsibility for finding solutions. Since then, no matter where I have been, no matter what else I have been doing, I have watched and listened, on the alert for clues. And though I know I have just scratched the surface, I have gained some insight into this dynamic which is so destructive to our movement.

If I were to condense and piece together into a composite picture the common features of the women-against-women experiences I have heard about and witnessed, I would get something like this:

The cycle begins with a clash of power, either overt or covert, on any scale, grand or humble, at an international women's conference, at a state NOW meeting, on the five-woman board of the local YWCA, or among the members of a feminist book club. Let's look at the book club.

The woman who started this club some years before has a strong history of feminist activism; this is not the first enterprise she has organized, or the only one she is involved in at the time. She is full of ideas and energy, is articulate and outgoing, gets women moving and things done, and so has come to be regarded as a leader in the feminist community. It's true that she has faults, but she is a committed feminist and trying to live her philosophy.

One day the local television station calls and sets up an interview with her. That night at the book club meeting she announces this to the group. A member points out that the decision about who would be interviewed should have been made by the entire group. Others in the group also feel chagrined about this. If there is enough either conscious or unacknowledged fear or jealousy or resentment of her already existing among the members, whatever the woman does at this point about the problem at hand is largely irrelevant: the cycle has begun. From this point forward the real motives of the players become more and more obscure.

The members split into two groups: those for and those against her *as a person*. But neither of these sides is really "pro" anybody; they are "anti" each other. The "sides" meet separately in private or over the phone, and pick out the many and egregious faults of the other side. They enjoy it so much that they go over them and the dangers they pose again and again, from every angle, remembering more and more incidents and more details, amassing more and more evidence against them. The more they find fault, the warmer the glow that spreads over them. Pumping up their feelings of superiority and righteousness in this way gives them a definite, but limited, high. They know from experience, though, that an almost unlimited high is possible from this activity, and these first warm waves awaken the craving for the truly super "rush." Because this craving is satisfied best and easiest in a confrontation, those who initially opposed the woman—by this time she has become a veritable monster in their minds—now seek to meet her face to face. They choose their moment and attack. Their unspoken and perhaps unconscious object at this encounter is to "break" her—to strip her of power.

The moment she exposes her vulnerability by trying to defend herself, they plunge their daggers in to the hilts; they say vicious things, and everything she says in defense is cruelly turned against her.

Some woman demurs. "I'm not comfortable with this attack," she says to the raging women. "This is not an attack!" they yell at her. She shuts up but she notices that there is a strange sort of excitement in the room, almost an exhilaration.

And then the woman under attack starts to cry. Immediately, the excitement which has been building steadily in the women seems to leap to its apex, hover there a second or two, then break into a shower of shivery tingles. Released from the tension, from the craving for the rush her "breaking" gave them, the women now become very mellow. They embrace the woman they were mutilating only moments earlier, they tell her they love her. But their abrupt about-face is inexplicable to her; for her nothing has changed. Only now, in addition to her feelings of pain and betrayal, she is totally confused.

The woman who has been told to shut up ponders all this. She knows she has watched something very important, and that the signal clue was the "buzz," the "high" of the attacking women. It's like watching a bunch of drug addicts, she decides.

I think she's right. I think trashing women *is* an addiction in every sense of the word, very likely including chemical. Every time we succumb to the need for the "fix" that talking against or attacking another woman gives us, we replicate and reinforce patriarchy's sadomasochistic pattern in our personal lives and in our movement. Sadomasochism, the very essence of patriarchy, is a habit, a deep habit — an addiction. There are very few women among us who haven't personally experienced the "rush" that comes from putting another woman down. If we are honest, we have to admit the pleasure of feeling "on top," superior, right for a change, after a lifetime of being viewed and treated as hopelessly stupid and wrong. Some of us can hardly get enough of this bogus freedom, this elation.

Also, part of being oppressed is struggling against the dulled-out feeling that comes from being repressed, suppressed, censored, invisible, inaudible, insignificant, beaten down. It gives many of us a need just to *feel*, to feel *anything*. We long for sensation, long to feel alive. And patriarchy, having set up the system calculatedly to ensure this dynamic, teaches us, encourages us from our mothers' wombs, to feel sensation, to feel alive, by feeling anger and jealousy and distrust and hatred for women; we have been taught that this is safe (whereas feeling it for men is *not* safe), that, in fact, antiwoman feelings are ultimately the *only* safe feelings.

Certainly these feelings bear the highest intrinsic as well as systemic rewards. The inherent rewards are feelings of being powerful, as well as of being "on the right side," which unconsciously means the men's side against women; the momentary feeling of not being like other women, not being a woman at all, not a slave like them, removed from the degradation of our caste altogether; the incredibly heady feeling of escape from the bondage of our gender. And I suspect also that as the cycle plays itself out, the excitement, the elation of being in the sadist position, the not-woman position, for just a little while is so great that the body produces some chemical substance, perhaps some endorphin, as it does with jogging and with eating disorders, on which we become physically dependent.

At the very least, I know that I have seen many women — and no woman is exceptional in this, *this* is the dynamic in which we are all caught — craving, working for, and finally achieving the rush, have seen them then riding the crest of that high until it gradually subsided into smaller, longer-lasting waves of pleasure. This explains to me how the most vocally angry women, visibly rancorous and terribly intent on hurting another woman one moment, can be embracing her the next. Why shouldn't they love and embrace her? She has just been the source of an incredible fix and they are soaring.

The pleasure is relatively long lasting — hours, at least — because now the attackers, having been able to hurt her (which provided the peak thrill), have proved her vulnerability, her weakness. In masculine culture, to be vulnerable is to be in the woman/masochist position and powerless. The one who "breaks" is therefore no longer a threat. Those who have proved themselves stronger, strong enough to break her, now "take" her power as their booty, and ingest it like a drug. The resultant high is the high that tops all others for women — and for men — in patriarchy. And as in any addiction, the inevitable hang-over later on never keeps us from doing it again.

One of the reasons this problem is so insoluble is that it leaves the women in both the sadist and the masochist positions in a double bind. The woman, or group of women, who has been "defeated" cannot petition the winners for a rehearing, or

57

for redress, or plead with them for mercy. Protest, and lobbying, and unkind treatment, and anger, and hate—these not only leave the situation unchanged, they exacerbate it, because sadists "get off" on these kinds of behavior; their pleasure in arousing painful emotions and feelings of powerlessness are only reinforced by them. In addition, those of us in the masochist position lose our responsibility with our power—both have been taken from our hands, willy nilly—and there is a thrill of freedom when we escape expectations, our own as well as those of others. As women are in the best possible position to know, powerlessness has its subtle delights, its uses, its ways of controlling others, its easy justifications.

The winners, those of us in sadist position, on the other hand, are now in the catbird seat. Bingeing on power, we have no motivation whatever to change the situation. It feels wonderful to control other women, to keep them in the position where we can tease and torment them—for their own good, of course ("they brought it on themselves"), and for the good of the movement. We are jubilant to have such a handy avenue to the headiest of all highs, the high that begins in fearing and envying another woman's power, that then progresses to where we need her humiliation to cancel out our own uncertainties about ourselves, and then quickly beyond, to where we actually crave it, *must have it.* And where out of this terrific lust to feed the addiction, we do violence to her. Basic to the perpetuation of the sadomasochist addiction we call patriarchy is that this high must reach near ecstasy level as the scapegoats show pain and fear, as they "break."

It could be argued that it is all right to go through this self-destructive, self-hating ritual time and time again if each time we learned a little more from it. But we don't. In fact, every time we go through it we become more addicted and even less able to see ourselves or the problem clearly.

The instant enough of us break this habit among ourselves, however, patriarchy will begin to wither. We must therefore take this ugly and ubiquitous phenomenon seriously enough, each one of us, to go out of our sadomasochistic minds right now and begin studying in our own lives how to stop getting our kicks from hurting one another.

There is no way to have genuine or productive communication once we have slipped into the craving stage of the sadomasochistic addiction cycle among ourselves. The least likely time for junkies to look objectively at their addiction and to want to do anything about it is when they are airborne. So we must delineate and anticipate every stage of this cycle *before* we get caught in it, while our minds are reasonably clear, and learn how to forestall it, how to outwit it *at any point* in its cycle.

Though I have a few preliminary thoughts on the subject of what to do, my fondest fantasy is that many women the world over will put their minds to it. The whole subject of women's internalized oppression requires and merits the most thorough and dedicated research possible, formal and informal. Each of us can do informal research in our own lives by coming up with and trying out possible solutions. Almost every woman has either personally experienced or observed this dynamic at close hand, and many of us will be involved in it again soon, if we're not at this moment. If we're not at this moment, we can try to think how to reunite the women in our community who have been alienated from one another in this way.

One sure way to at least disrupt this pattern is to refuse to give our co-addicts the fix. If we haven't been able to disrupt the cycle before the battering begins, when we feel ourselves begin to weaken under the assault, we can say, looking at our watches, "I have to leave now." Or as some Quakers I know say, "Now is the best time for me to leave." And then *leave* with great decisiveness, not allowing ourselves to be detained or held back *for any reason,* remembering that everything depends on our breaking our own habit and on not feeding other women's addictions. Leaving is not the ultimate solution, but at least it gives us time to think and to cool off, and it prevents our reinforcing the addiction.

Whatever we do, we must learn never to give the expected, typical response, but to think outside our limited repertoire, out of our addiction. Addicted persons are sometimes advised to carry an acronym about in their minds to remind them of things to do to disrupt their patterns, such as CSBS: change positions, suggest a song or a break or a moment of silence. Perhaps if we're in a group, we can suggest forming a committee to deal with this (since we must leave right now, glancing at watch), and so on. And then *we* for our part must refuse to form or join a side against them in which to talk and plot against them. We must put ourselves outside this pattern.

The continuation of life on earth depends on women's refusal of the sadomasochistic model, our refusal to act out the sadist role with women and the masochist role with men or women, and both with ourselves. The people on the bottom must always free themselves before anyone else can be free. So women must do it first because we are the only ones who *can* do it; those in the permanent sadist position depend every moment of their lives on the continual fix that position gives them. They are never going to change the power model in any way that cuts them off from it. Not to have it would seem to be death. They cannot remember ever having been without it any more than they can remember not being alive. And so it is like life to them, like poison to Rappaccini's daughter.

The theme of the women's movement is female is beautiful, female is lovable; its agenda is for us to love ourselves as women, to deeply honor and respect ourselves and *all* women: not just women we agree with, not just other Lesbians or other heterosexual women, not just white or brown or black women, not just poor or working-class or middle-class or upper-class women, not just "well-adjusted" women, or healthy women, or women who smell good and brush their teeth regularly, or women who have accepted Jesus as their savior, or women who worship the Goddess. *All women.* And not just to like them, not just to find them non-disgusting, tolerable, okay. But to *love* them — completely, passionately, madly. To be full of compas-

sion for one another, to be slow to take offense and quick to forgive. To conquer in ourselves the fierce pangs of competition
and jealousy, and to rejoice genuinely in one another's successes.

This doesn't mean we have to like the things all women
do, or agree with them, or ignore the difficulties, or deny that
what some women do is harmful. It means that we must learn
to know in our bones and blood that women are not the enemy.
It means that we must all stand together as the global class
called women or we will fail as individual Lesbians and Jews
and old women and women of color. It means that we must
give highest priority to hanging in there with one another *no
matter what* and working out our difficulties with skins of unparalleled thickness and the largest of hearts.

I believe women *can* love one another, *can* cooperate, *can*
trust, *can*, in short, rise above our conditioning. I believe we
are ready to practice what we know — that as we build one another up and rejoice in the achievement and triumphs, in the
gifts and beauties of other women, we ourselves grow more
gifted, beautiful, and strong. I believe that as we do this, we
will forge a sisterhood so mighty that nothing in the world can
stop us.

This is my dream. It is a dream in which we each remember that every woman born is us.

4

"They Need to Lose Weight Anyway!"

By the middle of 1981, the ERA had been in desperate trouble for a long time, and Mary Ann and I were talking seriously about a fast. Zoe Ananda, one of the fasters from California, later expressed to a reporter how we all felt. "I have stuffed one too many envelopes, licked one too many stamps. I have to do something of a deeper nature personally, make some kind of monumental statement."[1]

Several of us had been talking for over a year about how we needed something to rivet the attention of the public every day, day after day, upon the ERA, something — like the hostages in Iran — that would make people ask, "What's happening *today?*" Maybe a fast could accomplish that.

But where were we to do it? Misogynist Virginia, where the ERA had never even got out of committee once in nine years? Florida, where Dempsey Barron almost singlehandedly held the amendment hostage?

One night, Maureen Fiedler, a Roman Catholic nun whom I knew from A Group of Women and who decided to join the fast at the last minute, called me and announced, "The place to do it is Illinois. Their rule requiring three-fifths of both houses to ratify a national amendment makes them perfect!" The minute she said it, everything clicked into place. We'd agreed for some time that our focus had to be on procedure, not on personalities; this was less likely to turn our action into a battle of wills.

So Illinois it was. The Land of Lincoln. The only northern industrial state that had not ratified, and the one with the least democratic requirement for ratification. Perfect.

At the time we wanted to be associated with conventional religion. In explaining it to myself now, I remember again the intensity of the opposition's propaganda about the immorality of ERA supporters. We were manhaters, they shouted through the media, godless and perverted, murderers of babies, destroyers of society. In an attempt to render these red herrings as fishy as they deserved to be, much of what all of us did during the long campaign for justice was as reactive as this attempt to gain credibility through associating ourselves with patriarchal religion.

From the moment I realized that I was going to fast, I knew it would be wildly misunderstood — at least on a conscious level — by most people, whether they were for or against the ERA. It was being undertaken by women, after all, and everything women do partakes of our low status. All our acts are devalued simply because we do them; all our strengths are automatically turned into weaknesses. Also, on the surface, women's going without food would appear to be self-punishing and self-destructive, as if we were doing patriarchy's work for it by killing ourselves before they could get around to it, or by allowing their recalcitrance to kill us. In addition, fasting is extreme, and women are sedulously taught to be careful. I knew also that demonstrating so graphically that we were in total control of our lives would enrage practically everybody; it smashes so many icons all at once.

But most intolerably, a fast for women would be courageous. And though women have for centuries been programmed to be courageous in defense of men's happiness, to bear anything for men, we have been taught to look upon such courage on our own behalf as selfish, immature, and—especially—as ridiculous.

The problem with trying to ratify the ERA had always been that no one could take women seriously. Ironically, this applied as much to those of us working our hearts out to ratify the amendment as to anyone. We allowed ourselves to be persuaded by prestigious male lawyers to deny the very possible and highly desirable effect of the ERA upon reproductive and homosexual rights. By not having the courage to take the offensive and say, as is true, that the ERA could indeed insure *all* basic freedoms for women, and that the legislative intent and history should be written to reflect this determination—by thinking to make slave insurrection palatable to the slavemasters—we constantly and grievously betrayed women.

Since by fasting we would be repudiating all the cultural assumptions that command the public's notion of womanhood, I hoped that by associating ourselves with a familiar, presumably sensible, eminently respectable institution—the Church—we could allay the inevitable conclusion that we were insane. I also hypothesized that our being connected with organized religion—albeit liberal organized religion—would help the public understand the essential spiritual and non-coercive nature of the fast. What I didn't realize then was that this never works—hadn't worked, for instance, in the anti-war movement. The men in power simply said that the part of the churches that were pacifist weren't really part of the churches. Men can place a movement outside the mainstream because they *define* everything, which means that trying to associate a radical cause with an accepted institution can't work. In addition, the public doesn't associate religion with spiritual values anymore—and quite rightly so. On the whole the public doesn't remember "spiritual" at all. *That's* the problem.

The truth was that the fast was so shocking nothing could mitigate it.

At the time I was organizing it, asking dozens of women to participate and being refused by all but seven of them, I felt that eight fasters were pitifully few. Looking back, I am astonished that there were so many who had the courage to say yes.

We were an unlikely assemblage, disparate in every way but that we all wanted ratification of the ERA above all else, and felt we had been "called"—for lack of a more precise, less sectarian word—to the fast.

On the morning of May 14, Shirley Wallace, a "graduated" Mormon from Colorado who had been working in Virginia on the ERA for the past year, Mary Barnes, a brand-new Mormon feminist from North Carolina, my friend Mary Ann Beall, who was a Quaker from Virginia, and I set out together for Illinois in my little brown Honda. We left early in the morning, and spent the day steadily driving and steadily discussing our purpose, the philosophy of non-violence, the spiritual unity we needed to have, the certainty inside ourselves.

For hours we considered the four stages that Gandhi's writings prepared us to expect the legislators to go through in response to our fast.* He told us to assume that we would first be ignored, then ridiculed, then reacted against with extreme anger and perhaps brutality. And then, if everything went well, we might expect to convert.

Even though we were aware that there was probably not enough time left in the ratification period for the legislators to go through all of these stages and to come out converted, we also knew that we could not have begun earlier. I had realized

---

*I do not mean to suggest that any of us were under the illusion that Gandhi had had any feminist awareness. We knew not only that he had not, but that he was fundamentally and often shockingly sexist. We were also well acquainted with one of the most notorious proponents of non-violence in the Washington, D.C., area and knew that he frequently and brutally beat his long-term live-in woman friend. So we understood clearly why non-violence, as perceived by its male proponents, had thus far had no transformative power in the world. Their failure to make the intimate connection between private and public violence, between rape and war, renders most men utterly useless as peace activists.

that the fast would be considered so outrageous and laughable and offensive by some feminists, and all anti-feminists, that our only justification would be that it was a last-ditch effort. Our fast could appear to be remotely legitimate only if every other stone had been turned. Only a desperate situation could warrant what seemed such a desperate act, though in truth it was an act of strength and calm. So we had to wait until the ERA was down to the eleventh hour.

It was late when we arrived in Springfield, about 11:30 p.m. Dina Bachelor and Zoe Ananda, both from southern California, had arrived together earlier that evening. We all bedded down on the floor of the dusty old Kumler Methodist Church, which Rich Wood, a minister I had met that winter in Chicago, had secured for us, and slept, more or less.

In her journal, Mary Ann chronicled her thoughts that night: "[As I lay there] I remembered that warm late summer evening nearly a year before when a group of us had gathered at Sonia's house in Sterling, Virginia, to plan a series of demonstrations in support of the ERA. I could see Mary Wood's intense face as she read aloud the words spoken by Alice Paul when she left the Occoquan Work House after the long fast during which she and the other suffragists were subjected to much brutality: 'We have done this that women fighting for liberty will be considered political prisoners . . . God knows we don't want other women ever to have to do this again.' The air in the room was electric. Each of us knew deep in her heart that, before this long struggle was over, the unthinkable might be asked of her. We did not speak of it that night, but it was a constant presence looming before each woman, each hoping in her heart she would be passed by. Yet of the seven women in that room that night, four will be fasting here."

Maureen Fiedler arrived on May 15, reluctance itself. She had resisted the fast harder and longer than any of us, though only her conscience had ever tried to persuade her to do it. Up until the day the four of us left Virginia for Illinois, she had been committed only to doing the press work for us. After the fast, she wrote: "But I was not entirely comfortable doing only that. Now the enthusiasm of the Illinois Religious Committee for the ERA renewed the periodic nagging inside me urging me to become a faster. I was scared. Fasting was the last thing in the world I wanted to do — for the ERA or anything else. 'How can I?' I asked myself. 'I can hardly stick to a diet for a week; how would I last on an open-ended fast?' Yet the call was there, sure and strong. Gradually, my kicking and screaming inside subsided. Within a week, I answered the call and became a faster."

Three weeks later our last faster joined us: Mary Wood, a teacher from New York. She had begun fasting with us while still in New York finishing the school year.

We were all scared. We all had stories like Maureen's. In addition, Mary Barnes, Zoe, and Dina were smokers and caffeine addicts, so they were not only going to give up food, but coffee, diet soft drinks, and cigarettes at the same time. Fasting is hard enough all by itself without trying to become perfect overnight. We all wondered if we would be able to go through with it, we all worried about our health, and each of us confronted the fact that she might die.

Even in a relatively short fast such as ours there is ample time for the electrolytic balance of the blood to become gravely upset. A person fasting on water alone quickly becomes starved for potassium, the chemical that controls muscle function, including that of the heart. Without potassium, the heart can begin to fibrillate and even stop. When no salt is taken in to hold adequate liquid in the tissues, the volume of blood can become dangerously decreased, so much so that in any position but lying flat — and ultimately even then — the faster's too-scanty blood supply pools in the lowest place and the heart cannot pump it to the brain. Thin persons quickly use up their stored fat and start to destroy their own muscle and organ tissue; the liver becomes particularly vulnerable as the fat that normally surrounds it is used up and actual tissue begins to be eaten, tissue that can never be regenerated. Physiological weaknesses that might otherwise go undetected for a person's entire life-time may show up in life-threatening ways under the stress of fasting. Depending upon the person, any of these can happen fairly quickly and can prove fatal. And these are just a few of the perils we knew we were facing. We were not foolish to be afraid.

We were also worried about our spiritual health. We knew that to have the spiritual power that is possible from fasting we would need to love one another and in general to "purify our hearts."[2] Though it wasn't at all clear how to go about doing this, we nevertheless set about it in earnest those first few days. We told our stories, what had brought each of us to this point; we meditated together; we discussed and tried to work out our differences; we listened to and encouraged one another.

We also talked deep into the night about our purpose in fasting. I confessed that though I obviously wanted ratification of the Equal Rights Amendment and hoped our fast would soften the adamantine heart of the Illinois legislature, I had an equally passionate covert goal. In a discussion we had one night in the Kumler church kitchen, I called this goal "the be-ginning of the third phase of the women's movement." By this I meant that it was time for women to begin to be active rather than reactive. By fasting, we were defining our own param-eters, we were playing our own game and were in total control of it, as we could never be with civil disobedience. We were coming from our place of power, meeting the power-over-others mentality with power-over-ourselves. In this, we met as equals.

In that discussion, what I said most clearly, however, was that it was time for women to begin to understand how worthy we are—how worthy of sacrifice, how worthy of risk. Under-standing this is necessary to believing ourselves worthy of jus-tice. Regardless of what we know intellectually, so long as we don't really feel we deserve more than the crumbs society now tosses us, we can't figure out how to get more. Fasting was a symbol that was intended to directly educate the heart, even if the brain denied its significance. It would tell the women in this country how important they are. It would say, there are eight women in Springfield who think your dignity and your human rights are worth giving their lives for. It seemed to me that women needed desperately to hear that. That they couldn't possibly hear it too often or in too many ways.

I also wanted to provide women with a model for courage. I thought it was urgent that we begin to identify ourselves with courage, to expect it of ourselves and other women, and to see, in contrast, the bottomless cowardice of the men we have trusted to speak for us.

We quickly began to get ourselves organized. We wrote our press release, arranged our press conference, and had our "last supper" one night in the basement of Kumler Methodist Church with the press in attendance. In my journal the next day I lovingly recorded everything we ate, and then ended, "Over that meal we held hands and promised that we would remain faithful to one another and to this cause and to the immense task that we had set ourselves."

That night when we crept into our sleeping bags on the third floor of the church, we were as ready as we knew how to be for the ordeal ahead.

Then the hunger began. And with it the reaction of the public. It began closest to home. The congregation at Kumler forced the sympathetic pastor to evict us from the church ten days after we arrived, one week into the fast. We had no place to go, and I was weak and sick.

The national president of NOW stepped in at this point and rescued us. Although she personally considered the fast a poor political strategy, one that threatened ERA proponents' "credibility," she knew that the public associated us with NOW and she was wise enough to understand the political importance of presenting a united front. In addition, she was not an unfeeling person and we were truly a pitiful band at that moment. "Other churches may throw you out," she said, "but you still have the feminist church!" She assigned NOW members to help us find a place to stay. We ended up in the Ramada Inn, in rooms with showers and beds with clean sheets. It was better than going to heaven. And NOW paid for it.

On May 27, I wrote in my journal: "I suppose it's just as well that we left Kumler. We could not have navigated the stairs for many more days; I was already sleeping in the nursery on the ground floor."

On the first day of the fast, Dixie Johnson, a friend from Washington state, had turned up in the rotunda. She hadn't been able to dissuade me from the fast, she said, so she drove all the way from Spokane — her car windows advertising our cause in green shoe polish: "Spokane to Springfield: ERA or bust!" — because she knew we would need her help. We called her our "zookeeper." Two days after we moved to the Ramada Inn, our second non-fasting helper arrived — another Washingtonian named Kate McVeigh. Judy Rosenfeld from California became our final "eater," as we called our nonfasting helpers. We couldn't have made it without our three eaters.[3] They drove us about in our van (after lifting us into it), wheeled us in our wheelchairs, helped us in and out of elevators, up and down stairs, made sure we always had an abundant supply of spring water, ran errands, bathed us as we became weaker, and generally made it possible for us to do our agonizing work of embodying women's hunger for justice. We all did the fast together, though we did it in two modes: eating and non-eating.

And in those modes there we were, every day the legislature met, sitting in the rotunda dressed in white with purple sashes across our breasts, under a magnificent royal purple banner that proclaimed in gold letters the solemn truth: WOMEN HUNGER FOR JUSTICE. In the lower right-hand corner was the gold word DAY. We pinned a 1 to it the first day, a 2 the second, and so on. I remember when we pinned 21, 30. I wondered if I would last to 40. And if I did, if I would ever be the same.

In at least two ways, I know I'll never be the same, nor would I wish to be. What fear remained after the excommunication from the Mormon church and all the civil disobedience dropped away completely. I felt free of fear when I left Illinois. I had faced mortal danger, and I had faced it down.

And what I learned about hunger will be an ever-present torment to me until all people on earth have enough to eat every day. My journal entries nearly always begin with some rhapsody/requiem on the subject of food:

"May 31, 1982, 13th day of the fast. I hope I am never complacent about food again. I hope every time I sit down to a meal I realize what extraordinary good fortune it is to have food to eat. Rick and the kids had pot roast for lunch, and for supper he whipped up some vegetable-cheeseburger thing that the kids loved.[4] Oh my, everybody's eating!"

That included the legislators — constantly. Aides told us they'd never seen so much food consumed on the floor in their entire experience with the legislature. On those days when we sat in the gallery watching the proceedings below, it seemed to us that every mouth down there was chomping, salivating, gorging, burping, slurping. Our hunger seemed to be stimulating every salivary gland in town. We joked that grocery and fast food sales were probably hitting all-time highs.

June 2, 1982, my journal: "I'm lying here very weak on the morning of the fifteenth day of the fast, listening to the maid vacuuming the other rooms and to the sounds of the housekeeping and life going on around me. Through the open door are sneaking all the smells of breakfast from the kitchen. I'm thinking to myself, 'What an unutterable privilege for people to sit down to breakfast every morning. Almost everybody in this country wakes up every morning and just assumes they're going to eat. There it is — the food — waiting for them.'

"Yet I know that's just an illusion. All over the world, people are starving to death. Two-thirds of the world's population is dying of starvation at this very moment. Two-thirds! Think of that! Two-thirds of the people of the world have never in their entire lives had their stomachs completely full at one sitting. How we take this incredible blessing for granted!

"Dick Gregory says that 41 people die of starvation every minute. I remember the people I saw—lived near—in Africa, who had never had a full meal, whose life expectancy was 35. And I realize that although people in this country and in the Western world think the biggest problem in the world is competition between the two major bullies—the U.S. and the U.S.S.R.—actually, for most of the world's people, this is not the big problem. This is not a problem at all. For most of the world's people, the big problem, the overwhelming problem, the *only* problem, is hunger."

I lay awake many hours each night so tormented by hunger that thinking of my torment multiplied by hundreds of millions nearly drove me mad. When I thought of the agony of it, I had to bite my hands to keep from moaning aloud and waking my roommate, Shirley.

Although books on fasting and people who have fasted seem to agree that one loses the feeling of hunger after a week or so, I never did, not for a single instant. It gnawed at me incessantly; I was obsessed by food. At first we thought we should avoid all mention of food. We thought that if we talked about it, the hunger would become unendurable, so for the first few days, we didn't mention food at all.

That doesn't mean we got away from it, of course. There were those aides having to carry loads of viands through the rotunda constantly to feed the ravening herd in the general assembly. And from the very first day, the anti-ERA women faithfully carried out what we soon dubbed their "radical candy bar actions," which consisted of unwrapping Milky Ways directly in front of us with great ceremony and munching away on them. Then occasionally other "antis" would plunk themselves down, spread out an entire delicious-smelling meal, and picnic three feet from our famished toes. (These hostile acts of women opposed to the ERA bear many of the same earmarks of internalized oppression that I'd seen at such close quarters among "friends": horizontal violence, ritual torture, the necessity to wound the spirit.) We had to avert our eyes from bill-

72

boards, throw blankets over TV ads, skip whole paragraphs in books—even in *Dracula*, which I scrounged up somewhere, thinking that if there were one book that would be safe, that would be it. But no. Food *loomed*.[5]

Although we agreed not to bring the subject up ourselves, one day as Dixie was taking us to the park, Mary Barnes accidentally mentioned food. "Oops!" she spluttered, clamping her hand over her mouth. I said, "Let's just forget this. *Let's talk about it,* for heaven's sake!" And so for the next hour and half we talked food. We talked about every good thing we'd ever eaten or thought of eating. And what we'd eat right now if we could, how it would be prepared, and seasoned, what it would look like, how it would smell, and of course how it would taste. Deliverance! Such a relief just to give in and suffer it, to think about it openly and not try to repress it.

"So we do that occasionally," I wrote on June 5, the 18th day of the fast, "though we try not to talk about it all the time and we try not to think about it all the time. But every once in a while it does my soul good to listen to Zoe, who was once married to an Italian, give a blow-by-blow description of how she makes spaghetti. And to Mary Ann tell about the Greek food she knows how to make. Oh, it does your heart good just to hear it, and to know that somewhere someone is actually eating it at this moment. And that, Goddess willing, someday you will actually eat it yourself!"

Ten days into the fast we were also deeply into the ridicule and trivialization phase of public reaction. Bumper stickers jeered, "They need to lose weight anyway!" Newspaper articles lambasted us:

> . . . While Sonia and her friends truly believe they are starving themselves to show their complete dedication to this cause, many others look upon their sacrifice as another silly example of what ERA extremists will do to get publicity. . . . The best way to get ERA passed is by the tried and true democratic

73

method of letter-writing and phone calls to elected officials. We urge Sonia and her friends to stop fasting and start writing.[6]

An editorial in the *Illinois Times* portrayed us as "weak and forlorn."[7] In the *Chicago Sun Times*, the Speaker of the House called the fast "foolish," said it was "blackmail," and accused us of hurting our cause more than helping it.[8] Other legislators were quoted as saying, "I'm appalled. This is counterproductive. It will breed revulsion rather than sympathy"; "[the ERA] ought to go up or down on its merits and not on some sideshow." The article goes on to say, "Many lawmakers say the strike has become the subject of derisive comments and jokes."[9] An editor of the Decatur, Illinois, *Herald and Review* revealed his abysmal ignorance when he wrote: "This tactic is effective to offer the world messages [which] authorities try to block. . . . But what of the women fasting in Springfield? . . . Unlike the oppressive governments confronted by Gandhi and Sakharov, no one is preventing the seven women from offering their views on ERA in public or denying them a fundamental right to other tools of the lobbyist."[10]

But our champions had their say in the press, too. Larry Golden, of the Political and Legal Studies Department at Sangamon State University, praised our action as "a clear, disciplined sign of personal strength." And went on to say that "such action stands in direct contrast to the Illinois legislature, where action based upon moral principles is as rare as a cool day in a Springfield summer."[11]

In an early editorial, Sandra Martin placed us in the company of the great:

> Fasting is unladylike. Being a lady means playing the game by somebody else's rules. Playing by those rules, too many women have lost too much for too long.
>
> Rosa Parks ignored the rules.
>
> Dr. King and the civil disobedients of the sixties were told they were stepping out of line.

Gandhi was not afraid to heed the "still, small voice" that guided him in his outrageous ways.

Our suffragist grandmothers, whose hunger and marching and civil disobedience won women in England and America the right to vote, were perfect scandals.

They broke the rules. And they won.[12]

Letters were pouring in. Approximately fifteen per cent of them were negative, accusing us of being suicidal, hysterical, desperate for attention: "Don't you get enough attention at home?" We were told (sometimes by feminists) that we looked ridiculous and that women were ashamed. Members of women's organizations wrote to tell us we were hurting their image. Some letters charged us with standing in the way of ratification; some said we were the laughing stock of the country and no one could take us seriously. And a few were from angry women whose perceptions were that all women were losing respect because of us, insisting we weren't representing *them*.

We were accused of impracticality, imprudence, and bad taste, were criticized for not preparing correctly, for not getting medical permission, for starting at the wrong time, for starting at all.

But we were receiving far more love-mail than hate-mail. And women were saying just what I'd hoped they'd say: "Thank you for helping me realize how valuable I am." "It means a great deal to me that you are risking your lives for my human rights." "Thank you for your courage."

And we got hundreds of personal love visits and tokens. Mary Ann recorded in her diary on May 21: "Ethel Alexander, a legislator from South Chicago, came down today and sat with us for awhile. She apologized for not speaking to us sooner. She said she saw us come into the rotunda that first day but was unable to say a word to us. She said she sat on a bench around the corner from the elevator and cried.

"Tears were a reaction we often elicited. At the end of the vigil today, a young woman came by and handed each of us a single white rose tied with a purple ribbon. Tears were streaming down her cheeks. She was unable to speak."

Women often lined up to talk to us, and when they got to us, hugged us, or, when we became too weak for hugging, grabbed our hands, wept as they thanked us, praised us, or simply stood there speechless, their faces working, loving us with their eyes. The women of NOW were particularly supportive, standing by us and helping us in every way possible from first to last.

Frightened women, with only the illusory armor of the male god to protect them, were also drawn to us. On the ninth day of the fast, we were maneuvering my wheelchair into the elevator when three such women, looking very Middle America, approached Mary Ann and demanded, "Do you know that Jesus is your personal savior?"

She looked at them as if she had been waiting for them, took their hands, and said, "I am here, like you, in the hands of the divine spirit." "After their surprise wore off," she writes, "they were very open and caring to me. Often the encounters that moved me most were with those who were afraid and uncertain. These are women who have seen changes in their lives, and not for the better. They are afraid of what more change will bring."

We'd anticipated the negative response, so bearing it was relatively easy. But for reasons only feminists understand well, bearing the love was very difficult. Women are always so surprised when others love us. We are astonished at how much warmth and appreciation and understanding and affection others want to give and *do* give us. "Surely this can't be for *me!*" we think to ourselves. We can't believe we deserve it.

I had never been so gently cared for, so selflessly attended. I realized that this tenderness is what society teaches women to reserve for men, but neglects to teach men to return to women. I had never felt anything like it, and began to understand better why women turn to women for affection, for love, for companionship. I felt totally secure, cushioned in solicitude. I let go and forgot all other concerns but surviving from day to day. I knew I could trust the women around us to take care of everything else.

In addition, as fasters our emotions were so very near the surface all the time, especially as we grew weaker, that having some of the stimuli siphoned off by others was an incredible relief. We felt as if we had dropped our shields along the way. Our senses came quiveringly alive. Mary Ann writes, "My senses of smell, sight, and hearing became very acute. I could smell flowers a block away, color became lambent, and sound at times excruciating." Cigar smoke in the capitol was a constant torment to us; when we rode in a car, bumps felt like craters; and when Dixie turned on her blow-dryer, we yelped as if she were starting up a jackhammer.

Our amplified senses made life in the huge cold echoing stone cave of the capitol rotunda one physical assault after another—especially on rally days when hundreds of voices singing and shouting ricocheted from stone to stone all the four stories up to the dome and back down again. This increased sensitivity also made living together so intimately something of a feat in itself, like climbing Mt. Everest on roller skates. I marvel that we managed as well as we did, all so exposed and vulnerable, our every nerve taut and naked, though it felt at the time as if we were failing where we most needed to succeed—among ourselves.

Although we knew it would spell disaster, we came perilously close to a split on several occasions. From the first week we had difficulty getting along smoothly together, but since we knew that everything depended upon our cohesion as a group, we struggled womanfully with our wayward feelings. Even so, wild, unreasonable jealousies arose, tempers flared at the slightest provocation, paranoia skyrocketed. Disillusionment about one and then another of us ran rampant—though, I must make very clear, even in our bleakest, most fragmented moments, none of us seriously suspected any of the others of secretly breaking the fast. We trusted one another absolutely on that score. That may be what saved us from an irreparable rift.

We were trapped in habits of oppression that we didn't understand and therefore couldn't control. And though we parted amicably, if not lovingly, from Zoe and Dina—who thought of themselves as one "side" (primarily because they were Lesbians) with the rest of us on the other "side"—we have not recovered whatever tenuous feelings of sisterhood and love we began the fast with. It was too hard, what we went through, too damaging, too searing. We needed each other too much and we let each other down too hard, too often. And we didn't understand that we'd been socialized to act as we were acting— always, in all circumstances, with all women.

Weak and sad, I observed all this and tucked it into the pot already boiling in the back of my mind with the assault at the NOW conference and the coming apart of A Group of Women. I knew it was part of the same syndrome, and that it was deadly. I would have to get back to it. Something had to be done.

In the meantime, we had our work to do, a large part of which consisted of educating media folk. Reporters were always around us in the rotunda, but some were with us for a part of almost every day. We came to know them very well, to like and trust several of them. The price of our trust, and of their understanding us at all, was that they had to swallow the massive doses of feminism we continually pressed upon them.

Since we knew it was chiefly through reporters that we could hope to inform the public, we began by trying to get them to differentiate between hunger strikes and fasts. It took them many days to do so, and many more to believe we were sincere. The IRA's hunger strike, which had taught the world about hunger strikes, was still too recent. When we stopped eating, everyone automatically thought of Bobbie Sands who had died in an Irish prison. No one thought of Gandhi.

Again and again we had to explain to reporters the ways

in which a hunger strike and a fast differ, and that all they have in common is that participants don't eat.

Whatever success we had came from our patient, tireless explanations to the press. We began with the obvious. People on hunger strikes are usually—not always, of course, but most often—in prison. In the case of the IRA, they were people who had no scruples against using violence to achieve their ends. And because fasting is a non-violent approach, it was not appropriate for them. A hunger strike is far more "violent" in the sense that it is highly coercive. What hunger strikers are saying to the powers that be is, either you do what we ask or we'll die. It's a threat.

Of course what their threats do is cause even greater defensiveness in their opponents, make them even more solidly recalcitrant in their own position, cement them into a corner. It becomes a battle of wills and boils down to who's going to lose face first. There's a lot of face-losing potential in a hunger strike. Which is the reason they're not always successful, and certainly the reason Bobby Sands died. Margaret Thatcher had to prove she was a man.

We decided against holding the fast in Florida largely because we couldn't see how we could escape appearing—and being—coercive. One man there, Dempsey Barron, defeated the ERA almost singlehandedly. If we fasted there, we could hardly have kept from making him the target, and we didn't want to get his back up. We didn't want a battle of wills.

I knew from nearly half a century in the Mormon church the terrific value men put upon saving face. I knew that those men most afflicted with ego—and Dempsey Barron's is terminal—would kill rather than lose face, would rather die than lose face, since face is life to them. We could see that by focusing on Barron and backing him into a corner, we would be defeating our own purpose. It would look like a hunger strike—it would *be* a hunger strike, no matter what we called it—and it could well end up being a repeat of Bobby Sands and Margaret Thatcher. Dying wouldn't be useful.

I soon found a shortcut in clarifying the difference between that and what we were doing. I reminded reporters of the familiar fable by Aesop, the one where the wind and the sun argue about which is the stronger. The wind boasts that he is because he can whip the coat off the man walking down below. But when he tries to do it, he only succeeds in making the man hold on to his coat even more firmly than before. The sun, on the other hand, has only to beam down warmly upon him to make the man remove his coat almost at once.

As I wrote in my journal: "The fast is like the sun. It's an attempt to focus spiritual attention and energy upon the problem. It gathers all our passion and love together and sends it forth with authority into the hearts of even the most intractable."

We were concentrating upon the heart because all over the country legislators were being bombarded with intellectual, or pseudo-intellectual, arguments pro and con ratification of the Equal Rights Amendment. What it meant for the actual lives of women and men, and life on the planet in general was being obscured by the dust of multiple brainstorms. The problem, we thought, wasn't in men's minds, it wasn't in their logic — although we knew we were dealing with massive irrationality in dealing with power (which made any reliance on logic and reason absurd). The problem was in the heart. And, we reasoned, in the ERA campaign we hadn't insinuated ourselves behind those impenetrable shields that protect men's hearts. I no longer believe we can, or should, waste our time trying. But I had much to learn in those days.

"Maybe in the end," I wrote in my journal, "nothing we can do will persuade men to give up tyranny. Perhaps disaster will have to be their university. But we must try everything." Our first press release ended with these words: "Perilous times in human history demand extraordinary focusing of spiritual power and love. These are perilous times for women. This fast is our act of love."

Fasting is also a demonstration of faith in the persons one is fasting to communicate with, attesting to their ultimate

80

goodness and desire to be principled. The assumption of our fast, as opposed to the basically cynical assumption of a hunger strike (which is that people have to be *forced* to do right), was that those men had something of virtue in them, something honorable that could be appealed to, that, as the Quakers say, every person has light within that responds to the light in others.

This attitude appealed to us enormously because it seemed to go such a long way toward blurring the distinction between "them" and "us" which is necessary for the concept "enemy"— the cornerstone of patriarchy. It helps rid one's psychological repertoire of that classification. And causes one to see all people as having within them the desire—sometimes very, very deeply buried, I grant (so deeply it appears stone dead)—to obey principle quite aside from considerations of political consequences to self. We hoped that at least some of those men in Illinois, before they became morally expedient and gross, had been capable of caring about and living by principle now and then. Maybe some had even wanted to get into office at least partly to improve people's lives. Unfortunately, being in office has a way of recasting that motivation into baser stuff. But the person who set out with some idealism once is still inside somewhere—or so our hopeful theory went—and can be reached.

I have since come to believe, however, that legislators are perhaps the least likely of all men to have something noble left to appeal to. And that even if this weren't true, such "appealing" not only demeans and humiliates women, reinforcing our view of ourselves as vassals, but it also reinforces men's unconscious conviction that they are god Himself, or, at the very least, god's trusted stewards. Because it perpetuates the God/ worm paradigmatic thinking that is the basis of patriarchy, slaves lobbying their masters for freedom has always been a deeply lamentable, dangerous waste of time.

Early on some reporter said to me, "Well, you can talk about the difference between a hunger strike and a fast if you want. But it boils down to the same thing. All you want in either case is for those men to change their votes."

81

"Wrong," I replied. "What we want to happen to the legislators here in Illinois is that they'll be so moved and so touched when they see and understand the implications of what's going on in that rotunda that they'll say to themselves, 'I didn't take this issue seriously enough. I didn't understand that it was so important. I'd better think it through again.'

"If, by some miracle, we move into the conversion stage of this action of ours — if the conversion happens — when those men get onto the floor to vote, they'll have the courage to vote yes, even, perhaps, against what they and others perceive to be their 'best political interests.' That takes courage. And courage only comes from the heart — not the brain, not from political astuteness and sophistication.

"And since the heart is where courage is generated and since what we need from these men is courage, we have to touch their hearts."

The first step to reaching the legislators was to make visible the conditions that inspired the fast in the first place. Women's suffering in this country is as invisible as it is immense. As Larry Golden wrote in the *Illinois Times*: "The ERA continues to be portrayed as a luxury demanded by middle-class women who don't need it anyway. Lost in the discussion is the fact that the great proportion of poor people in the U.S. are women, and that women continue to be exploited economically and sexually on an everyday basis. The figures are staggering, as is the suffering. Such exploitation and suffering inevitably elicit strong, confrontative reactions. Indeed, it is amazing that we have not witnessed more such actions to this point. . . ."[13] This suffering is kept hidden for obvious reasons. In our present system, men succeed at the expense of women, always. They prosper, always, to our detriment. If large numbers of the population — particularly women — ever realized this, male supremacy would be threatened. To keep that from happening, the newspapers and television and radio and most magazines — all embedded in the male power system — ignore, or dissipate and dis-

courage interest in, or trivialize the consequences of being female in our society.

A hideous example of this occurred when a breezy, glib reporter from the *Washington Post* came out to Springfield to do
a story on us. For the "Style" section, naturally. One by one she
interviewed us in our rooms at the motel; I almost kicked her
out of mine. She did not want to hear anything serious. I had
nothing but seriousness to say. The ERA was going down; I
was risking my life. I was *serious*.

She not only wanted fluff and silliness from me, she
wanted raunch. "Does fasting make you horny?" she simpered.
I was so weak that the anger I felt at this frivolous, eminently
disrepectful question almost made me cry. I thought, "If she
should get a chance to interview Mrs. Shcharansky, who is 'important,'and 'serious' because she is fasting for a man's rights,*
I wonder if she would insult her by asking if fasting made her
'horny.'"

We were all frantic with anger when she left. Someone
called her in Washington and pled with her on our behalf not
to fluff and silly us, not to degrade us, not to smirk over us.
Though we had refused to answer insulting questions, we knew
the flippant mind that could be evident behind the whole story
and we waited in dread for the article to appear. To our relief,
it was less awful than she had been in person. It was less awful
than it might easily have been.

What the reporter who suggested that we use the "tried
and true democratic tools," such as lobbying, didn't understand
was that when lobbyists approach legislators and say, in an attempt to show the seriousness of the situation, "Sir, did you
know? Government statistics show that by the year 2000 the

---

*Soviet dissident, Anatoly Shcharansky, who has since succeeded in leaving the Soviet
Union, was on a hunger strike in Russia at the time, trying to persuade the government to let him emigrate. Though his wife was in the United States, she was also participating in the hunger strike.

entire poverty population of this country will be women and children?" the gentlemen shake their heads sorrowfully and say, "Oh, now that really is too bad." And probably they are sincere — for that moment. We believed when we began the fast that one of the reasons legislators felt no personal obligation to do anything about it, despite the appeal to their sense of fair play, their compassion, is, first of all, that they are neither women nor children, and second, that statistics are impersonal; they have no faces.

So we put eight women's faces down there in the rotunda. The beauty of a fast, we thought, was that it could make "abstract" suffering (who has ever suffered "abstractly"?) very concrete, very real. In our eight bodies there in the rotunda of the state capitol every day, the legislators had to confront the reality of the suffering they perpetuated. We represented the hunger of women in this country for justice, for dignity, for confirmation of our worth. We made that hunger human and individual and specific; we made that suffering particular and localized. And we hoped that upon seeing our faces, those men would not be able to toss ratification aside so lightly.

Physical hunger also speaks to a very particular and uncomfortable feeling everyone is well acquainted with. Everybody has been hungry enough times in their lives — even if not seriously deprived over a long period of time — to know how it feels. Those legislators had missed breakfast and sometimes lunch, too, when they had been harried. They knew with what gusto, with what delicious anticipation, they sat down to their evening meal on such days. They knew how good everything tasted when they were hungry.

So they knew enough to extrapolate: "What if I couldn't eat this meal tonight? What if I couldn't eat in the morning either? What if I had to go without food for a long time?" Our hope was that when they sat down to their dinners, spread their napkins across their knees, picked up their forks, and began to take that first bite, across their minds would flit the image of us in that rotunda, pale and weak, not having eaten for weeks. And that they would understand in their very cells what commitment women had, how important the ERA was to us, what a longing of the soul must have been ours if we were willing to dramatize it by going without food.

There were those who said (as there are *always* those who say), "Face political reality. The only tactic that will work is demonstrating that voting right on women's issues pays off for men's political careers." But because *not* supporting women's issues is in the interest of men who have so much more to give to one another in political careers than women can ever offer them, that tactic is doomed from the outset. We thought, "Why not try an appeal to integrity? It's certainly a novel approach, and what do we have to lose?" We thought, idealistically, that we might even gain when such a powerful appeal proved unsuccessful. Such a blatant exposé of the legislators' lack of integrity might make clearer to the public, clearer than anything else we could say or do, that it wasn't women lobbying against the ERA who were defeating it (as popular wisdom held), but men. Men were the ones who were refusing to vote for it and using the anti-ERA women as fronts — the classic configuration of oppression. It was men who were not being touched by women's suffering; men who were *causing* it, preserving their privilege at women's expense.

From the first people asked, "Is the fast working?" We could only answer that we were seeing some very interesting developments. At first the legislators tried to ignore it. That passed rapidly into ridicule. They began tittering a lot and making jokes, which shows how uncomfortable it made them. You don't have to have passed Psych. 101 to know that any time people giggle and have to make fun of someone else, it is because they are uneasy. Which meant the legislators were feeling exactly what we hoped they'd begin feeling: dis-ease of the heart.

This dis-ease led them into the next stage of reaction: anger. Oh, how they resented even a momentary disquiet, a momentary prick of conscience. How could they remain firm in their resolve to trade away their ERA vote if they *cared*? So they became angry and began to lash out.

On the fourteenth day of the fast, for instance, the Speaker of the House, a rank misogynist named George Ryan, dismissed the House for ten days — a completely unprecedented event, the papers called it "incredible." June was the last month of the legislature, and in the last month of the sitting of any legislature, as everybody knows, the work is absolutely overwhelming. It is during this time that they frequently meet around the clock and call special sessions. To take ten days off in the midst of this . . . ! Everyone was aghast.

And it wasn't lost on anybody why George did it. He feared those men's hearts were being touched by the fast. He counted on our not being in that rotunda when they returned in ten days. And if we were, well, we wouldn't have had that ten days to weaken their resolve. And he may have been right; that may have made a difference. So they all ran away from us, with George leading the pack.

But he had a surprise coming. We didn't go away. When they came back, we were still there, even weaker and wanner.

The governor also reinforced our sense that we were having the effect we wanted. In an interview with the *Chicago Tribune*, he said he was sure our fast was totally ineffective and in fact would cause legislators to change their votes from yes to no. (*He'd* see to it if *we* didn't, I thought at the time). We were jubilant. "Methinks he doth protest too much," we crowed. Would he have bothered to chide us if our tactics had been wrong? We didn't think so. If they hadn't been working, we reasoned, we would never have heard a word about it. Men think we are far more gullible than we are. Which is just as well, or they would be more cautious about revealing themselves to us.

About this time, Representative Mulcahey came down to our vigil, accompanied by a reporter, to tell us that if we continued this abuse to our bodies, he would change his vote to no.

We learned this from the reporter. Mulcahey never got around to telling us. According to Mary Ann's recollection: "He squared off directly in front of us and bellowed, 'God gave you a moral obligation to take care of your bodies and your children!'" He pushed his face aggressively into hers.

"A welcoming smile glowed on Maureen's face as she stepped forward and shook his hand. 'Representative Mulcahey, you and I share the same faith tradition. You know that fasting has always been an important spiritual witness for us. I'm sure you, more than many others, understand.' A look of uncertainty flickered in his eyes."

At this point, Mary Ann introduced herself to him, took his hands in hers, and told him that she did indeed love her children. That she had two wonderful daughters. "I'm doing this for them," she said. "His face began to harden," she wrote in her journal. "I said, 'Many years ago I nearly died when my eldest daughter was born. Since that day I have lived my life as a gift not to be lived for myself alone, knowing one day I might be called to give it back. Too many women in this country live in abject poverty and despair, and where they live and die no legislator sees them. I am here to bring you their lives, to help men like you become aware of the crucial urgency at the heart of the ERA.'

"'Well, my gut feeling is that your supporters are being turned off by this,' he rejoined. 'You can't do anybody any good if you're dead. . . . But I've got your message.'" And he didn't vote against us.

But Senator Forest Etheredge did, despite two secret (at his request) sessions with him at our motel. And when he voted against us, we held a press conference to point out that the uproar was proving that the fast was effective, and that it wasn't *our* lack of courage that accounted for the changed votes. Our press release said in part:

> We are here representing millions of women who hunger for justice. Let us suppose legislators

truly disagreed with the fasting of eight women in Springfield. Does that justify their compromising democratic principles by turning their backs on the desperate hunger of *all* American women seeking justice? Such lack of principled action only deepens our conviction that we are desperately needed here to continue our solemn spiritual witness to this legislature and to the governor.

When Lois Becker Frolova fasted recently in order to have her husband released from the Soviet Union, she was applauded by Vice President George Bush as a woman with "intestinal fortitude." Why, when women fast for the rights of men is it called "an act of heroism" and when we fast for women it is called "political extortion"?

The Etheredge affair had an interesting aftermath. Several months after the fast, a producer from the Phil Donahue show called to ask me the name of the Illinois legislator who had threatened to vote against the ERA if we continued to fast. Anatoly Shcharansky was still on his hunger strike in the Soviet Union, and Donahue was going to have his wife on the show.

"Forest Etheredge is his name," I told the young man on the phone. "But you're laboring under a serious misapprehension if you think he'll be opposed to Shcharansky's fast just because he was opposed to ours. Not only won't he be opposed, he'll be all over admiration for Shcharansky. He'll laud him as noble, brave, tout his fast as 'important.' What Etheredge found intolerable, you see, wasn't fasting, it was *women* fasting. Women having the gall to act as if their lives were as important as men's!"

The young man continued to be puzzled, and I began to get angry. "Have you forgotten sexism?" I demanded finally. "Do you really think that if you get Etheredge he's going to ask Mrs. Shcharansky the kinds of questions we were asked? Can you honestly imagine his asking her, 'Is your husband *crazy*?

No? Then why doesn't he just write letters and lobby? He probably just needs a little attention.'"

I said, "Look, you need to do a show on the differences in response to men's and women's fasting. More than that, on the differences in response to men and women when women are fasting for the freedom of a whole nation of women and a man is fasting for his own freedom. Maybe the reality of sexism will dawn on a few of your viewers when he is hailed as a hero, and the women who fasted in Illinois are dismissed as kooks."

The next thing I knew, I had a ticket to Chicago to do the Phil Donahue show with Mrs. Shcharansky, but she went back to Israel and the show was canceled.

Dick Gregory came out for five days near the beginning of the fast.

"Black people think this is a White issue," Dick told us when he arrived. "But they're wrong. I hope I can wake a few of them up to that." His having seven daughters may have helped wake him up to that in his turn.

So Dick came and fasted with us and sat with us in the rotunda. We held a press conference for him. "What these women are doing is dangerous," he told reporters. "Anything could go wrong at any moment." He said he'd been on many fasts and knew about many others, and that this was the most strenuous he'd seen. "Most fasters," he told them, "go into a well-ventilated room and lie down. People who are fasting are especially susceptible to germs and infections. These women come out here into the rotunda three hours every day and are jostled by the crowd, insulted, hugged, touched, crowded in upon. That's an almost inhuman undertaking." He said, "It's one of the most difficult actions I've ever seen. And, I repeat, it's dangerous!"

Dick taught us some things about fasting, did some media work for us, and gave us encouragement. On June 3, I wrote in my journal: "The best thing Dick did for me was to reaffirm the spiritual power of fasting. He said, 'This is bigger than you women here in Springfield. This is bigger than this nation, what you're doing here. It's an enormous thing.'"

When he left, he told us to keep in touch with him, and promised that he and his wife, Lillian, would fast on water with us to the end.

On Memorial Day, Dr. Lowery and the Reverends Brooks and Gills of the Southern Christian Leadership Conference joined us in a visit to the tomb of Abraham Lincoln. Each of the fasters placed a white flower beneath Lincoln's large gravestone inside the tomb, and Maureen spoke for us: "We are here because, like our Black brothers and sisters before us, we wish to be set free."

"You have our prayers, you have our love, you have our support," Dr. Lowery told us.

Earlier, when Reverend Osburn from the SCLC office in Atlanta called to make arrangements with us for Dr. Lowery's visit, he asked Mary Ann to reassure me that I should not fear my weakness and symptoms, but should hold to my faith and not be swayed. He told her he had experienced the same difficulties as I was then experiencing—low potassium, low blood volume—on a 48-day fast in a Georgia jail during the civil rights struggle. "Let her know that everything will be all right. I know, as I am a small person, too—just 120 pounds."

Ultimately, though one at a time each of our bodies sent us alarming signals, even collapsing on occasion and frightening us thoroughly, Mary Ann was the only one of us who nearly died. The rest of us found we had to take potassium or our hearts would stop, had to have some salt or our blood volume would plummet, had to be careful of our hypoglycemia, had to watch our uric acid levels, and be monitored for signs of damage to the liver.

But Mary Ann, who came to Illinois recovering from pneumonia, was hospitalized on June 18th, the thirty-second day of the fast, with a collapsed lung. When she became ill, we were all surprised; she'd been among the most energetic of us until then, lobbying, searching for living quarters, busy with tasks very much as if she were eating three nutritious, filling meals a day.

Mary Ann's life hung painfully in the balance for a week, during which, at one point, she died for a moment. But women need Mary Ann too much. We held her to the earth with our need.

Though in general our families understood why we were fasting, whether they agreed with us or not, they were worried sick about our health. My children begged me, "Mom, please don't die!" Fathers particularly had a tendency to become distraught. Dina's father, who was seriously ill at the time, threatened to fast until she stopped. My father scurried about trying to find legal ways to stop me. Mary Barnes's father commanded her to stop, and when that didn't work, threatened to come out and carry her home bodily. Dina and I are middle-aged women, Mary Barnes had been married for 10 years and had three children. "What's with these fathers of ours?" we asked ourselves.

A friend suggests that the fathers, and all the men, may have been acting as they did because in patriarchy women are their property and there we were acting as if we our bodies were *our* property. Of course, as she points out, our bodies aren't property at all but the current manifestation of spirit, and if they "belong" to anyone, it is to the universe or the goddesses or Life.*

After my second rush to the emergency ward, my mother sent a frantic mailgram to Ronald Reagan:

> I am Sonia Johnson's mother, and these women fasting in Springfield are in dead earnest. I'm terrified that she will die. I am outraged that women have to do this kind of thing to get justice. To fight to the death for rights which should be guaranteed them under the Constitution, as women did for suffrage. Please do all in your power to influence Governor James Thompson in Illinois to change the ratification

---

*Correspondence with Linda Barufaldi, November 1985.

rules for ERA from 3/5 to a majority and the women
of America will bless you forever.

If I hadn't been so weak during so much of the fast, I would
have organized a very different sort of action. My ardent fantasy was to plant dozens of women equipped with laugh boxes
throughout the audience in the gallery, women who would, at
a prearranged signal, periodically drown with laughter the
pompous circus down on the floor of the legislature. What happened down there daily became more ludicrous. Many of the
men were behaving like the small-time political hacks that they
were. How could we be taking it and them so seriously? Laughter was the only appropriate response.

I knew that the most appalling thing women can do is
laugh at men. I knew that women assure men they are powerful and important when we confront them with anger, build
peace camps near their war camps, march and shout and throw
ourselves in front of things, and are defiant. In these ways we
pay them homage, we give credibility to nonsense, power to
wickedness. What would truly demoralize them would be for
us to ridicule what is ridiculous about their behavior. To de-
tach ourselves enough to see clearly that we lose integrity when
we take silliness seriously, that we only encourage men in their
absurdity when we give credence to it. And it's not hard to
laugh. Men who consider themselves "important" take themselves so seriously that they are genuinely amusing.

But I did not have the strength to organize good, healthful, cleansing, revolutionary laughter. Though we would not
have won the ERA even if I had, we would certainly have won
a truer perspective and a greater measure of self-respect.

Of course, despite everything, we did not succeed. The
ERA went down in defeat in Illinois on June 22, 1982, but not
before those of us in the galleries had had the rare good fortune
to witness one of the most stunning performances in history.
Monica Faith Stewart, a Black legislator from Chicago's South
Side, stood and spoke with a feminist defiance equaled only by

Sojourner Truth. She, like us, knew the House would reject
the ERA. There was no reason not to tell it like it was:

> . . . . I don't stand here to petition your yes vote, be-
> cause what is your constitution to me? The Declara-
> tion of Independence was drafted by a man who, yes,
> was a founding father; who, yes, was a great econo-
> mist; but yes, he was a slave holder, and yes, for 37
> years, he went into the bed of his slave, who he
> thought was the perfect woman. Why? Because she
> was a slave. And so gentlemen, what is your constitu-
> tion to me?
> . . . . You can vote this amendment up or down;
> quite frankly, it doesn't make any difference to me.
> I think you are acting as people of your class and tra-
> dition have always acted, and you know what? It
> won't matter, because we've survived much worse
> than this. Back when I was in school, we had a say-
> ing, that if things didn't go the way you liked them in
> the classroom, we'd meet you outside at 3:15.
> And so, white males of the world, it is now 3:15.
> I represent the majority of people on this planet who
> are women, the majority of people on this planet who
> are of color, and you cannot have your sovereignty
> any longer. Why? Because I say so!

Up in the galleries, the applause fairly exploded as hundreds of us rose to our feet as one, stamping and shouting.
Overcome with admiration for her, and with gratitude, heart-
sick and angry and proud, we turned and wept in one another's
arms.

When the Illinois House defeated the ERA that day—*by
only five votes: 103 to 74 (the 103 votes were cast in favor* of the ERA,
but with Illinois' anti-democratic 3/5 requirement, we were the
losers)—national ratification was impossible. The long decade
of hoping and dreaming and struggling for justice was over.
We agreed that there was no point in continuing the fast. So

at our last press conference the next morning, we broke it officially, toasting one another and the press with grape juice in plastic wine glasses.

In the meantime, back at the motel, reporters wanted to know what we had learned from this. I said that what I had learned — again — was that women cannot trust men to represent us. We cannot work through men. "It's like trusting the slave-holders to represent the slaves," I told the scribbling pencils. Whatever lingering illusions I might have had about the representativeness of the government of the United States of America died quietly and forever that day. When the ERA went down, women all over the country lost their faith in God: how could a loving, just God not have heard and answered women's most fervent, most passionate, most righteous prayers? they asked. This did not trouble me. What I lost were the last wispy shreds of my faith in this system of government. And in the old ways of trying to change it — including fasting.

I also learned that ordinary women can do extraordinary things. Into the gloom of the day, this knowledge cast cheering sunshine. Look, just look, what we had done!

Eight months later, at a feminist think tank on the West Coast,* I found myself returning to the fast, finally able to distill from it what I had found ineffable at the time.

---

*See Chapter 6.

5

High Treason

Weighing not quite a hundred pounds and so weak I had to crawl up the stairs on my knees, I came home at the end of June 1982 to face my children's anger. As soon as I walked in the door, they began repaying me unconsciously with one crisis after another for having frightened them so badly and for so long with the specter of my imminent death.

I also faced the daunting challenge of beginning an aggressive campaign to try against all historical odds to turn NOW into a feminist organization instead of merely a women's civil rights organization. History tells us that the direction in which an organization begins is the direction in which it is most likely to continue, only intensifying as it goes along, which meant that NOW was most likely to become more and more conventional and mainstream each year of its existence — as indeed it has. I thought that if I were elected president of NOW, I might reverse that trend and help rededicate the women's movement to the search for feminist principles and how to live them.

I was so weak that the kids' acting out, combined with the

stress of the campaign, nearly overwhelmed me. I needed some sensible, down-to-earth help. I asked a friend from A Group of Women if she knew of a good, inexpensive, feminist counselor with whom I could have a few sessions and get things sorted out a little. She suggested another member of the group, Susan Horwitz, whose name was familiar but whose face I couldn't recall. Susan did re-evaluation counseling — "co-counseling," as it's sometimes called. And though I was pretty skeptical about re-evaluation counseling — it had an odor of the cult about it — it is an exchange of skills and is therefore free, which was very attractive. I set up an appointment with Susan.

That was in July. Susan was a gifted counselor, and with her support all through that summer and fall I dealt more confidently and effectively with the frustrations and difficulties of the NOW campaign and my relationships with my kids.

In the middle of the campaign, I received a phone call from Adele McCollum, a former Mormon patriarch's* wife, who is now an ex-Mormon and a Lesbian.

"All the Lesbians in New Jersey want to know when you're coming out," she said.

At first I thought she'd made a mistake and meant "coming up," as in "to New Jersey." I'm slow, but I finally caught on. "Well, I can't come out until I have something to come out about," I replied. "It's pretty hard to come out when you've never been in. And I don't see any signs that I'll ever be in."

"What do you mean?" she probed.

"I love us, Adele," I answered. "I love women. I much prefer our company. Probably because I have come to love myself and to prefer my own company. But the fact is, I don't find women sexually interesting. Though I don't want a male in my life, I still feel a zing when I'm around an attractive one. And I've never in my whole life felt a zing or anything approximating one around a woman, not *any* woman, no matter how

---

*"Patriarch" is the title of a high office in the church.

lovely, no matter how sexually attractive other people find her."

I told her I was willing to admit that feeling a zing around men and not around women is a patriarchally-conditioned response; that, in fact, the lack of such feeling for women is from a deadening to other women that the fathers demand of us; that the male zing is a trap and a lie; that "romance" is bunkum designed to ensnare us all deeply in society's shoddy value system; that "falling in love," as portrayed by the male-managed media, is a profoundly false and dangerous model for human relationships. I was willing to grant all that. But still, when I looked at women, I saw friends, I saw cohorts, I saw sisters, I saw collaborators. I didn't see lovers.

"No, no, no!" she laughed. "You've got it all wrong! That's not how it's going to happen to you. You're not going to look up one day and see this beautiful woman and feel a zing and fall in love and want to get married."

She went on to tell me how she thought it was more likely to happen, how it happens to lots of women. We will be working with a woman on a project, or in an organization, we see her often, get to know her well, feel comfortable around her, like and respect her. And then one day—if we're lucky—as we're working together, the thought comes into our minds, "I'd like to kiss her!" We're surprised, and glad to have been able to break through that ferocious taboo. But we're scared, too, because it's scary to defy taboos.

But then, if we're courageous enough, sooner or later we do kiss her, and we're on our way to discovering that breaking the patriarchs' law about loving another women does not bring down God's wrath upon us after all. In fact, quite the contrary. If we have chosen well, it brings a delight and an intimacy unlike any we've ever experienced—like that we always dreamed we were going to find with some man someday and never quite did.

I told her that sounded wonderful, but that it would never happen to me.

I was sure it never would. Being so sure made me feel pretty bleak, because I knew it meant that I was still so shackled by my patriarchal acculturation that I was very likely to go to my deathbed without ever having experienced the kind of closeness she spoke of. I would go celibate, too, because I was no longer willing to be sexually intimate without also being spiritually intimate, and I had come to a place in my development where no man could follow.

Rescuing sexuality from the patriarchal paradigm is not my mission in life — I wouldn't know where to begin — but rescuing myself from patriarchy *is*. My new life, this feminist life into which I've been incarnated without having had to die first physically, is all about breaking through the barriers of my conditioning to a new way of looking at the world and how to be real in it. This means that there is no possible way to get around the primary taboos that govern human interaction.

Because it has everything to do with the status of women, with keeping us in the state of dependence and servitude which is necessary for male supremacy, compulsory heterosexuality is at the top of the list of patriarchal imperatives, and homosexuality is at the top of the list of taboos.

I thought for years that bonding with women, making my primary identification with other women — the act ultimately most outrageous and maddening to the patriarchal mind — was sufficient progress for me. But I began to understand that essential to my going out of my old, joyless jail of a mind was my becoming genuinely open to loving a woman: not just affectionally, companionably, lengthily, and thoroughly, but sexually as well.

Coming to this realization was easy; regularly taking out my intellectual patriarchal garbage was a habit I developed early on in my new life. But I despaired of erasing the deep emotional imprinting of the fundamentalist Mormon church and of the America of the 1950's. I needn't have worried. Like all women, I was much more resistant to nonsense than I had thought — much more flexible, much wiser, much braver.

Looking back, I see that I was born just sexual, neither hetero nor homo. I know there are those who can remember coming out of the womb with fervent inclinations in one direction or the other, but not me.

Not long ago, while trying to recapture my earliest childhood memories of my mother, I suddenly both felt and saw myself at about six months old in her arms. She stood holding me against her breast in the bedroom of one of my earliest homes. I may have been nursing. From my position in her arms, I looked up into her face. She was so beautiful, so very, very beautiful. My heart nearly dissolved with love for her. And with sadness, because she was suffering. I could feel it as if I were she. I don't remember ever feeling love as overwhelming as I felt for her there in her arms. I have never thought anyone so beautiful as I thought her then, as she stood young and dark-haired and lovely and suffering in that room 50 years ago.

I loved all of her. I *was* all of her. She was me. I wanted nothing more than to be in her arms forever. I realized as the memory closed that I have missed her unutterably ever since I learned to walk. Missed being held against her, missed feeling her body against mine.

Is *that* perverted?

My children are all physically attractive to me, and were from the moment they were born. This doesn't mean I have felt compelled to engage in sexual behavior with them, but merely that I have always found their bodies delightful, loved to hold and snuggle and nuzzle them, often.

Is *this* perverted?

Sexuality is everything that inspires touching and caressing and holding and kissing and patting and smoothing the hair of and saying sweet things to, lonesomeness upon absence and joy upon return. It includes our physical and emotional and spiritual responses to all that is beautiful — in nature, in art, in one another, in ideas.

Though sexuality may be all this and more, about a year ago I wrote in my journal: "We don't know how to convey the best of what women's sexual experience is because all our words for passion and sexuality define *male* experience; men have had the privilege of naming, and we are left mute.

"Often—very often—books by women about women loving women sound hokey to me, wrong somehow. It must be because they're using male words and concepts."

In my early youth, boys and girls alike engaged in random sexual exploration; the sex of the participants didn't much matter. It was all just your basic Sex Education 101, a required course for everyone. Because of this, much of my early sexual experience involved investigating the fascinating and forbidden parts of my friends who were girls, as well as of my friends who were boys. Actually, I probably "played doctor" more with girls, because in those days girls pretty much played together, and boys played together, and the twain met only occasionally—in hide-and-seek, softball, bomb shelter, or "doctor."

And besides, our mamas, forgetting their own ambisexual childhoods, would let us be alone for long unsupervised hours with kids of our own gender.

In that little semi-rural Mormon town in Idaho, right under the noses of our parents, we lived, in a sense, in untrammeled nature, doing what seemed to come naturally—which was finding most other kids sexually interesting, girls and boys. Because of my youthful experience, I am strongly inclined to believe that in the best of all possible worlds, most of us would be sexually attracted to people on many more bases than gender. Gender, in fact, would probably come last, and might not matter at all—except when our purpose was to procreate. Unlike most other animals, who must rely on their instincts and sexual urges to guide them in mating, we can be guided by reason. Humans don't need overwhelming sexual desire in order to insure a continuation of the species. I know. I didn't get pregnant four times because of overwhelming sexual desire, and neither do most women. But in the meantime, this is far from being the best of all possible worlds, and in patriarchy gender has been *made* to matter, above all else.

I do not mean to imply that my youthful naivete lasted long.* By the time I was ten or eleven, I'd been thoroughly conditioned to believe that only boys were sexually and romantically interesting. Generic sexuality, as well as any sexual interest in females — or, indeed, any other kind of positive interest in us — bit the dust hard for 37 long years, during 20 of which married sex became less and less interesting and more and more lonely.

By the time I married, because of the crushing weight of guilt from the church, and also largely because of what were, in my pre-feminist days, incomprehensibly unsatisfying contacts on all levels with young men, something unrestrained and joyous had gone out of sex for me. And with every passing year I understood more clearly that though we were having what any sex therapist would have considered "good sex," genuine intimacy was impossible with my husband. We were both experiencing orgasm regularly and with no great difficulty, but the act meant very different things to each of us. Close in each others' arms, we could not find each other, and I grieved about it for two decades before feminism gave me the diagnosis. During those years, what I discovered was that few things are as lonely and boring to me as orgasm as an end in itself.

Back in 1980 the most exhilarating experience of my newly-divorced life was the discovery that I could be whole and happy without a man; that the fierce brainwashing to the contrary, which I'd sustained all my life, was not only composed of lies from start to finish, but was a total reversal of the truth: it's not women who need men, but men who need women. The slave never needs the master in order to survive and flourish; it's the master who needs the slave. One of the important offices of male culture is to keep this intelligence from both

---

*Neither do I mean to imply that in my adult life I have found that what we call "sex" with men is similar in any way to "sex" with women. They are not the same activity on any level, just as our relating generally across gender lines with men is not the same activity as relating generally with women.

master and slave, both male and female, because male supremacy depends on women's belief that we cannot do without men (though millions of us do it splendidly every day, everywhere in the world).

This all became so clear to me that I marveled constantly at how successfully propaganda had hidden it. Nothing seemed to undermine the authority of the myth that women can't do without men, including the well-documented and publicized facts that single men are less healthy, less happy, and die younger than married men, whereas single women are healthier, happier, and live longer than married women.

When the initial pain of being a principal in the world's most hackneyed plot — the wife of 20 years being dumped for a younger woman — subsided, I found to my delighted surprise that I could do very well without a husband, very well indeed. In fact, I began to suspect mightily that I could never be whole in a relationship with a man, any man — not at this time of the world, not in patriarchy.

I felt, in fact, that it would even be *immoral* of me to let a man figure centrally in my life in any sexual and intimate way. I knew that in such a situation, I could not help but be in constant reaction to his expectations and values, even if he were a "sensitive" man and struggling against the male value system himself. I sensed that such reaction would prevent my discovering, articulating, and acting upon my own female expectations and values. With the advent of feminism, to act out of my own center had become my basic morality.

I saw that emotional relationships with men are dangerous because they attach us — *fix* us — to men's reality, to patriarchy. In them we live in the thick of old, familiar, deadly patterns, either acting out or resisting our roles, never simply free to be — or to discover what we could be — without our chains and our fears. For those of us who must do the work of women in this time, it is too risky to continue to believe blindly that we can live with men without being drawn insidiously, inch by inch, back into the maelstrom.

I watched all the splinters of myself come together then, when for the first time in decades I did not have to try to please a man, did not think my thoughts and live my life always in relation to one, did not take my cues constantly from outside myself while ignoring my own authoritative inner voice. To have done so for so long, for other women still to be doing so — this seemed to me the most grossly unnatural way of being in the world, the most radically destructive of integrity. Why had I, why had we, lived like this for so long?

I'm not insisting categorically that women can't live with male lovers without automatically making concessions, though I think that on the whole this is true. Certainly, because of my 43 years of extraordinarily intense socialization, I knew I could not do it.*

I also knew I had work to do, that I had been born to do something very specifically female upon this planet, and I didn't dare compromise my female strength and integrity, didn't dare risk again giving it up in any of the thousand tiny ways I had been so thoroughly trained to give it up to a male lover.

Women's vision of how the world must and can be is just being born, and it is as difficult a birth as it is crucial to the world, fraught with dangers on every hand. Patriarchy is desperate to distract us from it, to keep our attention riveted on men. Daily it intensifies its campaign to frighten women away from one another, to persuade us that totally loving ourselves and other women is evil, to persuade us not to live in our own authentic ways.

Knowing that the purpose of feminism is to make the best of women's reality a global reality, to make the best of women's values the preeminent, guiding global values, it was not hard

---

*A quote from an article by Gloria Steinem in *Ms.* of June 1986, p. 42, "The Trouble with Rich Women," describes all women's dilemma in associating closely with men: "The closer we are to power, the more passive we must be kept. Intimacy and access make rebellion very dangerous."

to extrapolate the absolute necessity at this time in history for a critical number of women to become independent of men in every way, and independent of the culture that surrounds men like an aura; necessary for us to be independent enough to turn our entire attention to the creation of a new way of living — as womanly, as female-oriented a way as possible.

Because I understood this, I managed to keep the question of becoming emotionally involved with a man blessedly moot. I never thought of trying to meet one; the idea of "looking for a man" appalled me. I did none of the things that tell men a woman is ripe for romance. I thought no hungry thoughts of sex, gave off no musky "ready" aroma, glowed with no sheen of the huntress.

And it was no sacrifice, because I was never lonely. I was busy doing work about which I cared passionately and which kept me among interesting people much of the time. I was still being very much the mama to my four children, and I had wonderful friends.

But actually, all this is not what kept me from loneliness. I had been lonely as an adolescent, lonely all my married life, lonely with a husband and children, parents, brothers and a sister, and many friends. It took my becoming a feminist to learn that throughout that lifetime of loneliness I was lonely for myself. When feminism gave me to myself at last, that painfully insatiable loneliness finally ended.

The divorce added upon that gift by giving me the chance to discover how much I enjoyed my own company, how much I loved having myself to myself. It gave me another gift: an empty bed. I began to realize what a high old time I was having just going to bed alone every night. The unexpected relief of that took me aback at first. Right away, even while I was still grieving over the breakup of my marriage, I loved living without a man, and in particular I loved sleeping alone, feeling no pressure at all to be sexual.

To my great surprise, celibacy suited me. It gave me such incredible freedom, such a glorious, wondrous sense of wholeness. I relished every moment of being—for the first time in my life—sole owner of my body and my life. No wonder patriarchy wants all women to be married, I mused. It takes so much power from us.

I began to feel intensely protective of my body, my energy, and my time, my talents for caring and giving. Nothing could induce me to relinquish them again to someone who could not—who had in fact been *trained* not to—give me so much as interest on my principal, let alone make the same emotional investment in me as I could, and would be expected to, make daily in him. For the first time in my life I was utterly sure I deserved to be loved better than that.

What I thought all this meant was that I would have to do forever without the intimacy I had longed for and never found. I was not seriously dismayed at the thought of 40 years of celibacy ahead of me. Sex mattered very little as I rejoiced in my new intimate and loving relationship with myself. Finally having myself—the ultimate intimacy, without which none other is possible—I knew I could do without an intimate someone else forever, if need be (and need seemed to be).

I realized that now that I loved myself, I could love others better, was free to enjoy loving them without having to be "in love." Being "in love" seemed to me a torment, an addiction, a bondage. I viewed it then much as I view it now—as an aberration, a pathology necessary for maintaining patriarchy's sexual caste system—and I devoutly did not want to be "in" it ever again. I had yearned all my life to experience the *genuine* article, to *love*—which is a revolutionary act; not to be "in love"—its shoddy, exploitive, perverted, patriarchal substitute.

Although I felt a narrow chill around my heart at relinquishing my dream of a transcendent, numinous love, I reminded myself that having myself, being so happy in myself, I was incredibly rich. I persuaded myself that it would be a small sacrifice to give up hoping to learn to love here, at this time, on this planet, in the way I knew it was possible for me to love, somewhere, on some planet, in some lifetime; the kind of loving utterly lost to our patriarchal consçiousness and for lack of which all living things on this planet are now dying. In this life I would settle for transforming the earth with all the other life-loving women. That would be love affair enough.

I gave up my dream with so little struggle because I was accustomed to giving up my dreams, but also because it was taking me so long to realize that I might begin to make that dream come true right here, right now; that I might make a huge leap in my personal evolution by learning — *daring* — to free myself to love another woman. In those days, when I was still practicing saying goodbye to the dream because as yet it could encompass only a man, I often said, "Other women will have to pioneer sexual relationships. That's not what I'm about." And to myself I'd breathe, "Thank goodness!"

Two weeks before I left Virginia for the fast in May 1982, I was in Portland, Oregon, doing some speaking. Dixie Johnson, who had helped arrange the speeches and was escorting me from place to place, had learned that Mary Daly was also in town. Both of us were devoted fans of Mary's and neither of us had ever met her. Dixie was determined not to let such an opportunity slip by us, and she finagled matters so that one morning the three of us met in the restaurant of Mary's motel for breakfast.

We got there first, and ordered. Mary came in, walked over to our table with my book in her hand, laid it on the table, and before she even introduced herself, said, "I've just finished reading your book, Sonia, and I want you to know it's the most Lesbian book out there — except mine, of course."

"That's pretty intriguing," I laughed, "since I'm not a Lesbian."

"Yet," she said simply, as she slid into the booth.

Months after Mary's remark and three years after the excommunication and divorce, Susan walked quietly, shyly, unobtrusively into my life, and a little less than a year after that, Adele's and Mary's prophesies came true.

It happened one day as Susan and I were sitting in the kitchen, talking. Suddenly I realized I felt like kissing her. I could hardly believe that such an impulse had actually stirred in me, *me* of all people! I was euphoric. Maybe this meant that I could escape from patriarchy's heavily fortified prison of heterosexuality after all.

I was not, at first, overcome by desire, though I was nearly swept away by it as our experience together unfolded. I was not "falling in love," at least I was not falling into the patriarchally-induced coma called love, where women lose their identity, their autonomy, their survival instincts, their will, and their good sense. I simply recognized that I had learned to love Susan, as I loved my mother, as I loved myself, as I loved my children. And I felt the inclination to express it, in ways similar to those in which I expressed it to all of them: by touching, hugging, kissing, being physically close.

But in addition — and this was the victory — I felt the inclination to express it by making adult, sexual love with her.

I wanted my dream back — my dream of an intimacy richer and deeper than anything I had experienced, witnessed, or even imagined. I wanted after all to be in on every aspect of expanding the present dangerous limitations set on human love, which is feminism's quest. In the crunch, I couldn't resist my pioneer heritage.

I didn't say anything to Susan as we sat there in the kitchen. But later that afternoon, in the car on the way to the mall to shop, I told her I'd felt like kissing her that morning, and that I still did, not only because I had learned to love her; after all, I loved many women. But I wanted to kiss her because with her I had also somehow, miraculously, struggled free of my heterosexual straitjacket and was able — wonder of wonders — to feel sexually aroused.

From that moment to this I have never ceased to rejoice at being given this second chance at closeness, this new gift from my wise and expanding spirit to be physically intimate with women, the people I love most profoundly and with whom my destiny in this life is most inextricably interwoven.

I assured Susan that if she didn't like the idea, she should say so right away. Thank goddess, she said she'd be delighted if I should kiss her, and that she'd likely kiss me back. That evening I did, and she did. And that was the beginning of a close collaboration in all things. It was the beginning of an intimacy — on all levels — that I had stopped believing was possible years before, but had never been able to stop longing for. And it was the beginning of a sexual passion in myself I had not had intimations of since I was sixteen.

The struggle against the taboo of loving someone of the same sex had taken place unconsciously. I hadn't been aware of it at all. Who knows how long it raged in there or how fiercely. The important fact is that I was victorious over immense forces, and that I consciously chose to act on that victory. Having made the choice, I broke through the terrifying, albeit ultimately absurd, patriarchal barrier as if it were rice paper, as if it were no big deal. It was right and natural, as indeed such satisfactory, such exquisite loving would be in the ideal world. In our present benighted world, however, breaking through that barrier *is* a very big deal.

I am proud to say that I panicked only once afterward, and that only briefly. I really can't be frightened by bogeymen for very long anymore.

My discovery that I could love a woman and be physically and psychically close to her without any reserve was all I could have hoped for, but it didn't "make" me happy. For years, I had felt as if I were standing in the sunshine with all the colors of the spectrum beaming full upon me; I had been, and was, very happy. And peaceful in myself. I make myself deeply, forever happy. But being able to love Susan reinforces all that is strong and good and joyous in my life, and gives me even more zest. Being in some ways very different, we are able to teach and to learn from each other. Susan, for instance, is assertive and strong in situations where I would collapse at once. She has a fierce sense of fairness and of her own worth which has been dulled in me by years of marital subservience. She sees through cant and is characterologically unable to indulge in it herself. After years of being shut out of my husband's inner life and risking emotional betrayal at every turn, I knew the value of her honesty, her openness, her complete emotional trustworthiness. I felt the heady freedom possible only to one who has lived on a psychic mine field for 20 years. I trust I have been as valuable to her as she has been and continues to be to me.

And she is a wonderful lover, loving me the way I had dreamed of being loved all my life, loving me as only a woman knows how to love another woman. Perhaps I should say as only a woman knows how to love *anyone*. No wonder men can't do without us!

I know that woman/woman relationships can be as oppressive as man/woman relationships. I also know I could do very well, and forever, if need be, without any "relationship" at all. But loving Susan has been a profound education of the heart. I feel when I hold her as if I am holding myself, holding my mama, holding my daughter, holding all women, holding something inexpressibly beautiful and precious, something which has been lost and for which I have grieved and given up all hope of finding again. I feel connected with the best in myself, love myself extravagantly, feel whole and integrated, not split against myself as I did in marriage. I feel as if my work and my personal life are bounding forward hand in hand with double the energy, double the purpose, double the clarity and commitment. I feel incredibly augmented, widened and deepened, more of all that society had taught me to despise: more fully and gloriously female. But even now, or I should say, especially now, genital sex in and of itself—isolated from the rest of my life with Susan—means little to me. My hunch is that in the perfect natural universe, genital sex would be what it is at its best in this: just one of a myriad of ways of expressing and deepening an otherwise nearly inexpressible connection.

Heaven knows that patriarchy, in basing the entire power structure upon sexuality, in making everything contingent upon the gender one is, has muddled and corrupted sexual love almost beyond redemption. Patriarchy has killed off in many of us the rich, ripe sensuousness and voluptuousness that might possibly prevail in the perfect, natural universe if patriarchy were — oh lovely thought! — to drop dead this afternoon.

Or it could be that, in the perfect, natural universe, intimacy could be fully expressed with kindness, closeness, stroking, touching, hugging, decency, kissing, cooing, laughing, fondling, thoughtfulness, nuzzling, tumbling, generosity, trustworthiness, and goodness, with only an occasional foray into orgasm.

Or other possibilities. Or any combination of them.

Just recently I read of a study that compared the frequency of genital activity in a number of groups. Lesbians "had sex" (sic) far less often than members of any other group. That makes sense to me. Between women there is less necessity to maintain dominance through sex than there is with men. Because of our conditioning (and perhaps our "nature"?), women are more likely to be more affectionate, more tender, more thoughtful and loving toward one another more of the time — not just in bed — than men are toward either women or men, which decreases the urgency to establish some closeness, to make some kind of human contact, through "having sex." I know from my own experience that women don't need to experience genital activity with one another often or at all to experience genuine intimacy.

A woman in California also read this study and wrote to me: "It seems to me that Lesbian sex is such that it would be hard to fit it into these researchers' criteria (as in 'are we having it now?'). My lover's and my sexual expressions are much more along a continuum than anything I ever had with men. For instance, we might kiss deeply for five minutes, then go to work. Or we might roll around in bed and kiss and touch, then talk and cuddle, then get up and make breakfast, then get back into bed and cuddle and kiss and talk and touch some more. So is that all 'having sex' except the breakfast? Part of the problem with that research is that Lesbians don't just have one 'it.' Because our sex isn't goal-oriented (orgasm-oriented), it's hard to say when we're having it. On the whole, men just want to do 'it.' If it won't end in orgasm, they don't want to waste time with it."

I know I need hardly point out that not all Lesbians are perfect. I remember, in that phone conversation with Adele in July 1982, crashing up against my anger at the stereotyped behavior of certain women. I complained to her about some women I had watched at NOW dances ogling other women, looking them up and down slowly and suggestively — the male meat-market approach. I had been furious at this objectification of women by women, more furious than I had ever been at men for the same behavior.

I stormed to Adele that women should *know* better! We've been on the receiving end of that dehumanizing, degrading leer. I told her I knew that the most oppressed people most ape the ways of their oppressors, but that I couldn't help feeling enraged at such obvious disregard for the dynamics of oppression, at such open collaboration with patriarchy against ourselves.

She tried to calm me by reminding me that not all Lesbians understand the ramifications of this behavior because not all Lesbians are feminists.

But that was so ironic, so contradictory, it hardly made sense to me. Clearly we needed a different name for Lesbians who are feminists than for those who are not. Finding women sexually attractive has nothing to do with feminism; most men find women sexually attractive. But deeply admiring and appreciating women, dedicating oneself to their welfare, giving them and their values, their ways of being in the world, one's full, first, and total loyalty no matter what — this is the basis of feminism. I told Adele that to me, women who do this, whether they are interacting sexually with women or not, are Lesbians, but I didn't know what to call the others.

"How about 'gay'?" she proposed.

This distinction, which may seem artificial and even offensive to some, was, and still is, necessary for me. It is what finally allowed me to take upon myself the label Lesbian, and to continue to wear it. I could not do this with "gay," a word and concept with which nothing in my experience prepares me to identify.

111

Adele tried to tell me that day that loving women was different for us former long-time heterosexuals, but she didn't make clear how different, or in how many ways. She didn't tell me there may be almost as many varieties of Lesbian experience as there are individual women. It has taken me some time, for instance, to learn from experience that, as a newcomer, I don't and can't share the feelings of the old-timers. At first, when I discovered that I couldn't participate in their feelings of persecution (because they *were* and *are* persecuted), and of courage in being open, I castigated myself for homophobia.

When I casually mentioned at the 1984 West Coast Women's Music Festival that I loved a woman and the whole crowd cheered as if I'd made some momentous statement, I not only couldn't at first think what I'd said that could have elicited such a response, I even felt unaccountably sad. Thinking about it later, I realized that the response to my announcement was very complex — on both sides. Surely the primary feeling was one of happiness for me, that I would no longer have to be alone. There also seemed to be a feeling of reaffirmation, almost vindication; all oppressed people need evidence that the way they are is acceptable and desirable. The commotion may also have been a shout of celebration, because as dangerous as I was to patriarchy celibate, I was even more dangerous as a Lesbian.

But the applause hurt momentarily, too, because it seemed to invalidate who I had been before, which was a feminist of significant seriousness, commitment, and depth. I knew that any such feeling was certainly not intended by that very loving crowd. Nevertheless, I felt that at least a little of their welcome sprang from internalized oppression, the inner compulsion that encourages us to divide ourselves into factions, all equally certain of our inherent rightness and "purity." I felt, uncomfortably, that though I had been for many years deeply Lesbian in the ways that genuinely matter, it was only in having sex with a woman that I had become totally acceptable to them. Those women were claiming me now, now that I had

112

taken upon myself Lesbian oppression. But I had *always* claimed them, and I hadn't known until that moment that I hadn't been completely accepted in return. I was distressed by this evidence of the barriers we allow patriarchy to erect between us.

Intellectually, I understood very well the difficulty as well as the necessity of being visible, of proclaiming proudly to the world, "I am a Lesbian!" I understood it because I felt the same necessity to be visible and proud as a feminist. I recognized it as the first step out of the oppression. But whereas I felt passionate about proclaiming my feminism, I felt no corresponding imperative about proclaiming myself a Lesbian.

"You're afraid," I chided myself. "And ashamed. You're a homophobe." But though I'm sure this was part of it, it didn't explain it all. Only recently have I begun to figure out why I have trouble identifying with the feelings of other Lesbians. First of all, having been "in the closet" only during my campaign for President, and then primarily to the press, my experience of "coming out" of it was far less agonizing than it has been for some. By that I mean that I have never been directly and blatantly oppressed because of loving another woman. Of course, I'm very new to this. I'm sure it will come in time, and certainly this book will hasten it along. But no one has threatened to take my children from me, for instance, nor was my mother unduly horrified when I told her I loved Susan. Her feelings toward me didn't change when I told her; she knows I am a good person. In short, unlike my Lesbian sisters who have suffered years of the anguish of invisibility, of being disowned by family, of losing jobs and children, of being harassed by bigots, I have, as yet, felt little pain.

On the contrary, almost from the first I have been blessed in loving Susan. It has not been life-threatening to me in any way, on any level; it has only been life-enhancing. And I doubt whether, at this point in my life, *any* amount of persecution could cause me nearly the distress it would have in my youth — and therefore could now — if I had grown up with a fearful secret, feeling an incomprehensible, unmodeled, socially unacceptable *difference*, as so many of my Lesbian sisters did. My friend Linda Barufaldi suggests that this is not just because of my age, but because of my extraordinary experiences. "You had gone through the excommunication, the civil disobedience, and the fast, and lost your fear in a way that is almost unique in womanhood. I recall a story about Fannie Lou Hamer, the civil rights activist, saying a similar thing after she had been beaten within an inch of her life by cops—that the worst had been done to her, that they made a mistake in *not* finishing her off because now she feared *nothing*, not even death."

As it was, I didn't feel the slightest physical tug toward a woman until I was nearly 50 years old and my feelings about myself were pretty firmly formed and set. And I've felt it for only one woman. (I still don't feel a "zing" around attractive women, and may never. But then, neither do I any longer feel that way around attractive men. I must say it's a relief.) I doubt that public opinion can wound me now as it had power to wound when I was 16 or 20 or even 30. I am now a half-century old. I have by this time largely cut myself free of the weight and pull of other people's opinions—which is one of the graces of growing old.

And so, though I am grateful for their long, courageous struggle to be whole, which makes my loving a woman as easy now as it is, I can't share the feelings of life-long Lesbians or be thought to speak for them. Our entire life experience, as well as our Lesbian experience, has been so different it should hardly surprise anyone that our feelings about it are also different. But my experience is common, and becoming more so, and those who have had it will hear their voices here; in speaking for myself I know I speak for them, too.

This inability to share the intensity that a lifetime of oppression as a Lesbian often generates has made my education slow. For years, for instance, I was put off by the expression "coming out." Jargon always offends my sense of style. But I suspected that in this case homophobia might be adding to my aversion to the term. So I thought about it, and as I did, I realized that one obvious reason I didn't relate to it was because it was short for "come out of the closet," an experience I had never had and thought I never would have.

But even before Susan's advent into my life, I came to understand that "coming out" meant more than "out of the closet." It meant out of the mainstream, out of social approval, out of the known world into no-person's land, out of privilege, out of respect, out of a job, out of parenthood, out of a place to live, out of physical safety, out of the Constitution, out of favor with god, out of sanity. With this realization, "coming out" won my tolerance and respect.

I might be at ease and unthreatened about loving a woman, but I know it is not a casual matter. I know it is serious and important. But Lesbian politics — by which I mean the struggle for specific rights denied women because they are sexual with other women — are not my primary focus. Women's civil rights in general are no longer my focus. Feminism — the most inclusive and descriptive analysis of the human situation in written history — this is my work, and it includes *all* women, all life.

Most devoutly I do not want to be perceived as being on one "side" or the other, though I'm aware that this is wishful thinking. Patriarchy has won another round in pitting us against one another in the women's movement. If on the one hand a woman admits to being heterosexual, she earns the dismissal of many Lesbians, who perceive her as still shackled, still unfree, still giving her time and energy to men, not yet thoroughly feminist, oppressive to Lesbians. At the same time, many heterosexual women hail her as the perfect answer to the prevailing propaganda that all feminists are bulldykes. They are relieved that they can continue to identify with her.

On the other hand, if she admits to being Lesbian, heterosexual women have a tendency to view her suddenly as a traitor, as incomprehensible, and especially as weak-kneed: she hasn't had the gumption to hold on to her principles, but has been swept away by the ideological tide, which is bad, or by her gonads, which is worse. (The ideological tide being Ti Grace Atkinsons' assertion that "feminism is the theory, lesbianism is the practice." Having practiced feminism for years before I was what society officially considers a Lesbian, I can only accept this statement as long as it is understood to refer to all gyn/affectionate women,[1] women who put women first). The Lesbians, however, are apt to greet her with almost religious fervor, as if she were proving a hard-fought point. "You see, world?" they seem to say defiantly.

See what?

And the ambisexuals, the bisexuals among us, what about them? Well, being neither fish nor fowl (and one must be either fish or fowl in patriarchy; dichotomous thought doesn't allow for more than two choices), their existence is either ignored, or, if acknowledged, spurned. Neither Lesbians nor heterosexual women know what to make of them. Both "sides" feel betrayed.

I can't express how thoroughly I detest this acting out of our internalized oppression, how thoroughly I know that it bodes ill for all women, and therefore for all life, and how thoroughly and soon we must all go out of this mind.

On the fast, where the Lesbian/non-Lesbian split could have been disastrous, we inadvertently found a way to neutralize the tension that springs up around choices of sexual expression. While we were getting ourselves arranged to sleep that very first night in Kumler Methodist Church, I blundered into a conversation between Dina and Zoe, and overheard Zoe referring to Dina and herself as "radical lemons"—or so I thought. I burst into laughter. "Now I've heard everything," I gasped. "I know about radical feminists, but radical lemons! Really, even coming from California, that's too much!"

"What are you talking about?" Dina asked, puzzled.

It turned out, of course, that Zoe had not said "radical lemons" at all. Who would say radical lemons? What I had thought were insurrectionary citrus turned out to be "radical lesbian feminists."

116

'Well," I mused, when we finished laughing, "if you two are lemons, I suppose I'm a lime." And from that night to the end of the fast, we all referred to Lesbians as lemons and heterosexual women as limes. Though we hadn't thought it through or understood in advance the effect this would have on our relationships, it turned out to be the one best tension-reducer among us — and we needed all the tension-reducers we could get.

We needed them because as well as setting whole groups at each others' throats, patriarchy creates factions within each oppressed group, and sets members against one another. The destructiveness within the women's movement caused by distrust between women of different sexual preferences is as widespread and predictable as it is sad and unnecessary. But it is hard to polarize lemons and limes; they are too similar, their differences cannot be blown out of proportion and made the basis for suspicion and enmity.

From that night on we were simply lemons and limes, all equally tart, trenchant, piquant, and keen; all equally stinging and caustic to the taste buds of a public accustomed to blandness in women, to our being bread — mild, predictable, ordinary, and tame.

I have used the terms "lemon" and "lime" for this purpose ever since. They are great levelers and uniters, and make clear that what patriarchy would like us to believe are irremedial differences between Lesbians and heterosexual women are, in fact, hardly differences at all. Many lemons have been limes; many limes will yet be lemons. We are all sisters, and we are all under penalty of death. As Andrea Dworkin writes in *Right-wing Women*:

> One other discipline is essential both to the practice of feminism and to its theoretical integrity: the firm, unsentimental, continuous recognition that women are a class having a common condition . . . This definition cannot exclude prudes or sluts or

> dykes or mothers or virgins because one does not want
> to be associated with them . . . There is no real femi-
> nism that does not have at its heart the tempering dis-
> cipline of sex-consciousness: knowing that women
> share a common condition as a class, like it or not.[2]

I don't want to imply that calling ourselves lemons and
limes dispelled all tension that built up around sexuality in our
group, because it didn't; internalized oppression is stronger
than citric acid. Any time we had a serious difference of philosophy, we still found ourselves lined up as lemons and limes, not
because the matter really fell out that way, but because that
polarization was so strongly programmed into us.

All our designations for ourselves as women have been defined and attached to us by patriarchy: "mother," "whore,"
"Lesbian," "virgin." Since words are congealed energy and so
have a life of their own, in passionately rejecting or reclaiming
our "names," we add our energy and power to them, in addition to the energy and power of the men which already per-
meates them. In this way, the words become highly charged
with very contradictory and turbulent energies.

I am not saying that we ought not to use these words, only
that we must be aware and wary of the dangers inherent in taking into ourselves the fathers' female-hating energy which inexorably attends them, which is there whether we deny it or not,
and which subliminally buttresses our internalized oppression
and encourages division among us, whether we like it or not.
When we press the word "Lesbian" to our breasts, we are
clutching an asp, and for us to think that it does not bite and
poison us — does not reduce and limit us *in our own minds* nor
turn us from our sisters — is to be dangerously naive. This is the
reason, I believe, that Blacks dropped the term "Negro." Too
much damaging White energy clung to it, too much slave odor,
which would have continued to reinforce their feelings of inferiority, their internalized oppression as Blacks, even if they were
not conscious of it as it happened.

But the energy of the words "lemon" and "lime," needing to be neither rejected nor reclaimed, was simple and calming. In those difficult days, all of us being citrus fruit helped immeasurably to keep us from the fatal, irreparable split that patriarchy had set us up for.

Like most activist daughters, I have always tried to help my mother understand those concepts which over the years have come to mean most to me, and my motivation for being "scandalous" and making life difficult for her amidst the Mormons in Logan, Utah. But when she came for her annual visit in the summer of 1983, other events and other women took over the role of teacher.

The boxes were still stacked all over Susan's and my new townhouse and we were immersed in plans for Women Gathering, when we dropped everything, hopped into a borrowed van — Susan, Mary Ann Beall, Mother, my nine-year-old son, Noel, and I — and headed up to the Women's Encampment for Peace and Justice in Romulus, New York. A mammoth demonstration, including civil disobedience, was being planned for the first week in August. We wanted to be a part of it, and to get to the camp a little early, get situated, do a Gathering workshop, and find how we could help.

We arrived early in the evening. Walking to the house over the deeply rutted field in which we'd parked, Mary Ann turned her ankle and broke it, and the women put her in a tiny back room in the house for treatment. My mother and I went to visit her, and as we came around the back of the house, there in the grass at our feet lay three women, kissing and tussling and rolling about. My prim mother lost her savoir faire on the spot. She stopped in her tracks and gaped. The women on the grass took no notice whatever. I laughed and said, "Mom, if you don't shut your mouth soon, you're going to start drooling!" Even that didn't break her trance. She was dumfounded, stupefied, shocked to the core.

The next night, we sat in a meeting which at least one woman attended bare breasted (no men were allowed in the camp). She was a big woman and her breasts had much presence. My mother was uncomfortably aware all evening that a half-naked woman was in our midst. The culture shock for a 77-year-old Mormon woman was severe.

During the NOW campaign the year before, the Associated Press had sent a story about me over the wire, and my hometown newspaper had picked it up. In it, I mention reproductive freedom and Lesbian rights as part of NOW's agenda. Mom called me up right away. "Sonia," she moaned. "Do you *have* to say those things?" "Of course," I answered. "How could I *not*?" "But they're *perverts!*" she cried, which told me it was Lesbianism, not abortion, that was most horrifying her.

It made me angry, though I was still many months away from having cause to be defensive on my own behalf. "Mom," I said, struggling against my intolerance of her intolerance. "Let's talk about perversion. I'll tell you what I think it is. Think of Bea. You and I have watched her go to bed every night with a man who has psychologically abused her from morning to night for over half a century, a man she has neither loved nor respected since the first year she married him. To my way of thinking, that's perversion. Do you still want to talk about perverts?"

"How are the children?" she asked brightly.

"Everyone's fine, Mama," I said, grinning, and thought that she was unlikely to talk to me about "perversion" again for a long time.

Then at the Peace Camp, events threw Mom almost literally into the arms of a dozen lovely women — ironically enough, all Lesbians. Susan and I were arrested in nearby Waterloo, and Mom and Noel were on their own in a strange place with exceedingly exotic mores. Some friends of mine rallied to her aid and took her under their wings for the five days we were in jail. From the sound of it, she spent the entire time asking them questions about their Lesbian lives.

Some women worried about her sudden exposure to a point of view so alien and bizarre as Lesbianism was certain to seem to her. I said, "My mother is a wonderful, strong woman. Don't matronize her. Tell her what she wants to know. It can only do her good." I believe such information can do only good for everyone.

At the Gathering a few weeks later, I'd catch glimpses of her sitting here and there, on this step, at that table, questioning one Lesbian after another. Her greatest stumbling block — after God, of course — was simply understanding *why*. The women were very patient and loving with her. And finally, one of them said the thing that made the sun break through the clouds.

"Ida," she said, "think of it more as an affectional than a sexual preference."

"Oh!" Mom brightened. "Oh, I can understand that!"

And she told the woman about discussions women had had now and again throughout her life in which they commiserated with one another about not being able to show affection to their husbands without touching off a march to the bedroom. She knew that many women wished they could just cuddle and "smooch" without further expectations as they had before they were married.

She went home that summer a changed woman with no one to talk to about it. No one at all. She'd finally even been able to say the "L" word, but knew she couldn't breathe it in Logan or she'd be triple damned. (She was already damned for supporting the ERA, and for having had the nerve to give birth to me.) She knew that even her pro-ERA friends — and she had one or two loyal friends — would be horrified by any hint of what she had learned about non-patriarchal women's views of sexuality.

So there she sat, in that little self-righteous fundamentalist town with all those questions, all that new knowledge about women's lives racing about in her head, and no place to put it or any way to sort it out. So — she told me when I called — mostly she just didn't think about it.

When I went home briefly in the fall, I told her I loved Susan, and that I was peaceful and happy. She was deeply

troubled, but she knew there was no holding me with patriarchal reins any longer, so she didn't try. I talked of the affection-
ateness of it, the comfort, the companionship, the intimacy of
the soul, all of which she knew most women had been deprived
of in their marriages, as I had been in mine.

I wasn't saying that all heterosexual relationships are bad
and all Lesbian ones good. I was saying that what makes relationships good or bad is how people treat one another. The
majority of any kind of "marriage" leaves a great deal to be de-
sired, because the state of the art of loving is embryonic, and
will remain so until the great power imbalance that is rocking
the world is righted.

She was afraid word of my depravity would get out. What
the neighbors think is very important in Logan, Utah. Being
accustomed to being misunderstood and calumniated, I only
cared what the neighbors thought for her sake. Unfortunately,
her "Christian" neighbors have not been kind.

I must admit I do mind a little that the leaders of the Mormon church can now say to the membership, "You see? We
told you there was more to the excommunication than we could
reveal at the time. We did our best to protect her reputation.
But now, despite our efforts, the word is out and we can admit
that, yes, this is the reason we excommunicated her."

Nonsense, of course. Believe me, if they'd had the tiniest
inkling of even the slightest infraction of what they regard as
"morality," which is often profoundly immoral, they'd have
leapt upon it publicly so fast they would have appeared as mere
blurs to the eye.

But of course they can maintain that this propensity for
evil was evident and alarmed them even then, and that by defy-
ing church leaders and cutting myself off from the light, I
turned myself over to Satan. (I'm certain that Satan — in Christian myth *very* male — is horrified by the female power generated in strong Lesbian unions, and not only refuses credit for
them, but is working against them side by side with Yahweh.
Politics makes strange bedfellows.)

What I mind most, however, is that the brethren will now use me as even more of a whip to keep Mormon women in line, insisting on the outright lie that feminism is always the preface to Lesbianism, thus further preventing my sisters from risking the hazardous cliff-face and the promised land.

In my first book, *From Housewife to Heretic*, I stated categorically, "I am hopelessly heterosexual." When I wrote that in 1980, I was absolutely certain of it. I could have sworn it was true.

Fortunately, I lied. No woman on earth is hopelessly heterosexual.

The decision to throw in my lot with women completely, to give them my whole allegiance — the ultimate subversion in patriarchy — was deliberate and of the highest seriousness. I had known for some time that if I could outwit my patriarchal superego, I might open the windows of my spirit to incredibly fecund vistas, and I was aware that I was going to need that nourishment before I was finished.

A very successful businesswoman said to me, after reading this book and finding the Lesbianism "gratuitous": "A couple of years ago I made the decision not to chose Lesbianism as a lifestyle because I knew I couldn't be what I wanted to be in the corporate world as a Lesbian." And probably, I might add, not as a woman-identified woman, either.

It's funny how heterosexuals have lives and the rest of us have "lifestyles." To me, loving another woman, loving women, is not a "lifestyle"; it is my life. I couldn't be who I want and need to be and not be a Lesbian.

It gives me incredible hope for the world that I was able to give my love and trust openly to another women, despite the most consummate brainwashing with the twin patriarchal doctrines of revulsion for women and eternal damnation for refusing to worship men, and despite the fear of public outrage. It persuades me that other women also have the great good sense and the courage to do whatever is demanded by our planet's peril.

Though I'm not proposing that all feminists immediately become Lesbians, such a fantasy is most refreshing to the soul. Because it is the way of being in the world that is most destructive of male supremacy, Lesbianism is highest treason. For women to take our energy and attention, our sexuality, our primary loyalty, our deepest affinity out of the service of men and to bestow it all, all this richness, all our treasure, upon women, is the most powerful subversion of patriarchy possible on earth.

I'm not proposing that all women become Lesbians (although if they all became feminists the universe would swoon with relief). That is not the point. The point is that my life, and the lives of countless women like me all over the world, prove that the global patriarchal mind is dying, that we are rapidly growing out of it, leaving it behind to strangle in the dust.

Abandoning the patriarchal mind, we consign it to oblivion. So that, after all and despite everything, we and all other living things may escape with our lives.

6

The Think Tank

I ran for the presidency of NOW. The other candidates stood for reform and white gloves and making the men respect us. Because I didn't — and perhaps for other reasons as well — I lost.

And was left with the disquieting knowledge that the thousands of women across the country who had courageously set sail into the unknown, searching for routes to the new world, now had no hope of receiving help from the National Organization for Women. (Though it seems impossible, the other women's organizations were even more in thrall to patriarchy.)

I knew hundreds of these women personally, and had lists of hundreds more who knew me and wanted to be apprised of any progress I made toward expanding the map of the possible. Many feminist speakers and performers have such contacts and such lists, and like some of them — Alix Dobkin comes immediately to mind — I felt a responsibility somehow to link women who were on similar odysseys. And I felt a responsibility to imagine at least a first step toward freedom, as any of us should who knows the necessity to and can for even a second escape from the prison of patriarchal thought.

I had never at any time been interested in forming a new organization, and was even less interested in doing so at this point. Neither I nor anyone else I knew was clear enough about alternatives to existing hierarchical structure to avoid the same pits into which the feminism of the present women's organizations had plunged to its death. Of course, we all knew that centralizing power in a national office, usually around some charismatic figure, was the very essence of all that has gone so awry in the world. But it seemed to me also that *all* the ideas we had of any kind of organizing were patriarchal.

Take networks, for instance. Everybody was saying "networks." Like spiderwebs — loose, autonomous, but connected strands of silken power. "But," I thought, "a spider sits in the middle of the web, and out of one spider comes the strands. Now, if we could spin a web of ideas out of a *vision* that sat in the center . . . !"

"But that's just the problem," I thought. "Any feminist 'organization,' or 'network' or 'web,' presupposes a common objective, a shared and unifying vision of the planetary — perhaps even the cosmic — significance of the women's movement, of its purpose, its destiny, and how it translates in individual lives." I saw no evidence of such a vision.

Obviously, whatever we did would require the courage to dream a bigger dream than "equal rights" in a morally corrupt world system, a far more daring dream than women had dreamed for centuries. And it had to be a dream dreamed together. How could we dream such a dream together?

Goddess forbid that I should organize yet another "conference" to try to figure it out! I was afraid I might expire, flop right over into my stuffed chicken breast and peas, if I ever attended another conference — with a keynote speaker, panels, workshops, discussion groups. Perhaps I had to take part of the blame myself. After all, I had been that keynote speaker, on those panels, led those workshops, though I'd also been in countless audiences while others did it. And all in all, I had concluded that if you've been to one conference, you've been to them all, at least in getting any help in traversing the wilds of unexplored possibility, which is what I always craved.

What conferences like these *can* do at their best is to hearten and inspire everyone, make life more bearable for a while. This is obviously necessary and important work. But they are not places where women are incited to hazard outrageous and prodigious thoughts, nor stunned by visions of new and powerful ways to be women (as opposed to being female impersonators). Everything is careful and correct. Caution is the byword. Any dreams that slip through the security system are little dreams, pale, puny dreams. I often feel like leaping onto the head table and springing for the chandelier, just to wake everybody out of their conference-induced propriety/stupor. No, I didn't want to organize a "conference." But what other way could I begin?

"Begin on a small scale," I cautioned myself. "Get together a group of a dozen or two women first, a group to brainstorm. But which women? And how to brainstorm?"

Here my own hierarchical acculturation took over. "Why, the leaders of the women's movement, of course!" I answered myself. What I meant by "leaders" were those who had been there from the first, who had not been blatantly co-opted by the system, who, at least at one time, had seen clearly and had courage.

I wasn't alone in being blind to the patriarchal tendencies in myself. Susan had participated equally in the almost unceasing discussion, and she also hadn't seen the irony of our operating out of the very paradigm of power we were organizing at that moment to supplant.

So, blithely, we began to make a list of what we affectionately called "famous feminists." Or at least "important" women in the movement — writers, artists, academics, activists. After we'd tracked down their telephone numbers, I started talking to them about the "think tank" we were creating, the first meeting of which would be in San Jose, California, at a friend's ranch, over the weekend of February 19, 1983. (The term "think tank" should have alerted us immediately that we were still in the masculine mode.)

"All over the country," I told them, "feminists are feeling as if the women's movement has stopped moving forward, that it is making, at best, tangential, diffuse, uncoordinated, and unsustained forays, and that most organized feminist effort is going into shoring up a corrupt and dysfunctional political system. At this point, many of us don't know where to put our substantial energies and hope. We continue to work in electoral politics, to run rape crisis centers and battered women's centers, to organize against militarism, to teach, to write, to speak, but we do these things always feeling fragmented and powerless.

"We are asking for new ways of looking at ourselves and at the possibilities for transforming society — not for making mere cosmetic repairs. If there is discouragement, it's because we have thought the same ideas over and over again and cannot seem to step off the intellectual treadmill into some creative place.

"We need to get together and think. We need to bring the theory we have together in some way, and out of this wholeness, see the next step, see the way to begin, not simply reacting to the old system but acting to construct a whole new one."

If I sensed agreement up to this point, I took the plunge. "I think the women's movement is foundering in some very fundamental way," I continued. "This is not just a hiatus, a time between the ERA struggle and whatever comes next. The hopelessness and despair we feel cannot be attributed solely to our fatigue and need for rest. It means we have lost our moorings. Nothing appears to be on the agenda for the future but more frenetic effort to maintain the illusion that we are making progress. But the fact is, we are continuing, out of habit and because we have no vision, in a direction that has proved sterile time and time again, using methods that cannot — because they do not have inherent in them the power to — transform the world.

"And any other goal is too small. Any other goal is unacceptable."

Everyone I spoke to agreed, or at least I thought they agreed. (This should have made me suspicious at once, but I was laboring under heavy illusions.) Anyway, I *heard* agreement, though they might insist that they did not agree even then, as they certainly did not agree later on. Perhaps I simply assumed they would agree because what I was saying seemed to me so self-evident.

As I think back upon it now, it seems to me that they did undoubtedly feel a lack that they may have perceived me as addressing, a zero at the core, the center's not holding. Perhaps they heard me foremost with their despair instead of with their hope.

Whatever the case, I finally had a roster of those who were to participate. In the confirmation letter I sent them, I said in part that by assembling in San Jose, we were giving ourselves permission to stop and think. "We need to think out to the edges of this continuum. . . . to postulate Utopia. We need to make the sort of imaginative leaps that push out boundaries."

I asked them to begin the search, in the month before we met, for answers to such questions as: what is our vision of the ideal? Can any part of it be brought into existence in the near future? What do we need to change to bring it about? How can we make these changes? How do we get around the ultimate problem of vested interest and power? Can some kind of ongoing think tank for feminism be established? How can we involve many women in seeking the answers to these questions in a meaningful way? Can we conceive of a new method of affiliation that leaves behind some of the worst aspects of organizations?[1] Very good questions all, but not yet the right one.

Then, having got this far in our planning, Susan and I asked ourselves, "What are we going to do when we get there?" Fortunately, Susan knew a brainstorming technique called "think and listen." Months later when I was explaining to Mary Daly how "think and listen" worked, she told me that Nelle

Morton had described the same process in her 1972 essay, "The Rising Woman Consciousness in a Male Language Structure,"[2] only calling it instead, "hearing into speech," or "hearing into being." Finding "hearing into being" a much more felicitous description of what happens in this process, I immediately adopted that name for it.

The process itself is very simple — feminists will recognize it as having some of the best characteristics of consciousness raising (CR) as it was done early in the movement: no interruption or evaluation is allowed. With time and use I came to appreciate the very complex genius of this process. As a brainstorming measure, it has no peer, and it is the perfect mode for addressing questions such as those I posed to the women who were to meet in San Jose.

It works best in a group of three that has an hour and a half at its disposal. Everyone in the group has equal time to talk — in this case, a half hour each — uninterrupted and without evaluation. This is a revolutionary experience for some women. Being seriously and completely listened to, being genuinely heard, hardly ever happens to women in ordinary everyday life. Many women cry the first time they try this process. Their being so avidly heard in the present causes them to realize how deeply they have been wounded by being ignored and disregarded, shut up, talked over, and found inconsequential or amusing during most of their past lives.

It is also often the first time women have ever listened to somebody else for a half hour or so without responding, without murmuring, "Oh yeah?," "I see," "Um hum," "I know how you feel," at appropriate intervals. Or laughing, or making sympathetic noises. It is often the first time they have ever listened to somebody else without allowing their facial expressions to communicate understanding, puzzlement, disagreement, or a host of other reactions. It is not easy for women to learn not to respond. We are thoroughly conditioned to respond. We *always* respond. That is one of our roles in patriarchy — to be the responders, the chorus. Men talk, and we nod and say breathlessly, "Then what happened?" or "Oh, yes, I'd love to hear about your childhood rock collection!" Our children have legitimate needs for our attention. They need to have us laugh when they're witty or cluck with dismay when they tell us their woes. Our faces are infinitely plastic: we are required to register admiration, servility, sympathy, concern, sorrow, and understanding all day long every day. We almost cannot *not* respond by this time in our lives. We almost cannot allow somebody to set forth upon this quest for their own ideas in our presence without our solicitous questions and reassurances, our reactions stamped clearly on our visages, our oohings and aahings — we are such active listeners. When we first try to listen passively to others, some of us feel like traitors; we feel as if we're doing something illegal, as if we might be arrested for it any moment.

And because as women we have been taught to be primarily outer- or other-directed, we in our turn as speakers have come to rely on the cues our listeners give us, the little "I'm listening" noises they make, to judge where we are in their estimation, and where our discourse should move next if we are to win their approval, consolidate their sympathy, etc. Some of us become very disoriented without constant feedback. We even get angry; we feel as if a right is being denied us, even that we are being deliberately humiliated by being made to function without the usual social lubrication.

But in Hearing into Being, for every participant's sake, listeners and talkers must break their addiction to response and evaluation. The process works, if we will just give quiet attention and the speaker can just forget about us.

The reason for the nonevaluation, the nonresponse, is that evaluation and response make storming our brain's barricades impossible. Most of the time that we are conversing with people, we know we have to hurry and make our point before they break in to make theirs. Even as we're talking, they're judging what we're saying, how close we are to being finished, shaking or nodding their heads, and making impatient little gestures that tell us they're getting ready for their turn. Always being acutely aware of how little time we have before we're going to be interrupted, we focus very narrowly and exclusively upon the point we're making. We can't afford to extrapolate, to associate, to let extraneous thoughts claim our attention.

What's happening while we're concentrating and talking on this one subject, however, is that a lot of related material is emptying out of our mental files, as well as other ideas that are sparked simply by the fact that we're thinking, our mental sap is running. The mind doesn't just hand us evidence to support the one idea we're concerned with at the moment; we single it out from lots of other information. These other ideas, fragments of ideas, and musings are competing for center stage, but because we're so focused, we can't hear them begging from the wings to be let into the act. They seem irrelevant to our argument; they're not going to help us convert these people.

But when we are free to talk without threat of interruption, evaluation, and the pressure of time; when our listeners are attentive and interested, nonjudgmental, and not waiting impatiently for a chance to rebut or agree, or just to say their piece; when we don't have to defend what we say, now or ever; when we don't have to persuade anyone; when we don't have to elaborate upon it to help someone understand (because it doesn't matter whether they understand or not; this is personal, not *inter*-personal, communication) — when all these conditions are met, we move quickly past known territory out onto the frontiers of our thought.

Knowing that no one but us is going to say one single sound for that half hour, no matter what, helps us relax our minds. And when we relax, we can begin to hear and explore the other ideas that are clamoring to be heard. We begin to notice that there are hoards and flocks of them. We are astonished at how fast and how thickly they are rushing upon us. Sometimes we think, "Oh, I can't get all this organized. I can't talk about it because I won't be able to be logical; I won't make sense." But since it doesn't matter whether it makes sense, since

132

whether anyone understands it or not is irrelevant, we can say it however we can, however we want—stream of consciousness, free association, elliptical, disjointed. The important thing is that we are rolling, and pushing out the boundaries, beginning to explore our deeper mind where we know so much more than we know we know, so much that we never get to consider because we're always staying on the surface explaining the same ideas over and over again.

This is a powerful process. Being heard in this way lets us peel off layers of our minds, come closer and closer to what I call our wise old woman's mind. We may not have an epiphany in the first half hour, although every time I've been with a group doing Hearing into Being, most women have been amazed at themselves the first half hour. They have hardly been able to believe they are the source of such fascinating insights. But if exciting ideas don't occur to us in the first half hour, they almost certainly will in the second, and by the end of the third session, women realize that what they thought they knew, and how intelligent they thought they were, was the merest beginning.

The kind of free-wheeling thought this process aims for can only emerge in the absence of all interference, no matter how well meaning. Any evaluation, even praise, hangs us up at that level. Perhaps *especially* praise. Since a little praise whets our appetites, we tailor what we say to get more. We also fashion our discourse to bring down raised eyebrows, or to change looks of disagreement or perplexity. Almost every facial expression, except pleasant interest, detours us quickly right back into familiar territory.

Although Hearing into Being is of highest value for brainstorming, for coming up with many and varied ideas, for making connections, putting everything together and coming up with something new, from the beginning I understood and liked another aspect of it even more: it eliminates competitive talking, one of the major pleasures in men's culture. Samuel Johnson's dinner party talk may have exceeded the norm in degree, but not in kind (or should I say "unkind.")

I must confess before I go any further that I'd always loved to talk competitively myself. I thought I found it stimulating. I discovered instead that it was merely gratifying to my ego.

But Susan, who is intelligent and wise in non-competitive situations, simply cannot and will not participate in ordinary interruptive, judgmental, talk-to-win bouts of the kind that are staged throughout our society daily, including the women's movement. She was the first person I'd ever known to express such a severe reaction to what I initially and blithely termed "benign social situations." But because I knew that being shy didn't mean being stupid, I couldn't discount her point of view. In fact, I soon began to see the whole phenomenon through her eyes.

I became painfully aware of those women who sit in a group and say little or nothing, while usually no more than two or three of us carry on what we think is a scintillating conversation, doing 98 percent of the talking. I became alive to the daunting nature of constant interruptions in what we call "normal" discourse, the round-and-round-getting-nowhereness of it, the jarring of feelings, the defensiveness.

Suddenly I noticed that discussions of the sort that I saw raging at every feminist gathering I attended, every conference, every meeting, were *not* benign. How could I not have noticed how hierarchical this way of talking was, how much power-jockeying went on? I saw with dreadful clarity how completely we didn't hear one another, let alone hear one another *out*. And marveled that I had never noticed before how deadening discussion is on the generation of ideas, how genuinely conservative it is: we each trod our little track the whole time, trying to draw others onto it, conserving and protecting and defending and strengthening our positions. In such an environment no rigorous thinking could possibly take place, to say nothing of that incandescent, spiraling continuity of thought we call creativity.

It is almost universally accepted in our society that discussion — which is inherently inequitable — is not only wonderful for nearly all occasions, but is nearly always the most effective way to involve people. That each person involved is entitled to equal time, however, is *not* assumed. Discussion is based on the law of the jungle, the survival of the brashest.

Having recognized this, I was ashamed. There I was, a woman whose passion it was to free women of all subjugation, and I hadn't noticed how tyrannical competitive talking was to the 95 percent of my sisters who lost out in the first round, or who, like Susan, refused to play any more at all because it went against their feminist principles.

I am not suggesting that every woman's ideas are equally valuable every time, or that every woman needs or should take equal time. I'm saying that the time must be available if a woman wants it, that time as a resource does not belong more to those who have "proved" by publishing or speaking professionally or holding office that they have useful insights. Time belongs equally to all of us. Which means that if some of us wish to give our time—or a piece of it—to someone else, we must do it *only* from genuine desire, not from subtly being made to feel as if what someone else has to say is more important because she's better known, or is more confident and aggressive, or for any other reason. We must all feel that we genuinely *own* an equal amount of time, and are thoroughly deserving of it.

Hearing into Being answered the question of how we were going to go about thinking in our tank in San Jose. We would spend a major part of our time, in large groups and small, listening to one another on the questions I had sent out and considered critical at that time to any consideration of the state of the women's movement. It would be a good test of the process, too, and give us a chance to improve it before we used it again the next summer with larger groups of women, when we held our first non-conference conference.

Equipped with this one small but powerful tool, and our hope, we flew to California, all unaware of the fatal flaws inherent in our plan. Fortunately, I've never been afraid of making mistakes and I usually learn from them, so perhaps they're not mistakes after all. I can't think how else I could have learned what I learned from San Jose, and I can't think how I would have managed ever since without that knowledge.

We were a very impressive collection of women as we gathered in the central room of a friend's old Spanish-style ranch house that first morning. I began by restating my purpose for bringing us together: "Here is a place where we can really let go and crash about in our heads, expand, be incautious, irreverent, absurd. Here is a place where we can concentrate exclusively upon how the world would be if it were just exactly as we want it to be, without having to be 'realistic,' without having to deal with ours and everybody else's old perceptions of how the world *is*. (Who says it's this way anyway? We are, after all, living in someone else's dream. Is the patriarchal dream more "real" than ours?) Here is a place where we can see visions, and a particular one — please Goddess! — for women. The women's movement needs vision and a vision. Let's begin to weave this vision together here."

I went on to explain the process, stressing the necessity of not reacting to or evaluating anyone else's remarks, not just at the time, but during the whole weekend, so that everyone would feel perfectly safe in continuing to say whatever came to her mind. I explained the theory as clearly as I could, always underscoring how important it was just to listen, to hear, and to suspend the usual judgmental dialogue in our heads that is a major hindrance to the free flow of creativity.

So I was puzzled when this prohibition was flouted almost at once. And though we kept a semblance of the process going throughout the weekend,[3] few chose to give it a genuine trial as a brainstorming technique in small groups, as we had hoped. Almost immediately, nearly everyone began clamoring for topic groups, and spent most of their time that weekend discussing.

I had organized a "conference" after all, willy-nilly. At first I couldn't figure out why. These were brilliant women. I liked

and admired each of them, and as I write about them now, I
like and admire them still. No one was deliberately obstructive
or unpleasant. What had gone wrong? By bedtime that first
day, explanations were dawning upon me and several other
women who had been involved in the planning and who had
been as mystified and disturbed at the turn of events as I.

The process may have broken down because I had not
been sufficiently clear or persuasive about it, or not forceful
enough, not enough of a "leader." Or perhaps I had done too
much of the structuring of the weekend without asking the
opinion of the group, which always causes strong people to feel
rebellious. Another problem may have been that the process itself had no built-in mechanisms to remind us of its goals or to
point out when we were straying from them.*

It's also true that society rewards us constantly for left-
brained activity: judging, criticizing, seeing flaws in arguments, weaknesses in logic, reasons why it won't do. Those
who rely largely upon their intellectual prowess for their feelings of worth become threatened and angry when asked to suspend this habit for even a short time, as if they were being required to reject what they value most, as if they were being
asked to be stupid. (Or perhaps to be defenseless, since many
of us have chosen to protect ourselves with our brains.)

The dynamics became even clearer as I began to remember the one assertion that caused the most frequent breakdown
of the rule not to react or evaluate: that the women's movement
had washed up upon the shoals of lack of vision. Most of the
participants insisted that there was a vision, had always been

---

*Linda Barufaldi, while reading this book in manuscript, wrote about this: "A million
years ago when Emily Culpepper and I took over a theology class and made everyone
stop using sexist language, we wondered at first how we would 'enforce' this and still
have a discussion about something *other* than sexist language. We got party noisemak-
ers — the kind that unroll a long paper tube when you blow them. When someone said
'he' for God, we'd all blow the things, the person would correct her/himself, and go on.
I wonder if a device like this might work in a group that was actually committed to
this process."

a vision. Puzzled, I asked them to describe it to me. They had been in the movement longer than I, and, woman-like, I deferred to their greater knowledge and experience. But they couldn't describe it, and if these very intelligent super-articulate women couldn't describe it, they couldn't see it.

The women's movement was still sailing confidently onward, only in a less visible way, they contended. Women were doing wonderful things all over the country. But that's not evidence of either a movement or a vision, I countered. Women have always done wonderful things in our personal lives. Maybe not the same things as we are doing now, but strong, courageous things. A vision catapults people out of their personal lives into the world, forces them to be more than they ever dreamed they could be. It's not enough for women to think of their actions as benefiting only a limited, private domain, I said. It is absolutely essential that women envision ourselves drawn on a vast canvas with huge brush strokes, that we manifest ourselves planetarily.

About this time, some of them began to condescend toward me pretty heavily. I was new to the movement, they implied, and like all recent converts, brash and green. They could remember when they were like that. If I didn't know what the guiding vision of the women's movement was, it was because I still had such a lot to learn, was not perceptive enough yet, was too headlong and impetuous, hadn't a balanced view, misinterpreted the signs.

Everything they said confirmed to me the absence of both vision and hope. I could feel their despair viscerally; it drained me. It seemed to me that most of them had no real hope any more that women could do other than the little we were doing now. Certainly I could discern no sense of confidence among them that women could — and would — save the world. What I was seeing was burnout, an incapacitatingly powerless world view.

I was also seeing fear. Really hearing ourselves and other women, really taking ourselves seriously as women is a patriar-

chal taboo of extraordinary virulence. Any time it is in danger
of being broken, some terrified woman obeys the tyrant's voice
she has internalized and frantically tries to shepherd us all back
into the jail cell. She succeeded in San Jose.

Perhaps some of them were also defensive because they
were the ones who had been in the movement from the first.
If there were no vision, they were implicated. Moreover, perhaps some did not really want to change.

This is the main lesson I learned: when I chose these
women because they were "leaders" in the movement, I totally
overlooked the fact that "leaders" — in the patriarchal sense (and
so far that's still the only sense in which we really recognize
leaders) — acquire over time a substantial stake in the status
quo, even if it is in the status quo of a subgroup trying to
change the status quo of the main group. Leaders have found
their place. They are well known and respected, and make
much of their livelihood from the fact of their position in the
movement. What if some upstart comes along and changes
everything? What if the women's movement should really take
another direction? Where would that put them? Those in
power in any group don't want things to change. They stand
to lose their relatively safe and prestigious niche if other "leaders" come along. They resist change passionately, and are unconscious of their motivation.

Here I had being trying to promote change, and I had instead brought together women from the group least likely to
want change in the movement. Not all of those who came were
of that ilk, but there were enough of them that conservatism
became the group dynamic. Hearing into Being could be dangerous to the structures they had erected their lives upon.
Topic groups and discussion are not frightening; they don't
threaten the status quo. They haven't changed anything for
millennia.

Despite everything, I enjoyed that weekend. I enjoyed the
company, and the hospitality of my friend. Her ranch was glorious. On our walk one morning we saw four deer standing not

a hundred feet away on the hillside, standing quietly there as if they had come on purpose to give us a message, or simply pleasure, and then they bounded away.

I enjoyed learning what I had to learn from that experience. I had a much better sense of where we had to go from there. Though next time I'd gather women together who had no stake in preserving the lineaments of the present women's movement, I thought that first I had to find ways to identify whatever vision did exist, and then to create a new vision that could give us hope and direction, rekindle our passion, and enable us to do the impossible things we obviously had to do. I hoped such a vision could transform us into Amazons, Furies, Goddesses.

I never thought to question the necessity of a vision of the future any more than I thought to question whether it was even possible. More than that, it never crossed my mind that *trying* to envision the future might actually in some way keep us hooked to patterns that perpetuate patriarchy.

Though I think now that we can't know where we are going but must step out boldly anyway, I believed when I left San Jose that women could step out boldly only if they had a vision, a roadmap of the journey ahead. So I went home to work on creating that vision, that roadmap.

I went home with something else on my mind as well. Although for some time I had realized the ineffectiveness of civil disobedience in changing the system, when I went to San Jose looking for what to do next, I persisted in thinking in terms of "actions," some huge stunning action that would mobilize women, even though I couldn't really defend such a course any more. I was operating on contradictory assumptions because I couldn't think of where or how to move out of civil disobedience. I had already taken the step from confronting the system with anger and hostility, to the fast, an act of love and an appeal from the spirit to the spirit. I knew intuitively that I was moving in the right direction, but I couldn't see intellectually where it was taking me and I couldn't let go of "reason."

At the end of the San Jose weekend, I knew more surely than ever that civil disobedience — and non-violent direct action of all sorts, as presently defined — was now out of the question for me and dangerous for the movement. The group had helped me become very clear about this, though they hadn't been any clearer than I about where to move to.

All this simmered steadily on the back burner of my mind, and, by our last group Hearing into Being, I was grappling with it consciously. In transcribing the tape of that last meeting, I found that this is what I said to the group when it was my turn to speak:

"I learned something incredibly important on the fast in Illinois, though the full meaning of it is only now beginning to come clear. I'd always been a mystical person, and when we got deep into hunger — burning, bone-deep hunger — I began to feel a kind of reprieve now and then, vitality pouring into me from somewhere.

"Letters came that told me what the energy was that I felt flowing through me. I was physically feeling the love that women — and men — were sending me. A man in New Jersey fasted the whole time with us. A woman from some little church somewhere, maybe Methodist or Baptist, would say, 'We're fasting with you up here.' They'd say, 'We're sending you love, we're sending you strength. Can you feel it?' Well, you know, we could.

"People would say, 'How are you surviving?' And I would say, 'I'm eating the love that's coming to me. I'm drinking it up.' And I meant that. I wasn't speaking metaphorically or figuratively. *Something* was feeding me. It's inexplicable, as mystical things are. But what I know is that it is as real and as powerful — more so — than the things I touch, more powerful than anything. It is that which goes between us and transcends or defies time and space, and as we send it out is instantly available. Those powers are very real, and they sustain us, and we have to learn how to use them.

"Now, why can't I concentrate on that kind of power! I

141

keep coming back to it when I try to think of effective tactics only to run into the same old dead end. Then I think, 'Maybe it's got to do with this other power.' Why do I keep discounting that possibility? Why don't I learn? Why don't we learn to harness this other power, use it deliberately as women? It was overwhelmingly powerful. It could knock you down.

"Dick Gregory said something to us in the first days of our fast that I didn't understand until long after he'd gone. We were in this old church, and we were stewing about how the media wasn't presenting us accurately.

"Dick, who fasted with us for five days, sat there very patiently. Finally he said in a quiet voice, 'You women could go down into the basement of this church, lock the door, and not be seen or heard by anybody, nobody even know you were doing this. But if you did it with purity of heart, lack of hatred, love for the people about whom you're fasting, love for the women in this nation that brought you here, a light would come out of that basement that would be like a laser beam to the hearts of the people.'

"I remember thinking, 'Nonsense, they've got to know through the media, that's how it's done. Everybody knows that.' But toward the end of the fast I began to understand. We do, when we're pure in purpose and intent, and love — we do send lasers to one another's hearts.

"And that's maybe what I've got to start thinking about. Because it's clear that when I try to think of other ways to transform society, I keep slamming up against a brick wall. I must learn where the real power is and how to use it. I don't know how to learn it, but somehow I'm going to."

I went home from San Jose to start.

7

Experimenting with Our Large and Coherent Motion in Time

The San Jose group couldn't think of the next step to take because they couldn't really *feel* that anything except patriarchy was possible. Or if it was, they didn't know what it might be. I believed it was possible, but I didn't know what it might be either. We didn't even know what we wanted it to be. We couldn't talk about anything new because we could not imagine anything new.

Back home in Virginia, walking day after day down the country roads near my home, I turned the problem over in my mind, approaching it from various angles, seeing it in different lights, searching for clues. I thought about how, in the last decade or so, people in the West have been waking again to the role of the imagination in creating reality. The knowledge of this power, as old as human consciousness, had all but disappeared in those parts of the world where analytical, "rational" modes of coping gained ascendancy several hundred years ago. Ever since, those who persisted in the old ways have been regarded as ignorant and superstitious at best, and in league with the devil at worst.

But in recent years in this country, the idea that the image precedes the actuality, and, in fact, gives birth to it, has seeped back into awareness. We hear it with increasing frequency, sometimes in the most unlikely places. For instance, on ABC's televised all-male panel on nuclear war, which followed the showing of "The Day After," Elie Wiesel exclaimed despairingly, "Whatever is imaginable is possible!" He was lamenting that the warlords of the world, having imagined nuclear war, have made it possible.

That he should have expressed that principle in connection with nuclear war is hardly surprising. It is on that subject that most of the formal visioning in this country and others is being done. To counter the necrophiliacs, the biophiles of the earth — in groups and singly — are enlarging the possibility of a world without war by ardently imagining it. "Whatever is imaginable is possible" works as much for transformation as for annihilation, they insist.

As I searched for answers to the questions that the San Jose experience had raised in my mind, I thought about the imaginative process as it was being used by peace groups. It was then that the possible relevance of visioning theory to the women's movement struck me with great force.

What seemed clear to me then was that we must envision that world before it can come into being. The idea that every reality begins in the mind's eye, that every reality is built on a vision made good sense to me. I was persuaded that there was no other way but to envision what we want so clearly and in such detail — in panavision, in technicolor, in Dolby stereo — that we came to believe in it, which in itself would lead us to discover ways to move into it. We had to dream the new dream so powerfully and with such faith, I thought, that it would inform every decision we made, that everything we did would be dictated by whether or not it moved us in that direction. And we had to dream it in order to find the courage to do what history requires of us.

"Find me someone who knows how to do visioning," I demanded of Mary Ann. She told us about a woman named

Judy, and Susan and I went to see her. She agreed to come out to our house, as soon as we could get everything set up, to teach a group of us the theory of visioning and how to practice it. As it turned out, Mary Ann knew as much about visioning as Judy, but, womanlike, she had felt certain that someone else was more "expert." Nonetheless, we felt almost as if Judy had been "sent" to us. It was from her that we came to understand and to incorporate into our thinking a few hope-filled concepts from the New Age movement.

Having found Judy and visioning, we had only one more search to make before we were ready to try everything out on a small group of eight to ten women. We planned to use visioning and Hearing into Being to draw up the blueprints of the world we wanted, but we knew we weren't touching yet on the most basic problem of all—women's internalized oppression— and we set about figuring out how to come to grips with it.

All my experience in the women's movement had convinced me that the greatest barrier to our success is our hatred of ourselves and other women, our deep distrust and rejection of one another, and our profound and intractable belief—unconscious and pervasive, almost part of our DNA—in all women's inferiority. How can anyone who feels weak, frightened, ugly, and stupid believe she can create a beautiful new world?

What we needed was a process that would help us understand and rid ourselves of these dynamics. We needed a mirror to show us to ourselves in all our acculturated hurt and hurtfulness, and at the same time to reflect the nobility that has survived in us despite everything. We desperately needed ways to weed out the destructive habits, but also to completely redesign and replant our psychic gardens.

Once again we borrowed from re-evaluation counseling, this time a consciousness-raising ritual and an affirmation format.

Having found what we viewed as the last piece of the puzzle and assembled everything, we began to hold a series of small weekend gatherings at our home in Sterling, Virginia, where we refined and joined the theory and the processes that became the first Women Gathering.

We had worked so fast and with such excitement when we returned from San Jose at the end of February that, despite my heavy speaking schedule in March and April, we were ready to begin these sessions by the middle of May. For several months, every other weekend saw the house full of sleeping bags and stray socks and sleepy women.

An amusing story about these weekends began to circulate out of the National NOW office. A friend of mine from out of town was in Washington one afternoon and stopped in there to see an old-time NOW staffer whom she knew, and after they'd chatted a while, my friend asked, "What's Sonia Johnson doing these days?" To which the woman replied (as my friend tells it), "You know, it's really shocking. She's running a sleep-deprivation cult!"

I want to set the record straight. I always went to bed no later than midnight, and encouraged everybody else to do the same. It was all their own idea — the writing of those love poems, the feasting, the dancing, the other girlish hanky-panky. *They* may have been running a sleep-deprivation cult out there in the front part of the house, but I tucked myself into a back bedroom, stuffed my ears with tissue, and slept.

In June of 1983, I sent out a letter to about 2000 women, mostly from this side of the Mississippi, whom I had reason to believe were also searching for alternative ways to define, generate, and use power; women who as feminists knew that the personal empowerment of women is not simply preparation for some future revolution, but that it *is* the revolution. I briefly outlined the weekend, and, with San Jose echoing in my memory, I made a strong plea for anyone who chose to come to commit herself to giving the three processes a fair trial.

In the flyer we passed out at women's events, we announced that at the Gathering we would:

immerse ourselves in the dream — an act which in itself moves us toward it, "real"izes it;

affirm our powers to live the dream *right now*, not in some vague future time;

free ourselves of the patriarchal myths that bind us to *their* "reality";

discover the wise woman within ourselves;

out of our deep minds, think and plan the next steps to take;

demonstrate our commitment to women on August 26;

march together on August 27 in the Martin Luther King Memorial March.

And then, paraphrasing Ellen Bass's poem, "Our Stunning Harvest," we ended:

Let us gather in August
    With sisters
       With daughters
         With mothers
With all the wonderful, life-sweet women
and begin the gathering in of our stunning harvest.

One hundred sixty-five women gathered in Washington that summer, and for once (Goddess be praised!) August in the city was cool and dry. On the evening of August 23, after registration, we went to the gymnasium of Mt. Vernon College where we were housed to meet with the other members of our circles. We began by introducing ourselves and telling one another what gift we had brought to the gathering. For example, "My name is Sonia, daughter of Ida, and to this gathering I bring my hope for a new world."

Then we drew a line down the middle of a piece of newsprint, listing on one side all the things we could think of that we wanted in our ideal world, and on the other, those we most definitely did *not* want. Because most of us know what we don't want far better than we know what we do want, and because what we do want has so much greater power to move us out of old habits of thinking and acting, I suggested that we concentrate on the DO WANT column.

The lists, which were posted on the wall as part of our "living newspaper," were free-flowing outpourings written without discussion and without any attempt at consistency or consensus. We planned this "intentioning" for just before bedtime because we thought the internal tone it created and the ideas it generated could percolate through our unconscious minds all night as we slept, loosening the steely grip of patriarchal "reality" a little, and preparing us for the visioning exercise the next morning.

Here are just a few ideas selected from that first evening's edition of the newspaper:

DO WANT	DON'T WANT
women trusting one another	violence against women
women taken seriously	competition
shared responsibilities, communal nature-centered society	domination of one group by another
children's dignity protected by community	women fearing one another
	win/lose dichotomies
celebration of uniqueness, diversity	dress for success; careerism
	definition by sexuality
cooperative decision making	original sin
	power struggles
safe, effective birth control	denial of death
use of mediators instead of armies	dualism of mind and body
	conformity
self healing; holistic healing	jealousy
	isms: sexism, racism, ageism

celebration of uniqueness, diversity

cooperative decision making

safe, effective birth control

use of mediators instead of armies

self healing; holistic healing

respect for all living things

only necessary technology

psychic communication

acceptance of bodies; sensuality

food, clothing, housing for all

use of government for human needs

non-hierarchical social structure

positive images of women's sexuality

spirituality as catalyst for change

recognition of spirit in world

understanding and use of necessary, tangible, available magic

truth in media and textbooks

women's financial independence

teaching of feminist principles

women who are "junior men"

prescribed beliefs

linear time

experts

chemical waste dumps; nuclear waste

animal experimentation

war; nuclear or chemical weapons

scarcity mentality

withholding of knowledge and information

refined foods, sugar

waste of water

pesticides and herbicides

enslavement to motherhood

capitalism

exploitation, domination of nature

disdain for children

narrow definition of family

non-life-giving technology

repressive institutions: prisons, mental hospitals, AMA, national boundaries, churches

cigarettes, alcohol

styrofoam

ownership of people

nonsexist, free, and full
  education
clean water, pure air and
  soil
reliance on plant food;
  eating lower on food
  chain
solar economy, and other
  soft energy
mass transportation
touching
freedom from stereotyping
flexible work options
equitable distribution of
  world's goods
gift economy
death accepted as part of
  life

The next morning after breakfast, when everybody was seated as comfortably as possible on the floor of the gym, I told them about the thinking that had led up to this day. I tried to tack all the ideas to some coherent frame so that it would make sense and stay put, not slip away as soon as the weekend was over. In an hour or so, I tried to tell them all I'd learned, to bring them to the point I'd reached in my own thinking over a period of several years. This, in effect, is what I said:

"It wasn't until the ERA failed to pass last summer that I was able for the first time as a feminist to look out and see the women's movement whole. And what I saw made my heart quail. I saw the profile of a potential tragedy. I saw that we were in a perilous place in history, and more than saw it, I *felt* something perilous, as if we were at a juncture where something was about to go seriously awry in the world.

"It wasn't that I thought the women's movement had been a failure. I knew—I could see—what it had accomplished, and

I knew it had been magnificent in many ways. Perhaps its most revolutionary achievement had been to instate women into the consciousness of the race. That is a miracle in itself.

"But I also knew that that was only a beginning. I knew that the destiny of the women's movement is far larger than that, that it is to transform this planet, to spiral and loft the hearts and minds of the human species around and up and out of chaos and violence. And as I looked at feminists, I saw that we had either forgotten this task or despaired of doing it, and were drifting farther and farther from our moorings.

"Ever since the Mormons did me the honor of excommunicating me, I'd been meeting and talking to women all over the country as I went about lecturing. I knew that despair and burnout were the rule, not the exception, but I didn't really understand it very well. I had brought to the movement 43 years of the most immense longing, and megavolts of accumulated energy. In addition, the work I was doing was spiritually replenishing, so it took me a while to understand why and how the movement was draining the life out of women. I could see it before my eyes, but I couldn't understand it — and only partly because it wasn't happening to me. Usually the women to whom it *was* happening didn't understand it themselves.

"But when male lawmakers refused to pass the Equal Rights Amendment, I began to understand, from my own response, that what we were feeling was the futility of the methods we were using to try to make change. The women who had been working in the battered women's shelters and on the rape crisis lines saw that they weren't stopping the battering, they weren't decreasing the rape one iota; that, in fact, as their ministrations increased, so did the brutality. They realized that those broken female bodies were going to keep on piling up and piling up, and that the blood was going to continue to flow in rivers. And there was nothing they could see to do about it. It seemed as if the screaming in their ears was never going to stop. They simply could not live with their hearts being torn apart like that day after day. And so they said to them-

151

selves, 'I've got to get away from this pain and this fruitless labor.'

"There was also the sense that we might even be strengthening the patriarchy by actively giving it our energy, putting its victims back together so they could go out and be raped and battered again, taking on the responsibility of fixing what men break — hearts, hope, lives, doing our job in the patriarchy of cleaning up its mess, hiding its tracks, making it easier for men to go on battering and raping and maiming and killing us. We knew we could not stop them in the ways we were trying, and that in the attempt, the fire of our feminism was turning to ashes.

"The recognition that somehow, unwittingly, we were collaborating was very difficult to deal with. We saw more and more clearly that we were using all our energy to treat the symptoms, and had none left over to do anything about the cause. State and local funding for battered women's shelters and rape crisis centers told us subliminally that, to flourish, patriarchy *needed* these institutions. We were confused about how to help women without ultimately aiding their attackers more than we were aiding them. Though we could not stop caring about the suffering women we saw every day, we were utterly exhausted, and realized on some level that it was either them or us; that again patriarchy had succeeded in pitting us in incredibly painful competition for our lives against our sisters. The implications were desperately depressing. So we did what women do who are caught in the double bind so diabolically designed for us: we opted to save our own lives. We went home and turned our attention to our careers or our love lives or our children, and in this way tried to shut out the despair. Burnout is despair."

Since I gave this speech, I have come to believe that we never suffer burnout, we never despair, unless we are collaborating in some way. Burnout is not only physical exhaustion; it is spiritual and moral and emotional dis-ease as well. Doing the work of genuinely undermining patriarchy and liberating ourselves, no matter how difficult it may be, revitalizes us and fills us with joy. Rather than depleting us, truly transformative work leaves our bodies and spirits replenished and refreshed. This is always a dependable signal; we must learn to trust it.

We must re-evaluate the common assumption in the movement that we are not being effective in helping women unless we are continually struggling and striving and straining and exhausting ourselves. This attitude has loud overtones of the "nasty medicine" principle: the nastier the medicine, the more efficacious it must be. In my experience, the reverse is true. When I do my most seditious work, I feel light, relaxed, energetic, and happy.

"In addition to fostering despair in every possible way," I continued, "those in power take constant and careful readings on its depth and breadth. Every bit of propaganda they put out is calculated to reinforce our feelings that patriarchy is inevitable, that men will always have power over us, and that there is really nothing we can do about it.

"This is how they lie to us: 'Look, we've got the power. If you want any, you've got to get into our institutions, into our Congress, our Senate, into our corporations. That's where the power is. Joining us is the only way you can get what you want.' A compelling message to those of us who, because of our despair, can't conceive of any other possibility anyway. Despairing people don't hope — can't hope, can't see out of the small dark box that psychic pain traps us in, the box labeled 'status quo.'

"Knowing that we cannot trust the men, or any of the institutions presently on earth, where can we turn for hope and help? To ourselves as women and to one another, struggling for genuine faith in ourselves, in other women, and in our ability to create a new world together — and to create it in our lifetime.

"I say 'in our lifetime' because another lie the system zealously propagates is that if we work and work, maybe someday we can change things a little. But we can't expect to see the results in our lifetime. We have to be content with knowing that perhaps our children will benefit from our labors.

153

"Well, who said we can't change the world in our lifetime? Whoever said it is a liar. We *can* do it, and we must. If we don't, there won't be any more lifetime for anybody.

"We know a few things *not* to do. We know it is futile to try to solve old problems with the tools that forged them in the first place. We can't hope to solve the problems of inequity by working through an inequitable system.

"But can't some good come from, say, working for candidates who are saying the true words, injecting genuinely new ideas into people's consciousness? The question is, where are you going to find such candidates? They are so rare as to be practically nonexistent. And I'm not deceived any longer. Getting even 'reasonable' people elected — assuming we could find some who would run — is not how we're going to cause deep change, root change, radical change.

"There must be other ways. My inner voice insists that there are other ways.

"Women — conscious women — are the genuine pioneers on this planet, the true pathfinders. Somehow we've got to begin to believe that, believe that the world cannot survive now without us, believe that we are that important, because it's true. Our task is to save the planet. Nothing less. We were born at this time for this purpose and are standing in the midst of destiny. This means we have to be willing to grope and to trust and to make mistakes and not lose heart. And more than anything, it means that we must have faith in our inner voices.

"This is where the power is, inside us. The knowledge of what to do is going to come right out of us — each one of us. Not just one leader, or one group of leaders. We're in a new time when we understand the value of every voice and the damage done to the human spirit by hierarchy.

"But each one of us must understand how critical what we have to say is and what we think and feel is. Each one of us has to believe that we are as personally responsible for the direction of this movement as if we were its leaders. Because we *are*.

"I know that to have this new world where everyone participates with full responsibility and full authority, we have to begin living that way right now, this minute. The world we want isn't in the future; it's now. Because the means are the ends, insofar as we can be truly feminist, truly non-patriarchal people right here, right now, we are living in a new world.

"What this Gathering can offer are some tools to help us do this. These tools are processes — ways to find out how to proceed — and highly appropriate for feminists because feminism is itself a process. They're not cut and dried. Nobody in the world is an expert yet on the things we're doing, so whatever we do with them is just dandy.

"When you go from here, we want you to have something to take home and begin your own group with, in the hope that you will pick other tools and ideas from the rich supply that's beginning to become available. The three processes we're going to try out at this Gathering correspond roughly to what I think are the three basic questions.

"The first question is, 'What kind of a world do we want?' If we could step outside, snap our fingers, and have the world precisely as we'd like it to be in every respect, how would it be? A specific, concrete, sensory-rich, tactile, clear vision out of the deep intuitive center, *not* the theoretical brain — this is our treasure map, our source of hope and guidance.

"So the first thing to do is to relearn abilities that patriarchy says are irrelevant and that it scorns, those faculties which all human beings have but which women have developed to a greater degree. It's fitting that as women now begin to transform the planet, we use methods that are womanly, more compatible with our ways of being. The first thing to do is to reawaken our innate capacities to imagine, to remember how to dream. Oppressed people forget how to dream. And that's not an accident. One of the prime objectives of rulers is to kill the dream in those they rule. They make us afraid to aspire too much; they punish and destroy us for dreaming daring dreams.

"During 'Sisterfire,' the outdoor musical event for women

in Washington, D.C., we shared a table with a friend who was selling T-shirts. Most of her T-shirts bore slogans and pictures propagandizing for the goddess within, but one had emblazoned across its bosom: EXPECT NOTHING! 'Really, Margaret,' I said to her in dismay, 'would you call that a feminist slogan?' She looked a trifle shamefaced and said, 'I know, it kind of troubles me, too, but the woman who sold me the T-shirts told me I'd sell more of these than any others, and that it would subsidize the whole venture.'

"So I watched, and sure enough, that T-shirt sold out first and women lined up to order it. One woman ran up shouting, 'Oh, I hope you've still got one of those EXPECT NOTHING! T-shirts left!' I asked her 'What's the appeal of that shirt?' 'Well,' she answered, 'if you don't expect anything, you're never disappointed.'

"That's the voice of oppression. We expect so little, we dream so small: 'If we can just get some women in the Senate, some more women in the House of Delegates in Virginia.' What a small, safe dream to dream. But we've got to dare to dream the system-splitting dream, because we can't move into any space that we can't envision. We can only move as far as we can dream. That's our limitation, and we set it ourselves.

"The second process is called 'freeing ourselves from internalized oppression.' As we go through it, we'll entertain the second critical question: 'To have the world we've just envisioned, how would we have to change? How would we have to feel to do what we now have to do?' Knowing that we suffer only as much oppression as we are willing to bear, how can we become unwilling to bear it? How can we say to ourselves, 'I don't deserve this,' and *mean* it? Somehow we must learn to do that. The minute we do, it is all over for patriarchy!

"The third process is called 'hearing into being.' This process will give each of us a whole hour and a half—in thirty minute segments—to talk to our group without interruption or evaluation. Using this process, we'll think aloud about the third question: 'How can we make the changes that have to be made?' This may include talking about where we go from here, how we're going to keep in touch with one another in a non-hierarchical way that will keep us together, keep us all participating.

"We have to begin creating new ways of organizing society. Right here in the midst of the wreckage of the old order, we must build the new one. We can't go off to Australia and have a feminist community. This time, the new world is within us; it is not a geographical space.

"Now, why do we have any hope that what we learn to do here is going to make any difference? Look at us. We're beautiful and we're wonderful. But there are so few of us.

"All through history, the group exploring the frontiers of possibility, the group with the vision and the daring that paves the way for the rest to follow, has been small. Why did they succeed? What were the dynamics that allowed them to make the difference they made when they were so few and seemingly so powerless?

"Well, the answers are beginning to come, and some of them are coming out of the physical and natural sciences. You may have been hearing about them from New Age people. There are three ideas that are very instructive and hope-producing to me, very—as we used to say in the Mormon church—'faith-promoting.'

"The first idea, the theory of dissipative structures, won the Nobel Prize for physics in 1977. What it posits, in effect, is that every open system—and that includes our society—maintains the status quo by keeping each of its parts separated from one another, keeping them 'incoherent.' As long as the system is not all of a piece, but many disjointed pieces, it can wiggle and woggle and absorb lots of trauma without suffering much disruption. What it can neither absorb nor survive is coherence, unity among its parts.

"Let's look at this society. It depends upon women and all others of minority status *not* working together, not joining hands, perceiving our differences but not our overriding commonalities. All oppressed groups are trained to be wary of one another and to have trouble working together so that society's fabric will be lumpy and full of holes, giving the powerful lots of flexibility.

"Those of us who are going to begin to unify this dissipative, incoherent structure need to know that our work with it has two characteristics we can depend on and exploit. The first of these is that for a while, we won't be able to see that we've had any effect. We'll say, 'Oh for heaven's sake! Let's give up. This is not working.' But if we persist with total unity, even if there is just a handful of us, there will come a time when, all of a sudden, overnight, the system will flip-flop. The theory says systems don't change a piece at a time but that they stay the same until there gets to be a critical mass of agitation of the value system, 'critical' because it cannot be absorbed or accommodated. And then there's the flip-flop.

"The other characteristic we can count on is that this change only requires a few of us. This is true in physics and in the biological sciences; it is true in human history. The critical mass can be achieved by the minority—even a small minority.* How does that work?

"Well, there's another theory out there that helps explain this phenomenon: the theory of morphogenesis.[1] This hypothesizes that nature has no laws; that what we see in the universe are only habits. This is an infinitely hopeful point of view, because, while laws are immutable, habits can be broken, can be changed.

"Obviously, certain ways of thinking are habits. In the world at this time we have a patriarchal habit of mind. How do we break the world's habit of thinking patriarchally? You

---

*According to the *Washington Post* of November 26, 1985 ("Peace Group Tries to Look Beyond War"), Everett M. Rogers, a former Stanford University professor, believes that when approximately 5 percent of a population adopts a new idea it becomes "imbedded," and when the new idea is accepted by 20 percent of the people, it is "unstoppable."

might say, 'That's the hardest thing of all!' But it isn't hard, according to this theory, not hard at all. Take for example the story of crystals.

"New crystals are very difficult and very tricky to grow. To bring a totally new crystalline pattern into the world is arduous and time-consuming work. However, what scientists have noticed for a long time is that once they have managed to grow a new crystal in a laboratory, that crystal soon begins to appear in other laboratories and other countries in a fraction of the time it took the first scientists to develop it.

"For a long time they didn't understand (and mostly still don't) the wonderful phenomenon that was sitting right there in front of their noses just waiting to be discovered, because they were bound by their old habits of thought, by their belief in the old 'laws.' They went to extraordinary and preposterous lengths to explain it, totally disregarding the law of parsimony which holds that the simplest explanation is probably the closest to the truth. They speculated that maybe some scientist got a seed-crystal stuck in his beard, or in the cuff of his jacket, so that when he went to another lab to visit scientist friends, and just happened to wear the same jacket or not to have washed his beard, the seed crystal quietly shook out and began to grow. There's no end to the desperate nonsense we can think up to avoid having to change our way of looking at the world.

"What actually happens is that as soon as the new crystal — the new structure, the new thought — comes into the world, its next generation grows in a fraction of the original time, until enough have grown that the critical mass is reached. Just as soon as this happens, the blueprint of that particular crystalline structure is available to the crystal consciousness of the world. It has set up a new morphogenetic field, a new blueprint for form and behavior.

"The atomic theory of morphogenesis reminds us that there is no time and no space. It tells us that new ideas, new values, new structures don't have to travel across time and space to get around. Everything is right here, right now. The minute the crystal comes into being in enough force, enough generations of it, the critical mass is reached and its secret becomes available everywhere at once. Because there's no energy in this field, it doesn't take time to pass from here to there. Einstein disputed the concept of simultaneity until toward the end of his life. Then he admitted that, though he didn't fully understand it, all evidence proved its existence.

"Another example of morphogenesis is the story of the Harvard rats trying to learn a water maze. Although they were reasonably intelligent rats, they were having serious difficulty. So the experimenters kept running them through it until, after seemingly endless trials, the rats finally had it down pat.

"Each successive generation of these rats found the maze easier to learn, until the critical mass was reached, at which point the maze suddenly became part of rat consciousness — every rat could learn the maze in a bare fraction of the time it had taken previous maze-runners. Experimenters everywhere couldn't replicate the study with that maze any more; they had to throw it out and start with a new one. The habit of thought had changed. There was a new blueprint, and it was in every rat's mind. No rat born after that had to go through the process of laboriously learning that particular maze to know it.

"We're the first rats in the maze, and to us it looks impossible. Being the first generation of women to go through it, being the pioneers, seems unbearably hard. We can't see where we're going. We keep bumping into walls and receiving dreadful shocks and misinterpreting cues. But because we won't give up, because life depends on it, we will ultimately set up the morphogenetic field that's going to make the habit of non-patriarchal thinking available immediately, everywhere, all at once, over the entire planet. Then every generation of women — or men — won't have to go through what we're going through to get where we are, or where we're going. Won't, that is, if we dare to change our direction and stop crashing against the same barrier that the women's movement has been crashing against for a hundred years in this country — which is the totally unfounded and dangerous belief that we can work through the system to replace it, that we can use patriarchy to make patriarchy extinct.

"The most famous account of morphogenesis concerns some monkeys on the islands around Japan.* For thirty years primatologists had been studying them. Then, in 1952, on one island they began feeding the monkeys yams — dropped them in the sand on the beach for them to eat. The monkeys loved the yams, but found the sand gritty to the teeth and gustatorily unpleasant.

"One day, a young female monkey named Imo took her yam down to the water and washed off the sand. In the next few days, she taught her mother and siblings and friends how to make lunch more enjoyable this way.

"During the following six years, all the young monkeys learned to wash their yams. Adults did, too, but only those who imitated their offspring. As Ken Keyes tells it in *The Hundredth Monkey*:

> Then something startling took place. In the autumn of 1958, a certain number of Koshima monkeys were washing sweet potatoes — the exact number is not known. Let us suppose that when the sun rose one morning there were 99 monkeys on Koshima Island who had learned to wash their sweet potatoes. Let's further suppose that later that morning, the hundredth monkey learned to wash potatoes. *Then it happened.*
>
> By that evening, almost everyone in the tribe was washing sweet potatoes before eating them. The added energy of this hundredth monkey somehow created an ideological breakthrough![2]

---

*The veracity of this story has recently been disputed. But since there appears to be no way ultimately either to prove or to disprove it, I choose to assume that it is to one degree or another another evidence of the same phenomenon as the rats and the crystals, and therefore useful.

Next the truly amazing and most hopeful phenomenon of all was recorded. The moment the critical mass of monkeys was washing yams on Koshima Island, whole colonies of monkeys on the other islands and on the mainland began washing their yams, too — *instantaneously.* That they were now yam-washing creatures had become embedded in monkey consciousness. Enough of them had thought and behaved in a particular way that they had changed the habit of monkey thinking. They had set up a new morphogenetic field.*

"That's what we're about: setting up a new morphogenetic field. It isn't beyond our capacities. If monkeys can do it, surely we can do it. I believe women are the ones who are going to figure out how.

"The third theory out there that I find exciting and hopeful is holographic theory, the central idea of which is that the whole exists in every part, that from every part the whole can be reproduced. For example, if you take a pebble and drop it into a pool, as the ripples go out, they form a particular pattern. Now, if you were to lift out a pie-shaped piece of those ripples, you would see that from that piece you could reproduce the entire ripple pattern.

"Scientists are now conjecturing that the brain is holographic, that from a very little piece of it, the entire brain can be reproduced. They're also saying that the universe is holographic; each little piece of the universe holds the pattern of it all, and from each piece the whole universe could be reproduced. So we have holographic brains interpreting a holographic universe.

---

*Recognition of both morphogenesis and critical mass appears more and more frequently. On November 6, 1985, for instance, *The Washington Post* ran a long article in its "Health" section about the growth of resistant bacteria. David Monagan, the author, concluded: "If so much as a single bacterium happens to hold some antibiotic-stopping gene, that code can leap throughout an entire colony, so that a new generation — which can occur in as little as 20 minutes — can be immediately equipped with resistance to that drug."

"Like the other theories, this one is beginning to flow over into and to affect the thinking of those who want to change society. Starting from the premise that every individual is a hologram of her/his society, we can expect that from you and from me we can reproduce our entire culture. And insofar as a critical number of us create a new pattern in our pie-shaped wedge of ripples — ruffle the water by changing our feelings and thinking and behavior — we can create a whole new pattern in society.

"These theories are interrelated, substantiating and reinforcing one another. They are sources of hope in a time when hope is draining out of the world through a thousand wounds. They help us understand why, all through history, small groups have spurred the greatest change. The vast body of any movement is always lethargic and reformist, seduced by the trappings of the old society, and therefore in despair. That's why little groups like ours are as essential as we are small. Without us, there is no hope, no change, no chance for life.

"So we must stop minimizing our importance, but believe and make real in our hearts the difficult truth that we are indispensable to the life of our planet. Us! Not just women. You! With your name! You very specific individual person. Me. That's our destiny. There aren't very many like us — just *enough*. We can't spare any of us. *We're* the ones we've been waiting for.[3]

"So where do we begin?

"I remember the Bible story about Joseph, who was sold into Egypt. His older brothers hated him because his father openly favored him. Joseph was insufferable about it, and unwise: he was a younger brother in a violent time, romping about bragging about his dreams of ruling over his brothers. In those days, people believed mightily in dreams, and the thought of this young puppy lording it over them galled his brothers unutterably. They plotted to kill him. 'If by stealth we destroy the dreamer,' they mused, 'what then shall become of the dream?'

"Martin Luther King is dead because he had a dream that was beginning to change the system, not just Black civil rights. As important as civil rights are, that's a small dream, the kind of dream oppressed people dream. Dr. King was beginning to dream a world of peace, a world without poverty, a whole new world. So they killed him.

"And his dream died with him. It was too new and unfamiliar a dream, and too few were dreaming it for themselves yet. For many, he was still the source. They had faith in him and in his dream — that it could be real in the world because it was real in his mind and heart.

"He died when Black people were just beginning to have hope — the first step toward freedom for the oppressed. They had just begun to understand what we're beginning to understand: what men say is 'reality' is *not* reality. There is no objective reality. Reality is what we accept as real. What we collude with. What we bestow the name 'truth' on when we say, 'Okay, I agree that you're real. I'll agree to your values. I'll say yes to you.'

"The system killed King because he was saying, "No, I won't agree. You're not real. The world I envision is the real world. I say yes to *it*.' The next step would have been making that new world real, so they hastily killed him.

"That's why each of us has got to be the source of the dream. So that by stealth no one can kill one dreamer and destroy the dream. Each of us has got to own this dream. Each of us must long for its realization, touch it, smell it, breathe it, live at least half our lives in it. Refuse that old nonsense, that old nightmare called patriarchy, *by thinking and behaving as if it had already disappeared from the earth.*

"This is how revolution happens. I don't think we've ever seen a true revolution, at least not in written history. We may be the first we'll ever have heard of. This may be the first genuine revolution of the human spirit on planet earth.

"Let us resolve to envision our way out of patriarchy and into a just, free, merciful and life-loving society. Let us resolve to dream it together and not stop until it is planetary reality."

For three days at that first Gathering in Washington, D.C., we faithfully tried our processes. Hearing into Being and affirmation were particularly powerful. The following perception turned up in Susan's journal of one of her Hearing into Being sessions at the Gathering: "Consistently having hope keeps far more pressure on the system than acts of civil disobedience. Patriarchy cannot survive prolonged hope. There is enough hope in this room now to dismantle it. A small group of men created the atom bomb. A small group of women, guided by hope, can uncreate it."

In my notes from the same session, I found this hypothesis: "Maybe — if, as Sheldrake[4] postulates, there are no natural laws, just habits — men may not be biologically impossible after all. Because if genes contain not laws but habits, the habit of testosterone can be broken. Perhaps men have been conditioned to pump vast amounts of testosterone into their blood over the centuries in order to do "manly" things. If such pumping is just a habit, men should be able to reduce the amount of testosterone in their blood, through biofeedback, for instance, the way diabetics can learn to control their insulin levels, and also by helping establish and living in a society that no longer values force and violence, in which such overproduction of hormone is recognized as not only an anachronism, but pathological and calamitous."

Many other insights came out of those sessions. A couple I copied off our "living newspaper" were: "the step toward the new female paradigm is to put a gift economy in place of the exchange economy," and "the Italian word for power, 'potere,' means to be able to, to have capability. This must be the meaning of power in the coming society."

Of the three processes, affirmation is the one that is so absolutely indispensable to the health of feminism and therefore to the health of the world that it must become for all of us, not an occasional ritual, but a way of life. Its whole purpose is to jolt us up off the bottom of the lobster bucket, out the open door of our jail cell. Through it as in no other way I know we can escape from the self-hatred and powerlessness in which we have been so thoroughly schooled, and from the resulting spiritual paralysis and cruelty to ourselves and other women — the results of internalized oppression.

Early on, in those first days of trial and error at my home, we discovered that affirmations, to be genuinely change-producing, needed to be about characteristics of ourselves, not about things we wanted to do or goals we wanted to reach, and — though we developed no coherent theory then to explain why — we learned that they needed to be stated in present tense, *as if they were already reality*. So during the Gathering affirmation process, we talked about how we wanted to *be*, knowing that such affirmations tear up our negative beliefs about ourselves by the roots, and we did it as if we were the way we wanted to be that very moment.

To plunge right into the heart of the problem, we asked each woman, "What would you most like to believe about yourself but find the most difficult." When first asked this question, most women needed to talk a little about themselves before they began to focus down to their deepest worries and yearnings. As each woman talked, members of her group listened very carefully to her, concentrated upon her. They could make suggestions if she was struggling to find or to phrase it; usually, each woman tried out two or three before she landed on the one that felt right.

One of the signals that a woman had found a powerfully healing affirmation is that she found it difficult, almost impossible, to say aloud. Many women began to cry, or to laugh with embarrassment. But as they repeated their affirmation, it began perceptibly to change in them whatever it had been that hurt or embarrassed.

My very first affirmation in our practices many months before was, "I am a wonderful mother!" — what I most needed but found virtually impossible to believe. It took me several sessions to be able to say it proudly and with conviction. I cried a lot at first, and had to talk a little about how heavy motherhood is in patriarchy, how fraught with guilt and loneliness and pain. I am living proof that affirmation works, because even now — years later and with no more practice of this particular affirmation — I not only *know* that I'm a wonderful mother, I *feel* it in my bones — and that is something akin to miraculous.

At the Gathering, we spoke of affirmation as recording over the old tapes patriarchy set playing in our heads to maim and incapacitate us when we were born female — tapes that for many women have been playing continuously and almost exclusively ever since. Operating on this assumption, we thought it was necessary for the message we record over those old tapes to be *extravagantly* positive, extravagant enough to drown out and drive out the loud, lying, over-learned message underneath. This meant that it wasn't enough to say, "I'm smart." To contradict with strength the feeling of stupidity with which patriarchy has so undercut our confidence, we encouraged one another to say things such as, "I'm absolutely brilliant!" Or, as one woman shouted, "I'm a fuckin' genius!" Our theory was that our ugly, destructive feelings could only be swept away by hyperbole, by superlatives, by very vigorous, very intense language. Words are congealed energy. By controlling our language, men have sucked our energy from us, the energy of our belief in ourselves. Using passionate, puissant words could give us back some of that stolen energy. "So let's use them!" I encouraged everyone. "The biggest, most vivid, most luscious, gorgeous, lavish, radiant, stunning words in any language to describe and heal ourselves."

And women did: I am riotously fun to be with! I am completely lovable just as I am! I am a hell of a leader! I am a brilliant star! I am absolutely gorgeous! I am in complete control of my life! I am totally self-confident! I am an incredibly important person! I am a winner!

Because we taught affirmation as fabulous accounts of our genius and beauty, some women worried about the literal "truth" of our statements. We answered that the *feeling* we were seeking by affirming ourselves *is* the truth. Whatever we must say to gain a *true feeling* was true. To say "I'm a genius," to affirm that, to insist on it, to shout it, may not make me feel like a genius, but it will certainly give me the feeling of being not stupid, perhaps even of being intelligent. And that I am intelligent, that we are all intelligent, is the absolute truth.

Since we knew the women couldn't get together often, we urged them to affirm themselves alone and in small groups. "Each one of us," I told them, "every morning when we awake, should go to the mirror, look ourselves lovingly in the eye, and brag aloud to ourselves about ourselves, something like:

"Good morning, Sonia. How did you get so beautiful? Did you practice all night? Just look at your lovely eyes, brimming with wisdom and humor, with all those gorgeous wrinkles around them. You look vital and healthy and alive — perfect! I'm so glad to be you! So brilliant and funny, playful, passionate, and dedicated. I'm proud at how well you've supported yourself and your kids for so many years in the insecure career of free-lance feminist. You're something of a marvel, dear friend, and I love you very much. Never forget that you can always count on me, no matter what. Now go and have a wonderful day. No one ever deserved it more!"

I often suggested to women in other audiences during that time period that since we are the stuff myth is made of, we should create epics, sagas, legends of our victories, our gifts, our incredible lives; in speech and writing and song rhapsodize about ourselves. Just to show how easy it is to do, and to demonstrate how not to care what our paeans sound like to others (and to remind myself how marvelous I am), I occasionally took something I love about myself and mythologized it off the cuff right there at the podium:

"As women are wont to think of our gifts, I once thought of my gift to speak as something independent of me, something that was only using me as a vehicle. But no more. This gift is *me*, nothing separate. It is attached to my flesh, flows in my veins and arteries, with my blood infuses every organ, every muscle, every cell. It comes out of my life, out of who I was before I was born, out of the longings of my soul, out of the passion of my heart. I am a voice for women — for my sisters, my loves — who have no voice, to whom no one listens. From 5000 woman-years of rage to be free, my voice soars. When I speak, I speak out of the lustiness of my woman's body and mind, out of all women's richest womanhood combined. My whole soul is full of language to honor women's wondrous ways. When I speak of women I am a bird flying, a tree standing against the storm, a dolphin dancing in the sea. When I speak I am all women who ever lived loving me. I feel their smooth arms and tangled hair. I smell their lemony fragrance, taste the tears on their cheeks, kiss their sweet smiles. When I speak I am diffuse — all women of all times. When I speak I am one individual woman, a particular woman. When I speak, I know my name. I know who I am."

I believed then, and still believe, that since we have been so diminished, so inexpressibly smallened and uncreated by phallocracy, we have both an obligation now and the unparalleled opportunity to create ourselves, paint ourselves onto the global canvas with boldest, broadest strokes, most brilliant colors; to portray ourselves as giants, collossi — magical, incandescent, powerful almost beyond imagining — lifting the world out of misery in our hands mighty with love. Goddesses together.

At the Gathering I urged us all to do this often, actively: every day to ourselves, at least once a week with others. I knew we had much to contradict, but I believed it could be done. I insisted that we could quickly substitute another recording. And that doing so, changing our feelings about ourselves, was the most important work on earth, the primary work in the redemption of all life.

Visioning was the problematic process. Though something about it felt awry to me, and though this feeling grew with time, it seemed to work in our lives. Ever since Judy had come to teach us about visioning, I'd been using it often. Susan, my children, friends — all of us have stories to tell.

169

Susan's favorite story began one Sunday afternoon, around the time of the fast and before I knew her. She and a friend, Leonard, were talking about what they were going to do next with their lives. "If you could do *anything*, what would it be?" he asked her. Without a moment's hesitation, she answered, "I'd be Sonia Johnson's press secretary." Three months later, she was my press secretary.

My favorite visioning story is about how I sold my house. I'd been trying unsuccessfully for a long time. It was a beautiful house but 6000 square feet and out in the country. I wanted something small, snug, and close in, and so, apparently, did everybody else. Despite my agent's active and aggressive campaign, it didn't sell, and I was beginning to feel desperate.

Then Susan, my daughter Kari, and son Noel, and I went down to see Barbara Deming in Sugarloaf Key. One evening as she and some friends were sitting talking to us, I told them how anxious I was becoming about selling my house.

"What you need is a little magic," Barbara told me. "A little help from some unacknowledged natural laws. Are you willing?" Was I willing! "Okay, then, first draw a picture of your house and a picture of a woman and a man and cut them out." Kari drew the house while I drew the Steins — as we called them because I drew the man's head so concave that I had to fill it out with a yarmulke — and we handed them to Barbara.

She placed the house beneath one of her plants, picked up the Steins and began walking them about the living room, talking for them all the while: "We really need a good house," she had them say as they walked. "Oh, here's one. Let's go in and see it." Pause. "No, it's just not right somehow. We'll have to keep looking." And on around the room until they came to our little paper house under the plant. Ms. Stein stopped and said, "Oh, honey, look at this house! I have a wonderful feeling about it. Let's go inside!" And Mr. Stein answered, "I'm excited, too. I think we may have found it!" So they walked into my house, took one look, and said, "This is it. This is our house, the perfect place for us. We'll buy it!"

Then Barbara brought the Steins and the house over to me, folded the house over the little paper people and said, "Now, take these home and do this several times a day." I promised and carried the Steins in their house carefully home to my house in Virginia.

I began at once. I roped Susan in, and even tried to get my real estate agent involved. One afternoon when she was there, I walked into the kitchen with the Steins in my hands and said, "Ruth, these are the Steins. They're going to buy the house."

She looked at me quizzically. She looked the Steins up and down, then said to them scornfully, "I know you're just imposters!"

"Stop!" I shouted. "Really, Ruth! Don't you know you can't mess around with magic like that?"

She thought I'd gone quite mad.

Along with this ritual, I practiced my new visioning skills. In my mind's eye, I saw the Steins arriving, liking and buying the house, and us happily ensconced in our new home. I envisioned this in rich sensory detail—colors, odors, emotions, sounds—at least twice a day.

I saw us leaping into the air, dancing, whirling each other around with glee at the sale. I saw myself in my rust jacket, nodding my head, smiling, shaking hands, feeling the pen in my hand and happiness in my solar plexus as I signed papers at the settlement. I saw us packing up particular objects in each room, the yellow moving van driving up, heard the men's voices as they worked. My most powerful image was a bold shiny new SOLD sign out on the front corner of the lawn where the old weather-beaten "For Sale" sign had languished for so long.

As I sat quietly with my eyes closed going through this process, I also called out in my mind to the people who should buy the house. "You're looking for a house just like this one. This house will make you very happy. It's the house you need. Listen to my voice and follow it here. Come looking for houses today in Broad Run Farms. You can follow my voice right up to the door." And so on.

And as I spoke, I saw them being drawn by my voice toward the house, turning their car around, heading for Broad Run Farms. Not being forced, but trusting my voice because it reached only those whom the message fit, those for whom it was true. I sent the image of my house out there, knowing there was no space or time between human minds.

I also knew it was important to cut my emotional ties to that house which I so loved and where such momentous events had happened in my life. I suspected that my ambivalence about leaving it had complicated the selling of it. So I began saying goodbye to it and to that era of my life, daily envisioning myself leaving it, and soon my heart was also ready to go.

Four or five days after we returned from Florida, I was working in the library when Ruth, my real estate agent, appeared in the doorway, her eyes practically popping out of her head. "You're not going to believe this," she whispered, "but the Fleckensteins are at the door!"

"Of course!" I replied as I stood up. "And it's about time!"

The Fleckensteins didn't buy the house, but a few days later the Grubers did. It took us just over a week to lead them to our door. And then all the rest went smoothly along according to plan. I stopped believing in coincidence about then.

My son Eric has a favorite story about visioning. He used to have difficulty taking tests. Not because he wasn't intelligent, but because tests seemed to him most alien things (he was quite right, of course). Shortly after the Gathering, he had to take a welding test in order to become certified to do certain kinds of welding and upgrade his job qualifications.

As he was worrying about it, I said to him, "Eric, you've got a week until the test. Several times a day, for about five minutes each time, close your eyes and see yourself taking that test. See it from beginning to end. See yourself walking confidently into the room, picking up the torch, welding all those seams, inch by inch, doing it perfectly, calmly. Then imagine that when you're finished, the supervisor comes over, looks at your work and says, 'I've never seen better welding in my life. That's the best seam that's ever been welded in this test!' See him put it under the X-ray and gasp, 'I can't believe it!' and call everyone to come and see a perfect seam. See them signing your certificate, slapping you on the back, shaking your hand. Then see yourself going back in and doing it all over again."

I told him about those people who win sweepstakes and lotteries by visioning, and about the studies showing that athletes — runners, for instance — after they reach a certain level in their training and skill, improve more by envisioning themselves running than by actually getting out on the track and doing more of it.

So Eric decided to give it a try. And he not only passed the test; the man in charge came up to him afterwards and said, "I've never seen a seam welded better than that in all my experience. I can't weld that well myself," and he slapped Eric on the back, congratulated him, and called other people over to see!

During my campaign for President of the United States, one of my objectives was to win federal primary matching funds, something no third party or independent candidate had ever done before. Because getting these funds would be such an anti-system coup, everybody said we couldn't do it. But Susan and Julie (our treasurer) and I thought some anti-system magic might work in this case and so we set about systematically imagining money flowing to us from everywhere.

I remember some of our images, though not who created them. We saw a postal service truck drive up in front of the house and three postpersons begin unloading bag upon bag of business reply envelopes on our porch. We saw ourselves and dozens of volunteers opening these envelopes and filling dozens of boxes with checks, which a relay team then rushed to the bank.

That just warmed us up. Next we saw the windows open and funnel-shaped clouds appearing in the sky outside — clouds

173

which were really money, swirling cyclone-like right through our windows and piling up in the corners, then in the middle of the floor, then filling the room, the kitchen, the bedrooms. We saw ourselves shoveling it into dump trucks to haul it to the bank, which took on extra employees and stayed open all night for weeks counting and sorting and stashing away.

In our minds' eyes we envisioned ourselves submitting our request to the Federal Elections Commission, saw them nodding their heads over it, saw our first check arriving in the mail, which meant we'd qualified! We'd done it! We saw ourselves hugging one another and laughing and celebrating our victory by taking everyone out to dinner and dancing until dawn.

And we *did* do it! Money *did* pour in from everywhere. Looking back on it, it seemed as if we did it with ease, though I know that wasn't the case. Perhaps it seems that way because believing it was possible made it *feel* possible to us the whole time, while to everyone else it felt obdurately out of reach.

Now, I believe that it was feeling as if we had already succeeded that worked the magic, and that the images were only important insofar as they generated that feeling. Then, I lay the prime importance at the feet of the images themselves. Perhaps that's partly why something about visioning made me a little uneasy. Without being able to put my finger on it, I felt that it wasn't going to change women's lives deeply or permanently enough. I didn't suspect yet that because I hadn't gone sufficiently out of my patriarchal mind I was caught in a fundamental error in my thinking.

So I reasoned with myself that my vague feelings of discontent probably stemmed from my longing for the *one* idea, the simple, elegant idea that would suddenly make everything clear, and warned myself that such an idea probably didn't exist. I'm not sure what I personally expected from visioning — certainly it seemed to have worked for me (though not always, nor always so spectacularly) — but I continued to feel as if I were overlooking some key, missing some essential connection.

For three years I felt that way: practically on top of an idea but unable to grasp it. And then in August 1986, in Dobbs Ferry, New York, sitting with four friends at breakfast, I finally made the breakthrough I'd unconsciously been working and waiting for.

But first I ran for President of the United States.

8

Drowning in the Mainstream

"You must be out of your mind!" some not very tactful folks gasped when they first heard I was running for President. "Not yet, but I'm working on it," I laughed, though I was perfectly serious. The campaign had all come together—in my mind and in the doing—from here and there, like a bouquet of wild flowers.

Looking back, I can see that it all began that day in June 1982, when the Illinois state legislature voted down the ERA, dooming all chances for national ratification within the time limit.

For the eight of us fasting there in Springfield, this was the 37th agonizing day. Our physical weakness made the pain of the defeat, which would have been difficult for us to bear in the most robust health, very nearly unendurable, but that didn't stop the reporters, ghouls that they were, from pursuing us back to the motel to ask us how we felt about it. How did they *think* we felt about it?

As I sat there on the grass in the cheerful noonday sunshine, listening to us talk about how our hearts were broken,

I had a sudden realization. I understood finally that our political system doesn't work for women, and, most significantly, that this is not merely an oversight. Not just, "Aw, shucks! We forgot to set things up right for the girls." I knew that in fact the system is deliberately set up *not* to work for us, and that the Democrats are as implicated in this, are as much a part of patriarchy, as the Republicans.

If anyone had asked me any time in the five years I had been a feminist if the Democrats were part of patriarchy, I would have been surprised at the naivete of the question, and would have answered at once, "Why, of course!" But I had been a part of the National Organization for Women—which is very pro-Democrat—and didn't realize until that moment in Springfield that I was in serious disagreement with their political views. On the spot, I moved to a higher level of inner coherence. The knowledge that the Democratic Party was essentially the same Old Boys' Club as the Republican Party suddenly dropped, hard and unyielding as a stone, from my head down into that place in me where I know viscerally and forever the implications, the soul, of the facts.

The facts that suddenly came together with meaning were that we had watched as many Democratic as Republican legislators vote against the ERA, that as many Democratically-controlled legislatures had voted it down as Republicanly-controlled. I remembered speaking for Minority Plank 10 at the Democratic National Convention in Madison Square Garden in 1980. That plank, which instructed the Democratic National Committee to withhold financial and technical support from any candidate in the country who did not support the ERA, won by acclaim. It was a voice vote and it nearly lifted the roof off the building. I'm certain that nothing else in the history of the party has been more obviously the will of the body.

But we had no sooner left the convention than it appeared that the Democratic National Committee had never heard of Minority Plank 10. They went right out from Madison Square Garden and that roof-raising vote, and all over the country

177

supported with money and technical assistance, candidate after candidate who had no intention whatever of voting for the ERA. Indeed, many of them had voted against it in the past.

Glancing back over history, I realized that the Democrats and the Republicans have been in power about equally in the last 150 years, and that women are still on the bottom of every-thing. I realized that, although the Democrats have better rhet-oric—and when they're in power they toss us more and bigger crumbs—they never make a place for us at the table, and they don't intend to. They intend only to neutralize our radicalism by throwing us a few sops.

Surrounded by sunshine, but darkly shadowed by knowl-edge of the deliberate institutionalized evil against us, I re-solved there on the motel lawn never again to give any of my time or energy, any of my precious woman's stuff, to either of those two parties. I swore to myself that I would never again willingly or knowingly collaborate with the patriarchy, never again be an accomplice in my own oppression. Not for one more second of my life.

When I had recovered from the physical effects of the fast and looked out over the women's movement to see what was going on that I could put my energies into, it didn't take me long to realize that there was no place for me. The great center body of the women's movement—the women's organizations, but particularly NOW, which I loved, which had taken the place of family and church and friends—had become almost exclusively the handmaidens of the Democratic Party. They were all drowning in the mainstream.[1] Thousands of strong women giving all their energy, all their time, all their wonder-ful creativity, all their freshness and vigor, to the very system that was destroying women and all life on earth. A system which without their help would fall apart. The irony made me miserable.

But I knew why feminists were being co-opted. I knew how lost and empty I was feeling about the defeat of the ERA, and how deep the grief and feeling of failure went.[2] We had

worked for a decade with all our strength. We had done everything we knew how to do. And we had failed.

So all the old messages of patriarchy came rushing back,
only, now, redoubled in strength: "You're inferior/you can't do
these complex things; leave them to the men/you're not smart
enough/you can't learn it right because you're female/stay out
of politics; it's no place for women."

And we were feeling, though not consciously thinking,
"Maybe they're right after all. Maybe we *can't* do it. Maybe we
are inferior."

And then, right at that moment (as it always happens in history when the powerless are at their most vulnerable) came the
seductive voice of the powerful — the voice, in this case, of the
Democratic Party — saying, "Oh, we're so sorry this happened to
you. It breaks our hearts. Because, of course, unlike those other
guys, we're your friends. And you're lucky you've got friends like
us, because we've got power and can help you. Now if you'll just
stop rampaging around and getting out of hand, stop being
'coarse and pushy' [as the *New York Times* called NOW during the
1984 presidential election], stop being wild-eyed, bra-burning
dykes! — if you'll just be nice and good and join us, we'll give you
some power. And *then*, you can change the system."

Ah, how sweet that sounded to our ears. But what we
didn't realize was that they were giggling behind their hands as
they said it, because they knew that our getting into the system
and trying to stay in it would change *us* far more than we could
ever hope to change *it*. Once we were in there — and under
their thumbs — we would learn quickly that we had to conform
even more if we wanted the privilege of being re-elected.

It must be amusing to men that they can so readily persuade us to put our prodigious energy and creativity into keeping them on their thrones. The irony must be delicious to them:
women bolstering up the moldering, putrescent corpse of patriarchy as it drips with the blood of millions of their sisters.

Men in power strive to get the strongest, most dangerous
women to join them, because as long as we are where they can

179

see us, imitating them, working for their favor, acquiring a stake in the status quo, we are not fomenting revolution. They like us to think they have the only game in town, and they're delighted when we strive for nothing more than to play it. Because they own and control that game, they make all the rules, hold all the cards, win every time. As we saw in Illinois, when we begin to look as if we just might win a round, they simply change the rules. Since they devised the game and understand it perfectly, we can never best them at it. And they know it.

Where they don't want us is outside their game, not respecting or honoring it, not pouring our energies and time into it, but away somewhere on our own, out of their sight and control, playing our *own* game—a game of our own devising, which we control, the rules of which they have no say in making, and don't know for certain, or understand. A game they can't see well, because we're not right under their noses but instead, off somewhere else doing our own work of initiating a new sane and loving order upon the earth that signals the end of their reign.

We are infinitely less powerful and dangerous within the system than consciously, designedly outside it. Men know this or, believe me, *none* of us would be in it at all!

We know this as co-optation, a classic ploy used throughout history to render potential rebel leaders docile and "safe." And we're certainly not the first group to be so seduced. A couple of years ago, I was on James Farmer's radio show in Washington, D. C. Farmer was one of the leaders of the civil rights movement 20 years ago. As we chatted before the show, I asked him where he saw the Black civil rights movement now. His eyes filled with tears. "We don't have a movement any more," he said. "They gave all the leaders important jobs in the government. They bought us off."*

Co-optation implies blindness to the real dynamics of power. It also speaks clearly of insensitivity to genuine evil.

---

*"All of us but Dick Gregory," he added.

If I were to differentiate between the radical feminist mind and the mind of the women's rights feminist (the one who responds with such alacrity to invitations to be a wallflower at the Old Boys' Club dance — anything to be allowed inside the door), I'd say that the women's rights-ists look at the pie of power and say, "This is basically a good pie; as good a pie as we're likely to get in this world, certainly better than the pie in most countries. The only trouble is that it hasn't been cut up equitably. So what we have to do is get bigger slices for women and minorities and all those who have had to make do for so long with such exceedingly slender slices."

What happens when we get bigger slices of the pie is chronicled briefly by Ellen Goodman in a column right after the 1984 election entitled "Sisterhood May Be Losing Out to Equality":

> The question — What has happened to that always tenuous bond called sisterhood? — goes wider and deeper than any one election. There was a time, and not that long ago, when women began to focus on what they had in common, what they had suffered in common. There was a sense of community created out of this fresh awareness — out of anger, too, and a belief in change. A certain population of women thought of themselves as women first, and found some self-conscious assurance in the slogan, "Sisterhood is powerful."

> Today much of that energy has been dispelled in the best possible way: by success. The head of steam from women has been dissipated by new opportunities . . .[3]

Many professional women content themselves with the few crumbs they've been tossed. They have gained a little respect as professionals, and are afraid of tampering with a proven "success" formula. What patriarchy terms "success" for women, however, is our most fearful and frightening failure to

181

establish another reality on this planet by determining to live by feminist values.

Radical feminists look at the women's rights-ists' pie of power model and say, "That pie is rotten! It will poison anyone who touches it. What we have to do is bake a whole new pie from a whole new recipe."

As Elizabeth Oakes Smith tried to make clear in her address to the Woman's Rights Convention in 1852:

> My friends, do we realize for what purpose we are convened? Do we fully understand that we aim at nothing less than an entire subversion of the present order of society, a dissolution of the whole existing social compact?[4]

What women have needed to do for well over a century is to wash the men and their value system right out of our hearts, to go out of our 5000-year-old minds.

We are trapped in these minds by lies. At least three major lies about power are inherent in the seduction called co-optation, and these are ancient lies, cunningly crafted to keep us obedient and malleable. The first is that, under certain carefully specified conditions of worthiness, the powerful will give the powerless some of their power.

Can anyone think of a time when that actually happened? It has never happened, and it's not going to happen. The powerful squat over their stinking piles of power, waking and sleeping, every nerve alert and twitching. It is simply not on the patriarchal agenda to give up even one real atom of it to women. Rather, the entire effort is toward steadily increasing the store — at the expense of women and of all life on the planet. Nevertheless, though one would think females might have noticed and remarked on this extremely strong male habit, the lie that slaveholders are anxious to share power with the slaves somehow remains one of the father's favorite and most potent strategies with women. Everywhere in the country, women are eager to join men in public office, in corporate office; avid to serve patriarchy.

Praise and scorn are major tools of co-optation. After we lost the ERA, for instance, major news media crowed disingenuously that finally the women's movement had come of age. They congratulated us on learning how to play the male political game. We were praised for losing! Red warning flags sprang up in my mind when I read those honeyed words. I knew that deception is *always* involved when the powerful praise the powerless. We must understand this phenomenon, this trickery. Men will always and only praise us for doing the *wrong things*, for reinforcing the status quo, for perpetuating their privilege.

Like children with all-powerful parents, we long for the approval of powerful men — the *real* human beings. For too many centuries we have so depended for our very lives upon their good will that over time our deepest sense of self has become almost inextricably dependent upon their opinion of us. Having perfected our dependency, and operating on a visceral understanding of behavior modification, it is small wonder that now men can manipulate us effortlessly and shamelessly with praise and scorn.

The humiliating part is that we are so easily and completely taken in. They crushed the radical women's movement of the early '70s with scorn and abuse. Women, the most deeply oppressed people on earth (which means the most dependent on the favor of their oppressors), have not been able to stand up under withdrawal of approval from the minions of the system — Left, Right, or moderate.

We will know we are being effective against patriarchy when we are again attacked, belittled, and laughed at, when we are told that we are brainless fools, doing everything wrong, will never get anywhere acting like this, are obviously wanton, unattractive to men, hateful, strident, vicious, and our own worst enemies.

Or when we are studiously ignored. At the moment, patriarchy has little to fear from us. We are on our knees before it, slavering for just a little approval, just a small chance to join

the game, to stand behind the men's chairs and whisper suggestions about how they might play their hand, having no cards
of our own to play, even when it appears that we do. Women
in policy-making positions are only there on sufferance, only
there so long as they prove that they have no intention of playing any other but the same old ugly game called patriarchy.

We will have to abandon our patriarchal mind to find our
own game, and we will have to do it soon.

The second lie, which is very closely connected to the first,
and which as females we hear from the moment we're born, is
that power is "out there" somewhere. Men have it. They can
pass it around to women they like, just like any other commod-
ity. And so if you'll just get in line, and stay in line, they might
pass you some.

The truth of the matter is, of course, that the locus of all
power is within us. There is no other source. Nobody can give
it to us and nobody can take it away. We awaken to it ourselves, and claim it, or we believe the lie and abdicate.

The patriarchs—male and female—make abdication
likely by obfuscating the nature of power, defining power for
us in such a way that we don't recognize that that longing for
dignity, that passion for justice and *more* than justice, that sense
of connectedness and wholeness, that courage in our own
breasts, signals power of a kind and magnitude they cannot
even comprehend. It is a patriarchal reversal to define power
as that which dominates and destroys. In reality, "power" is a
positive creative force. Patriarchy has none of it. Because men
cannot create life, they specialize in death. They compensate
by destroying.

The third lie of the fathers about power is that there is a
scarcity of it. The strength of this nurtured delusion was
thrown into bold relief for those of us in the campaign when
Geraldine Ferraro became the Democratic Party's Vice-Presidential candidate. Angry, desperate letters began to appear at
my campaign headquarters, pleading with me to drop my campaign so as not to deflect women's votes away from her.

Equally irrational reporters asked me every day from then until November, "Why are you still running now that Geraldine Ferraro is out there?"

I always answered, nonplussed, "Did you ask Gary Hart and Jesse Jackson this same question all those months they were running against Walter Mondale? Did you say, 'Really, Gary, really, Jesse, why are you running? There's already a man running!' Or did you ask Fritz, 'Why are you running for President, Fritz? We already have a man in the White House?'"

Even though we weren't even running for the same office, Ferraro and I were instantly perceived as in competition for the very same sliver of the pie. This mentality of tokenism is necessary to keep our present system intact, and will not, cannot, give way in patriarchy.[5]

So in addition to the potent lie that there is only so much power, and only in the amount and of the kind men choose to give us, in patriarchy women are presumed to be clones. Slaves must be dehumanized, must be stereotyped by slaveholders to justify slavery. The assumption was that because both Geraldine Ferraro and Sonia Johnson were women, they were the same, would say the same things, appeal to the same people, have the same goals in running, have a similar ideological impact — if on a different scale (since it was clear that Ferraro was going to get far greater exposure). So why did I continue, when by doing so I would hurt the movement? Why didn't I just go home — and bake a cake, or something?

There are always many roles for women, despite male views to the contrary. Ms. Ferraro and I were playing two very different ones. But of the two of us, I was the free agent. I was not competing for a piece of the patriarchal pie, but was operating out of a different kind of power altogether. I waited for no one to choose me, but chose and empowered myself for ten months of a 13-month campaign. From the beginning, I told the Citizens Party exactly what I was going to say if I ran; on the whole, I think they were more uncomfortable than not about what I was saying. I knew they might not nominate me, that if a "progressive" man chose to run against me, I would very likely lose. But I thought of the ten months I'd have to promulgate radical feminism nationwide before the convention, even if they ultimately chose not to nominate me, and knew that I couldn't lose. Ten months was not much time to plant essential, urgent ideas in enough minds to make a difference, but it was better than no months at all. I had to try. So I got right down to work and said exactly what I knew had to be said, as passionately and persuasively as I knew how to say it, every minute of my campaign. As far as I ever heard, Ms. Ferraro and I seldom, if ever, voiced a similar opinion.

From my life in the Mormon church, I learned forever about institutionalized power and lies, about their intimate connection, their symbiosis, their utter dependency upon one another.

I knew that the feminists working so determinedly and well for the Democratic Party, like the women in the churches, believed the lie that the party belonged to them, too. They thought this was *their* party; why should they be driven out? But of course, it is *not* their party, any more than those churches are women's churches. The men in charge of both political parties and churches — which are twin chapters of the Old Boys' Club — are delighted to have persuaded women to think so, however. They get our labor, get it almost entirely free, and our reverence, though now and then we kick up a little ruckus to get some attention. So long as women believe the monstrous lie that these fiercely male institutions include us and belong in some measure to us, we play prettily and pitifully into our own destruction.

In the late summer of 1982, when I looked out over the women's movement and saw us crashing upon the reef again, I finally despaired. I thought to myself miserably, "We've forgotten who we are. We are not going to succeed after all."

But that thought was unendurable. My whole life means women are going to succeed, are going to establish a regenerative value system upon our planet. Because I couldn't negate the purpose of my life, or deny the vision that sustained me, I fought against despair as against death. And informed with all the knowledge I had stored up, equipped with every tool at hand, I campaigned for the presidency of NOW, I began research into empowerment processes for Women Gathering, I intensified my speaking schedule. But still despair lurked just under the surface.

Despair did not merely feel miserable, it was impolitic as well, and I knew it. I knew that as long as we have hope there is hope, and the moment we lose hope, there is no hope. This makes hope the quintessential political wisdom, the first and basic program of the women's movement. But even knowing this, I couldn't banish the fear — which is so vast a part of despair — that we would continue to be enticed by lies to collaborate against ourselves, as we had for centuries, and fail in our purpose.

Then, in the spring of 1983, needing to do something definitive about this state of mind, I decided to go down to Sugarloaf Key in Florida and meet Barbara Deming, whom I knew only by correspondence and telephone. She was thought by many who knew her to be among the wisest of women, and I hoped that her perspective on the direction of the women's movement would cheer me and that we might conspire together.

As I sat reading on the plane, a woman came up and tapped me on the shoulder. "You're Sonia Johnson, aren't you?" she asked. I said yes, and she said, "Well, I've just come from an executive committee meeting of the Citizens Party and your name keeps coming up as a possible candidate for president on our ticket. Would you be interested?"

"Oh, no!" I laughed. "That's not what I do!" (As if it's what everyone else does, just not me.) "But there *are* women who do that sort of thing. Call one of them," I said, and promptly forgot all about it.

Two or three days later as Barbara and I were preparing lunch in her kitchen, I suddenly remembered the incident on the plane. "You know, Barbara," I said, "the most amusing thing happened to me on the way down here. You're not going to believe this! Somebody actually came up and suggested that I run for President! Isn't that funny?" And I started to laugh.

Barbara turned and looked at me with a most serious face. "Well, you're going to do it, aren't you?" she asked.

It took my breath away; the perfect feminist response always takes my breath away. It's stunning to be taken seriously as a woman. It hardly ever happens. And, too, I was embarrassed at being caught red-handed in my own sexism. What was I laughing at? What was so funny about that? Look at who *is* President!*

So I went home a better feminist, but no more inclined to run for President. Then a half dozen members of the Citizens Party began to call me from here and there around the country urging me to do it. I didn't want to do it, but then, who would? Who needs a whole year of having everybody think you've finally gone over the brink?

Besides, I was vastly disillusioned with the electoral system, vastly ignorant of the nature and history of third-party politics, and vastly skeptical that *any* party would want me as their spokesperson if they knew what I spoke. In addition, I couldn't see clearly how to organize a national Presidential campaign upon and around feminist philosophy, how to bring feminism to bear upon all the urgent problems of our time and illuminate them, though the challenge of it excited me. The excitement itself hinted that it needed to be done.

Several well-known women's rights advocates had been proselytizing the flock and writing books about the gender gap, about the mighty power of the vote. I knew that women hadn't even gotten the vote until it was nearly useless, until the choices of candidates had been narrowed by financial and military interests to the point where no matter who seemed to win, these interests actually won the election, and the status quo would

---

*As this is being written, Ronald Reagan is President of the United States.

not only grind inexorably along, but would intensify. I knew that only a semblance, a mirage, of choice exists in our present system.

As Benjamin R. Barker writes in an *Atlantic Monthly* article entitled "Voting Is Not Enough":

> The real choice we face in the coming years is not between Republicans and Democrats, or between the supply-side and the welfare state, or between hawks and doves; it is between an ever more meaningless and weak form of democracy in which we periodically rubber-stamp the bureaucrats and politicians who govern for us and over us and in our stead, and a strong democracy in which we reassume the responsibilities of self-government.[6]

As I turned feminism and politics around in my mind and investigated the third-party phenomenon in this country, I began to see electoral politics from a different perspective. Immediately and irrevocably, the myth of the two-party system broke down. I learned that, though many believe there is something sacrosanct about having two parties—and two parties only—in this country, perhaps going so far as to think that the Founders even decreed a two-party system ("Isn't it in the Constitution?" I've been asked by people who should know better), in fact, political parties did not appear in this country until the Federalists and the Anti-Federalists turned up in the election of 1797. There had been two elections before that in which there were no political parties, and another in 1828 when all four candidates were Democrats, all running without party endorsement. In the 49 presidential elections conducted through 1980, there were 18 two-party elections and 18 three-party elections, one one-party election, eight four-party elections, and one five-party election.

I came to understand that we have never really had a two-party system in the United States and should thank our lucky stars that we haven't. It is true that there are two dominant parties. I can't call them "major." For 15 years I taught university students about "major" and "minor" writers. Though the designations are often questionable, the theory is that "major" writers are distinguished by the presence of genius. Because the two big parties are always the guardians of the status quo, they cannot afford genius. The men who run them are men for whom the system works — for whom it is deliberately set up to work: rich, white, heterosexual men. They have no motivation whatever to change a system which has made them lords of all they survey, and that makes the one man among them who is elected President King of the World. Left to themselves, the two big parties, with their principal desire not only to keep privilege but to increase it, would merely deepen the inequities present in the system — the rich getting richer, the poor getting poorer, the industrialists and militarists having freer and freer reign, as we have seen more clearly than ever in the Reagan administration.

Though this is the strong trend, the two big parties have fortunately never been left entirely to themselves. The trend has been hampered somewhat by the truly "major" parties through our country's history — parties which, though small, have a certain limited genius.

It seems tautological to point out that change necessary for the well-being of those for whom the system was designed *not* to work is never initiated from within the system, but this truth remains inexplicably murky to otherwise clear minds. Because essential change is strenuously opposed by those in power, the burden of rectifying injustices and imbalances always falls upon those outside the circles of power. They exercise a kind of power history books ignore — or historians censor.

Though the League of Women Voters and the media operate on the untenable and ahistoric assumption that the ideas of Republican and Democratic candidates alone are worth hearing in an election, the truth is that alternative candidates have far more often launched significant, vigorous new ideas into mainstream politics than have their larger, better-known cousins: the abolition of slavery, for example, and most labor reforms — the Socialists' eight-hour workday, minimum wage, social security, child labor laws, workers' compensation, unemployment insurance. Many items of the Populist agenda of 1892 were ultimately enacted into law by both the Republican and Democratic parties. Major portions of the New Deal programs of Franklin D. Roosevelt derived from platforms of the Progressive Party in earlier decades.

Alternative parties can accomplish this because they are uniquely able to think more about principle than about power. This makes them better able to see problems, and because they have nothing to lose, to think of creative ways of solving them. They are the risk-takers, the conscience, the ideological governors that — just barely — have historically kept the big parties from plunging into an abyss of total mindlessness.

Alternative parties are reformist movements, anti-system movements on some levels, limited rebellions and foments — safety valves for the system. I am absolutely certain, however, that if any one of them came into power, nothing basic would change because the power-over, dichotomous patriarchal paradigm still rules their minds. Their being *out* of power is their strength. Although other kinds of organizations and groups function to address specific ills — environmental and nuclear, for instance — these traditionally function within the two-party system and therefore threaten the status quo far less, so that they have far less potential for bringing about reform than strong third-party movements.

As I thought about the difficult new concepts I wanted to introduce to the electorate of the United States, I saw clearly how the sting must first be removed from them by familiarity. New ideas must be so often and so reasonably explained that they no longer sound alien and extreme, or as dangerous as they are. Their common acceptance then usually forces the sluggish and corrupt system to adopt them — or, more often, some watered-down version of them. But the system cannot adopt feminist ideas without destroying itself. So any moves it makes in the direction of equity and justice are infinitesimal, agonizingly slow, and undercut in a dozen ways. At the present rate, for example, women will not have equal representation in state and national legislatures in this country for nearly 900 years.

But, I reasoned, even if feminist ideas will never be adopted in any useful way by the system, nevertheless easing their sting by repetition and familiarity through a national campaign could help change the morphogenetic field, the entire global paradigm.

Although I came to realize that political campaigns can, on the rarest of occasions, be genuine instruments of change, at the same time I understood that this can only happen when candidates have no expectations of winning — and no desire for victory. Then they can use the time and energy they would have spent moderating and modulating and compromising and equivocating to win votes concentrating instead upon the task of winning acceptance of certain principles, upon the victory of ideas. And although I knew that the ideal third-party campaign was generally considered the one which, by threatening to lure away huge numbers of votes, throws the traditional parties into a frenzy of re-evaluation, the option to concentrate upon principle rather than votes began to seem highly legitimate and desirable to me.

"Sonia," I said to myself at about this point in my thinking, "you have an idea which must not just seep, but *leap* into global consciousness." The possibility of such a campaign began to seem real, even pressing. Although I'd been speaking all over the country for four years, my audience had been limited. Feminism not only deserves to have, but, if we are to solve the seemingly intractable problems of our times, *must* have the largest possible forum. I knew that third-party candidates get little media coverage and small audience turn-out compared with big party candidates, but even so, the message would get out far more than it would otherwise. And what else could I do that year that would be as useful?

192

There were other reasons a feminist had to run for President, of course. I remember sometime in May 1983, when we were having the first big media blitz about the possibility of a woman as the Vice-Presidential running mate on the Democratic ticket, how distressed I was at what the nation was watching in the media. There before us were images of highly capable, strong women on their knees in classic slave posture before that great bevy of disdainful Democratic candidates, pleading, "Oh, please, let me be your Vice-Presidential running mate. Please give me permission to take myself seriously. Please give me just a little bit of power, will you? Open up the door for me just a crack. I promise I'll be good!" That we thought we had to grovel, that we thought there was ultimately anything to be gained by abasing ourselves in that way, had been making me feel sick for some time.

I thought how, for many people, the kind of campaign the Citizens Party was talking about could whisk that demeaning image right out the window, and replace it with images of women taking *ourselves* seriously — if *we* don't do it, nobody else is going to. Images of women not asking permission of anybody to act human, to do what we should have been doing from the beginning. Women demanding, "What is this Vice-Presidential nonsense? Women should be President!"

I wondered what we'd been waiting for. For the men to coax us? For Fritz and Ronnie to say, "We're so boring that watching us may plunge the whole world into a coma before November. We have no new ideas, and we've made the most horrific mess. Please, women, take the reins from us and guide us back to sanity"? Or have we been waiting for a *dea ex machina*? Waiting for something outside oneself to give the signal for action is a slave attitude. I knew it was time to stop waiting.

Every feminist alive knows that the public's view of women in our country's history needs serious reform. I saw that a feminist campaign could bring people up against the realization that if there had been even a semblance of democracy in the United States in the last 200-plus years, at least some of

our Presidents would have been women. And if there had been
genuine democracy, more than half would have been. It would
make clear that we can't call ourselves a democracy without
rolling on the floor in perfect fits of hilarity.

In addition, just to have a woman's name on the Presidential ballot in at least half the states (which was the Citizens
Party's goal) could make a difference in how voters viewed
"women's role." It was important for people to walk into the
voting booth and see for the first time in living memory and
in a national election, a woman's name on the ballot, a woman
they could actually vote for for President of the United States.
A shift of consciousness could come about just by that one inclusion. I decided that was worth the whole campaign. It became clearer and clearer that it had to be done. And it became
clearer and clearer that no other feminist was going to do it.

It seemed significant to me that it had been exactly 100
years since a woman had run in a national Presidential election. Belva Lockwood, a staunch and active Republican for
many years, attended the Republican National Convention in
1884 with Frances Willard, and argued in vain for a more feminist platform. The men laughed them both out of the hall. At
that point, Belva became convinced that there was little reason
to believe that the Republicans would ever support a national
drive for suffrage.

In a storm of self-determination, she contacted the Equal
Rights Party of California and urged them to include a strong
feminist plank in their platform. To her surprise, they wrote
back asking her to be their candidate in the election.[7]

> Belva was a smart woman. She had gotten her-
> self into the National University Law School in
> Washington, D.C. over the objections of most of the
> faculty and administration. In fact, she was never of-
> ficially admitted until the end, but was tutored for the
> most part by one supportive faculty member. Never-
> theless, she was the first woman to argue a legal case

before the Supreme Court, and that in defense of a black lawyer being denied admission to the bar. She knew her politics.

Anyway, Belva accepted the challenge of the Equal Rights Party and immediately set about to develop a platform emphasizing suffrage, the placement of women in high government offices, and the extension of full citizenship rights to all, regardless of sex, color, or class.[8]

Although Susan B. Anthony and Elizabeth Cady Stanton were not supportive of her campaign,[9] viewing the race as untimely and a dilution of the energy of the suffrage movement, Belva was not daunted. She understood politics better than they. In essence her campaign said that, even though it was in the interests of the two big parties to support suffrage, until they understood sexism their analysis of the other problems facing the nation would be inadequate. This is exactly what needed to be said a hundred years later in 1984.

But I didn't want to run for president. I knew I could count on being wildly misunderstood even by the majority of feminists, many of whom were having an all-consuming if ill-thought-out courtship with the Democratic Party. In addition, I'd been an aberration in the women's movement for some time — almost from the day I walked out of the Mormon church into the dream. Although I think of it as being a pioneer, and understand that it is a necessary role — indispensable, in fact — still I know what it looks like to others of a more cautious bent, which is practically everybody. This makes it heavy at times, and wearing. I'd been fulfilling it faithfully for four or five years by that time. Obviously, I was fit for it. But I thought I deserved to be spelled; someone else should be the deviant in the women's movement that year and give me a rest.

Sometime during the last day of the Gathering, when for a moment I held the microphone, I mentioned to the assembled women that the Citizens Party had approached me about running for their nomination for President of the United States. I told them that I was going to check it out when I spoke at the Citizens Party convention in San Francisco the next week. "But I'm going to give them such a ferociously feminist speech," I said, "that they'll probably back off in great haste and never come near me again."

I told the women that I wanted them to know I was thinking it over, but that the odds of its coming to anything were very slight. Despite my assurance that no party — left, progressive, liberal — really, in its heart of hearts, wanted to be represented by a feminist, my announcement exploded like a bomb. I could almost hear the shocked reactions: "I can't believe it! All the time she was being so persuasive against working within the system, and showing us other ways of transforming society, she was considering running for President!"

I can hardly blame them for perceiving this as grossest hypocrisy and ultimate perfidy. I should have taken the time right then to explain why I was even considering such a course. But it seemed so unlikely to me to come to anything — and if it did, so clear that it would be a course treacherous to the system — that at the time I thought explanation was unnecessary. I rapidly recognized my error. I had been turning this possibility over in my mind for months. That such a campaign could be used for feminist purposes was clear to me by then. But the women in that room had just had the idea dropped on them out of the blue. At first scent, it had to reek of compromise, even duplicity.

As I felt their dismay, I promised them silently — having given up the microphone — that if, by some unlikely chance, I decided to run, I would run on the most revolutionary platform ever proposed in this country or any other. Revolutionary in the true sense: replacing with life-giving values the decayed and crumbling foundations of the fathers' failed experiment.

9

"Now, if I Were President . . ."

Though the determined few from the Citizens Party pressed me for six months, almost everyone else I spoke to about it warned me not to run, said it was politically unwise, had many and varied but almost always negative reasons why it just wouldn't do. But they agreed on one point: "Not *this* year!" they shrieked in crazed unison. "*This* year we've got to beat Reagan!" I had to climb up a mental stepladder in order to look out over their terror, to disengage myself from their nearly palpable, brain-numbing panic.

I marveled that, in their fear, all these intelligent women and men had retreated even deeper into the old mind and lost sight of one of the most obvious of all metaphysical laws: we never get what we want by joining in the politics of fear and reaction which demand that all voices, all creativity, all imagination be conscripted against what we *don't* want. The only way we get what we want is by working directly, with all the energy and longing of our hearts, for what we *do*.

I knew that since "reality" is what we pay attention to, concentrating on Reagan, as so many otherwise reasonable persons were doing, would only succeed in making him more and more real, larger and larger, stronger and stronger. After all, negative energy is also energy. If we gave him our energy, if we watched him and thought about him — obsessed about him — if he dominated our thoughts and actions for an entire year, there was no way on this green earth that he could be defeated. We would *make* him invincible.

(And this is what happened. By the end of his campaign, Reagan positively LOOMED over the United States. This should hardly have surprised anyone. *Everybody*, for and against him, had been imagining him, lavishing energy and thought upon him.)

Mary Ann and I had several discussions about the curious fact that we are always in danger of becoming like those we hate or are in conflict and competition with. This is one reason the Democratic Party is becoming less and less distinct from the Republican Party. We pondered why it was that so few people seemed to be acting out of an awareness of this phenomenon.

The week following Women Gathering, I went to San Francisco to speak to the Citizens Party at their convention. I wanted to get a look at them, having heard many ugly stories about the Left and sexism. Their literature and constitution sounded good to me, but I was deeply distrustful of rhetoric. I remembered the Mormon church and how its leaders "love" women. I remembered the Democratic Party and its broken promises. And I also wanted this group to take a close hard look at me.

I began my speech to them by telling them how excited I still was from the Martin Luther King, Jr. Memorial March the week before, and that I was excited because an amazing thing had happened on that march. A group of men — Black, white, Hispanic — from some union in Pennsylvania marched next to our group of women for awhile. They came alongside us as we were singing, "We are gentle, angry women, and we are singing, singing for our lives" (substituting different adjectives each time: visionary women, strong courageous women, and so on and on). Right away, as they began marching at our side, some unexpected sound made me turn and look over at them. I could hardly believe what I saw. There they were, wearing hardhats, looking tough in sleeveless T-shirts, singing blithely along with us, "We are anti-patriarchal women, and we are singing, singing for our lives." I stared at their mouths. I nudged others and several of us began staring at their mouths. They couldn't be but they were — singing with us that they were anti-Reagan women who were voting for their lives! They were not laughing or smirking or making a joke of it, either; just looking as unself-conscious as if they had always sung songs about being women-loving women.

I told the Citizens Party that this inexplicable event had made me feel hopeful in a way nothing else could. Because I knew that the day that men in general no longer define "man" as "not a woman" is the day the system will have flip-flopped in earnest. The singing hardhats were evidence of a new morphogenetic field in the making; they belonged in a new paradigm.

I talked to party members about the necessity of having a vision of this new world that informed all they did, a vision that hadn't come out of the intellect alone. Such dreams are difficult to dream, and I told them I knew that. They are difficult because patriarchy has always said, "Forget intuition. That's women's stuff. Forget the deeper mind in there. Forget your DNA, and all the richness underneath and above and outside what we tell you is real. Reason is the important thing."

But of course the most momentous scientific and philosophical breakthroughs have not come through reason or logic, but out of the deep mind. Einstein said that many times he got his answers in dreams, not from sitting there thinking it over. They came out of that intuitive, that symbol-making place where we genuinely live and which really motivates us. If there is anything we should know by now it is that we are not motivated by what we think but by what we *feel* — all of us, all the time.

I talked to them about means and ends, reminding them that in the best of all possible worlds, we would all know that the means are not separate from the ends, and would behave accordingly. As an example, I pointed out that *how* they held their convention was *what* they were doing; that they couldn't hope to do sexist things there, racist things there, power jockeying there and expect to have any other reality than the same old dreary, destructive mess.

I told them that one reason I'd come to San Francisco to be with them was that I knew the major question of the convention was whether to run a Presidential campaign, and if so, who to run, and how to do it. I wanted them to know that I'd come to urge them to do it. I understood all the objections to this plan. I understood them from the point of view of the organized women's movement, but they were similar to objections from the Left, the liberals and the progressives. I warned them that because of the fierce reaction against Reagan, they couldn't count on support from the women's organizations no matter who they ran.

Looking back, I see how true a prophet I was. In their panic to defeat Reagan, liberals, radicals, and progressives made 1984 the most politically repressive year we have experienced in a long, long time. No one was allowed to speak unless they spoke for Mondale. Any voice that tried to point out the obvious—that Mondale was a preposterous choice for the peace and anti-nuclear and non-interventionist movements—fell upon ears deaf with dread. Hardly any discussion was allowed. Everyone was expected to drop their scruples and fall, lockstep, into line behind the Democrats.

We were expected to do this regardless of reason, regardless of Democratic Party policy or tradition or history, none of which merits loyalty by any genuinely humanitarian group in the country. The pressure was so great that even the Communist Party buckled and backed the Democrats (though they ran their own candidates, too, heaven knows why). It was surreal. A person had to become terrorized and desperate and out of control herself to understand why everyone around her was behaving so irrationally, had so totally lost perspective.

I don't know how many times I heard the argument that we had to defeat Reagan before he filled the Supreme Court with right-wing extremists cited as a reason for everyone, en masse, to throw principle and integrity overboard. Few seemed to realize that dishonoring their own stated values and goals by working for an unenlightened candidate *had* to affect the outcome negatively.[1] Almost everyone separated means and ends about as far as I've seen them separated, and forgot, in the breach, that how they were acting couldn't be separated from the society they wished to build, that how they were acting *was*, in fact, the society they were building.

They also forgot that to the degree that they concentrated their energies and will against something, to that same degree they created it around them. Paradoxically, when the Left began to shout that all those who did not vote for Mondale were traitors, they participated in bringing about the very world they fear, the world Reagan and his cronies are busy creating: a world with little diversity and less individual and political freedom. (When anyone tells me I have no choice, I am instantly wary. I know that to the degree that I accept that dictum, I *won't* have a choice.)

But that was all still very much in the future. Speaking to the Citizens Party in the fall of 1983, I had other problems on my mind. Nineteen eighty-four was being touted by some feminist leaders as the year women's vote would make the difference in the election. The general hope was that by November 6, this "gender gap" would have widened into a mammoth chasm into which all misogynists would plunge and be dashed upon the rocks, and that no politician would ever again dare to discount women. I feared we were setting ourselves up for a fall.

But the problem was thornier than being discredited if we were wrong. I reminded the Citizens Party that the promise of the gender gap was an illusory promise. All it promised, even if it existed, was that we could substitute one party for the other. I didn't have to tell members of a third party that the Republicans were not the only villains who determined U.S. politics. Better than most, they knew that all major world wars were fought under Democratic administrations, that Truman bombed Hiroshima and Nagasaki, that Kennedy and Johnson gave us Vietnam and greatly revitalized the arms race that Truman had initiated. I didn't have to remind them that F.D.R. sat in the White House for years knowing that Jews were in the ovens in Germany and didn't do anything to stop it, or that for at least the past 60 years every President has had nefarious dealings in Central and South America, has encouraged investment in South Africa. Knowing this, what could we imagine it would mean even if it were proved that women vote differently as a group than men? That women are soft touches for empty liberal rhetoric? That they might be influential in putting a Democrat instead of a Republican in the White House, in perpetuating the deception that there is a saving difference between one set of patriarchs and another?

"There comes a time," I told them, "when a group must arise that has some kind of historical perspective, the courage to see out beyond the gripping panic of the present moment, the ability to see currents in history, to take a wider view." With this perspective 1988 did not look as if it would be a better time to run a candidate than 1984; matters were clearly going to deteriorate steadily if something didn't interrupt the pattern. I knew that when we keep acting out of terror of the imminent, we lose the courage to do what we would have the wits to do for the long run, what we would do if we believed there were time to do it. And so we fulfill our own prophecy of doom.

I knew that those who were saying that 1984 was a bad time to run an alternative candidate were forgetting that there is never a better time to do what needs to be done than the present. Never. Certain risks are essential. No great achievement was ever won without enormous risk. The risk is an integral part of the achievement. Sometimes I think we can tell how important it is to risk by how dangerous it would be to do so.

It is impossible to calculate the risk to our shaky democracy if alternative voices do not make themselves heard, somehow, in every possible arena. I knew the Citizens Party found it hard to believe that their small group could be that important. It's difficult for us to think — any of us — that we can really be the one that destiny is waiting to use as a tool. It's always somebody else. It's always those folks in the news, those guys in the history books. On the contrary, it's always *us*.

I assured them in San Francisco that day that people who thought as they said in their literature they thought, were tools of history, tools of whatever it is — this great longing of humankind to stay upon this planet, to stay here peacefully, to take evolutionary steps forward — they were part of that, and they must not discount themselves because of their size and the small importance they were accorded in the political world. I reminded them of the theory of dissipative structures that holds that it is always small groups that set off systemic changes. If their voice wasn't heard during the coming election year, they would never know what might have been. If they hadn't said to themselves, "Now, let us be *reasonable*."

I told them I'd come to urge them to run a woman candidate, not to be self-serving, but because one of the noblest features of their dream — at least as outlined in their literature — was that it portrayed a world where women were something other than we have been for nearly 5000 years. If this were not just rhetoric, it behooved them to have integrity and to begin transforming the world at once in this small way. If they were going to be true to their progressive roots, I couldn't see any other alternative for them, couldn't see how, with the kind of dream they said they had, they could justify *not* running a woman.

Then I delivered the ferociously feminist portion of the speech, the portion designed to make the war against women visible. At the end, I made the men honorary women (for the moment) and had everyone stand and sing that they were gentle angry women, non-patriarchal women, women-loving women.

Afterwards, I sat out in the foyer to be available for anyone who wished to stop by and get better acquainted. I was besieged at once by males who, one after another, asked nearly the same question: "It's good to talk about feminism, but can you talk about the other 'issues'? If you run for President, you'll have to talk about economics, and foreign policy, and issues other than women's rights. Are you aware of that?"

Each time I somehow recovered from these slaps in the face, and answered mildly that of course I knew that Presidential candidates have to talk about those issues. I wanted to talk about them. Fortunately, feminism *includes* economics, foreign policy, and all the others. Of course, this didn't reassure them at all. And all the while I was carefully noting their condescension.

The women had their chance to reveal their priorities and level of consciousness, too. Several of them descended upon me to bemoan the fact that I had made their men very uncomfortable, and surely the best way to set things right would be by working *together*.

"But the men aren't working," I pointed out, "and they won't work on this problem until they're made distinctly uncomfortable. Discomfort always precedes change, and accompanies it. That's why change is so hard. It won't hurt the men to be uncomfortable, just as it doesn't hurt whites to be made uncomfortable about racism. Don't be so protective of them. They can take care of their own feelings, and should start doing so, the sooner the better."

One woman approached me with tears in her eyes, her lips trembling. Taking hold of my arm, she looked beseechingly at me and pled, "Please, Sonia. Don't polarize men and women!" Though I could hardly bear to begin at the very beginning *again*, I explained as patiently and briefly as I could that feminists are not polarizing men and women; we are making patriarchy's intentional polarization of the sexes visible, and shining light upon the reasons for it. Some people always assume that if you mention a problem, you caused it.

These experiences were not reassuring, either to them or to me. Clearly, feminism didn't have an exactly Amazonian grip on the Citizens Party. There were, of course, exceptions to this mode. While one member was rushing around madly hissing to anyone who would listen that he would *not* be an honorary woman, a bearded gentleman was embracing me in tears, thanking me for opening his eyes and asking me what books he needed to read. (He read them, too, as I discovered when I met him later in the campaign.)

Still, sexism prevailed, and as the day wore grimly and predictably on, I went from angry to murderous. Toward the end of the day, I had had enough. I asked for the microphone in the session then in progress and withdrew my name from consideration as a candidate. And I told them why. This was not the party it said it was. No one would have thought to ask a man the questions I had been asked, in the manner in which I had been asked them — as if I were a somewhat dense child. Nor did the women seem to understand their oppression, either in the world or in the party.

I went home convinced that what I'd heard about the Left and sexism was as true as ever. Though that fact was dispiriting, I felt vastly relieved. Because of it, I wouldn't have to undertake the mammoth venture of running for President; it gave me a respectable way out. But I was also a little sad. Now millions of people who would otherwise have heard at least a fragment of radical feminist philosophy would have to wait a little longer. And I had a feeling there wasn't much longer left to wait.

I had no sooner arrived home and unpacked, however, than several Citizens Party members turned up on my doorstep to ask me to rethink my decision. I didn't need much urging. In retrospect, I saw that I wasn't as deeply disillusioned by the sexism of the party as I'd initially supposed because I'd certainly had cause to expect it. I had been told by the women in the party who had worked with Barry Commoner during his 1980 Citizens Party's Presidential campaign that he was a thorough-going male chauvinist. I had known that a party that really meant business about women's liberation simply would not have chosen him to represent it.

Even if I hadn't already had good cause to suspect rampant misogyny, previous experience would have made me suspicious. I had never found a mixed group — and still haven't — that was organized for something other than to fight women's oppression that was not sexist, and thoroughly so.

A factor weighing in favor of running for its nomination was that the Citizens Party was a small party, a new, developing party, still flexible enough to change dramatically, I thought naively. And it was true that some political party in this country, no matter how small, needed to understand what the women's movement was all about, even for a few months, when clearly none of the others, regardless of size, had ever had a clue.[2]

Finally, I agreed to run. And the minute I did, I had one of the most extraordinary experiences of my life. Most girls in this country don't grow up having fantasies of themselves as President of the United States, though some rare ones might. But I can promise you, good little Mormon girls never *ever* have this fantasy. And since I had been a good little Mormon girl, it had never entered my mind in all my 47 years even to imagine myself as President.

Now suddenly I did have to imagine it, not because I thought there was a hope of being elected — I knew the chances were infinitesimal, if they existed at all — but because I knew I couldn't project the image of a woman taking herself seriously if I didn't take myself seriously. If I didn't believe I could perform adequately as President, I would convey this to the people in my audiences, the reporters, everyone. We wear our perceptions of ourselves on our skins. How could I go around this country talking about women's taking ourselves seriously, about everyone taking women seriously, if I couldn't do it myself?

I knew the women in my audiences weren't going to be fools. They would be able to tell if I really believed I could do the job, felt capable of it, worthy of it. Since a large part of my agenda would be to encourage them to feel that way themselves by watching me feel that way, I knew I really had to feel it, really had believe it, had to be able to see myself being President. Not believe that I could win, but believe I *should* win because I could do the job better than any man running. (That last part, fortunately, was *not* hard to believe.)

I also knew that reporters — and everyone else — would ask me: "Why are you running for President?" and then, often hoping more to make me look ridiculous than really wanting to know, "What would you do if you were President?" And I'd have to say what I'd do about foreign policy, about the economy, about human rights, about the environment. For women's sake, I'd have to surprise them with sensible answers. So I asked myself, "What *would* I do about all those things?"

That's when I had the extraordinary experience.

The minute I started to think what I'd do, I realized that I *knew* what to do, and that most women I knew also understood what to do better than any man we've seen try to be President in our lifetimes. I'm not just saying this for effect.

I had a dream during this time that I was in an international chess competition — though I find chess thoroughly masculist and excruciatingly boring. Feeling sure and powerful, I first beat the British, then the Russian champion. And I thought, "There's nothing to this after all!" The mystique was gone.

My dream helped me realize how thoroughly and deliberately the office of President has been mystified. Of course, we know that men in power always want us to think that their jobs are incredibly difficult, that they take extreme intelligence and skill, and certainly can't be done by just anybody. But even in a system that so adores mystification of male work, the job of President of the United States has been excessively befogged.

We are taught to believe that *that* job is absolutely fraught with complexity; that matters of state are so perilous that only the most astute minds should be allowed near them; that it takes a special kind of genius even to begin to grapple with statecraft, maybe a political giant born only once in a generation. The truth is that if Ronald Reagan — and most of his predecessors — can even go through the *motions* of being President, it has to be a simple job.

Looking back over that array of mediocrity, it becomes clear that the job looks difficult only because it is being done by men who don't know how to do it, primarily because they don't understand the basic principles of interacting effectively with other people. Even doing dishes can look awkward and can turn into a mess if one doesn't understand certain basic principles.

Because of the hierarchical mentality which imbues jobs at the top with incredible mystique, ordinary citizens feel humble and awkward and stupid in the face of the "great" ones. We think, "Who am I to say what the President should or shouldn't do? He has a unique gift for dealing with political matters, and lots of experience. I'm just a secretary (or a mechanic, or an accountant, or a teacher.) He also has information I'm not privy to, and can therefore see the whole picture. We'd all be better off leaving these important decisions to him." (Women never feel comfortable telling men what to do anyway, and Presidents have always been men.)

Many of us feel reluctant to believe our own judgment anyway, even if we have the audacity to exercise it. So we feel relieved and let off the hook when some elected official takes over; we are quick to abdicate our responsibility as citizens in a democracy to understand and take action on matters that concern our country and our lives. Finally, because we have been convinced, and happily so, that statecraft is too far beyond our comprehension, we stop thinking about politics altogether and join our neighbors in their apathy and ignorance.

After my own heady experience of breaking through the myth of presidential genius, I wanted everyone to experience the liberation and burgeoning personal power I felt daily as I studied the President's job. To counter the deliberate disempowerment inflicted upon us by this system, I thought how each of us should stand before our mirrors every morning first thing (after affirming ourselves), look ourselves squarely in the eyes, and say, boldly, "Now if *I* were President, I'd . . ." and tell ourselves what we'd do about the latest bit — or blockbuster — of mismanagement in the White House.

We'd soon see that we have very good ideas about what ought to be done in that office, what can be done, and how to begin doing it. We would say for instance, "Hey, just a minute. There must be far more effective ways of reducing the deficit!" And we'd vow that as President we would make the connection between the deficit and the military budget clear to the people of the country, and immediately take other steps to reduce and finally eliminate the military budget altogether.

Because we're not jaded politicians, we aren't encumbered with preconceived judgments that certain solutions are just not possible, that they won't work, that they can't be done. On the contrary, with our fresh points of view we see that some ideas that would be discounted and rejected out of hand by "politicians," are highly possible, that they will work, that they can be done. Because we don't censor ourselves before we consider new ideas, because we trust ourselves, we don't dismiss the seemingly impossible, the apparently naive, with the customary, "That's not the way things are done." We have too much evidence that how things are done is not just ineffective, but downright dangerous.

As we increased in confidence in ourselves as President, our tolerance of the genuinely shoddy jobs that are done in that office would decrease sharply. In our lifetimes we have witnessed incredibly bad jobs of being President. Think of Roosevelt, Truman, Kennedy, Johnson, Nixon, Ford, Carter, Reagan. Is there any one of them we couldn't president circles around? Nearly every man who has somehow blundered into the Presidency has planned or waged war, diverted resources from human needs to the war machine, actively increased suffering in poorer, darker-skinned countries, further exacerbated tensions in the Middle East, sanctioned atrocities in other countries and perpetrated them in this one, done little or nothing to alleviate and much to increase the deepening hunger, violence, inequity, and despair at home and abroad. Because they have not understood the basic principles of the use of power, they have all been singular failures. What have we got to show for 200-plus years of being "the greatest democracy in the world?" Look at us. Look at the world. This mess didn't happen in a day or a year. Men in power all over the globe have been working at it assiduously for over 5000 years. How could any of the rest of us possibly do worse, or even as badly? We've been at the nadir for at least a century. There's no place to go but up.

I chose to announce my year-long, non-violent direct action to help change all this on October 24, 1983. I couldn't have picked a worse moment for press coverage. U.S. troops had invaded Grenada the day before. The media would have had no room for anything else for the next week even if, on October 25th, the day after my announcement, a truck hadn't run a barricade and blown up American troops in Beirut. Together, those events dominated the media for at least a month. That I received any coverage at all is amazing.

The week after my announcement, a group of about 25 women and men working in various ways for peace met for the weekend in a little hideaway in the Maryland woods. I think of it as the Halloween Peace Party.

Despite my weariness and my skepticism about the usefulness of meetings of this sort, I went. And lay awake in my bunk the first night wondering why. As is true in most progressive groups, the participants' consciousness about peace and nuclear issues, the environment, racism, Central America, and related issues was very high. And totally in the pits about the women's movement. We had introduced ourselves to one another that day, and had taken turns describing our present and proposed projects and what we most needed to get on with them successfully. I liked the group, but I saw that we were going to skim across the surface of the problem again, and I chafed at the waste of time that represented to me.

But the next morning, something interesting began to happen. The leader told us as we gathered that, early that morning, a woman claiming to be a channel for beings from another planet had visited him at the retreat. After they'd talked a while, she asked if she could speak to any of the rest of us who were interested. He said that of course we were not obliged to pay any attention whatever to this, but that if any of us were interested, we should know that from his long experience of investigating such phenomena, he considered her to be among the most credible persons claiming to be channels.

Naturally, we all wanted to see her, so the next morning began with the woman — I'll call her Ann, not her real name — sitting at the head of our circle telling us how she became a channel for extraterrestrial beings. Then the drama began. "They" told her she'd talked enough and they wanted to begin. "They" were five or six people (mostly men, I gathered — certainly Moka, the spokesperson, was male) whom she could see only dimly but could hear very clearly. They stood behind her right shoulder, she told us. Our eyes all shifted to her right shoulder. Nothing there but the bricks of the fireplace.

The "group" began by telling us what wonderful people we were, and how beautiful, and how glad they were to get this chance to talk to us. Early on someone asked why we could not see them. "Ann has a very pure spirit," they replied. If we would prepare ourselves as she had done, they assured us, they would be delighted to use us in this way.

Then they got down to business. Our main job — theirs as well as ours — was to lessen fear on this planet. They told us we have been thinking in too small a way, and must now begin to think galactically. "Come play with us among the stars," they ₰ bade us. "We're asking you to stretch and stretch and stretch to become a part of the universe. It's time for your globe to join us."

The way was simple, they said. All we had to do was to be perfectly positive. "Your world is filled with negativity."

Where they came from, they said, they communicate with the spirit, not with the voice or the brain. "Don't think dark thoughts. Center yourself in your spirit," they advised us, "not your mind. Turn off your brain. Work and join hands with us to create a positive field."

The first step in being totally positive was to believe that peace can be attained, and to be able to imagine it: every child with a smile, every person filled with love for others. Image it, they insisted: every person with a radiant face, every person in touch with their god-ness. They promised us that every time we imaged the world transformed into a world of peace and love, we were creating that world. "What you image, you create in your life," they said.

"Image Andropov filled with love; don't feed his negativity. Spread the word. Have others image the world radiant . . . thoughts *create* . . . you have the power within you to create this world whole. . . . thoughts are electricity. They can transform."

Instructions for how to take the second step followed: "After you get your own positive self in line, image situations in your own personal life to be the way you want them to be and they will be that way. . . . Image your parents as loving you totally, caring for you utterly. . . . Do not fear a holocaust, or hunger."

And then the third step: we were to take this information out into the world, to tell others never to image dreadful things, to "breathe them out;" not to image children hungry or running from bombs, but to see happy children playing together. And that any time they inadvertently imagined a holocaust, to immediately image a meadow full of peace.

They assured us that we live in a lucky time because there is great incentive to be positive [otherwise we die]; that they'd like to come and teach us but there is too much fear among us; that there are millions of them, in thousands of small ships, come to help us.

And although there are negative forces out there, too, we are not to think of them, and the minute we find our minds wandering to them, we are to image their spirits being bright and pure within them, or see them as tropical fish or beautiful flowers. "They can't feed off that," they said.

Then the spokesperson said, "How does it feel to know you have such a huge back-up team!" The tears that came to my eyes caused me to realize how helpless I'd been feeling. It felt wonderful to believe even for just a moment that whole civilizations were gathering to help save this beleaguered and beloved planet.

Someone asked why all these people from all these other planets were interested in what happened to us. Moka, the leader, answered that we are all the same family, made from the same material, all part of one another, and that they and the others feel very close to us and love us. The predictable answer, completely consistent with their philosophy as far as we'd heard it.

They were playful and positive and loving and quite delightful, and gave me hope. Whether they were "real" or not was immaterial; the feeling was real, and that was worth a lot.

At the end of the session, I went up to ask Ann a question, and got in on a conversation that began to turn the whole experience very sour very quickly. She was relaying a message to one of the men from Moka. Moka wanted to meet with him and the leader of our group and one or two other men later that day to impart more instruction. The woman standing at the man's side asked if she could attend the meeting, too. Ann put that to Moka, who replied that she could, since she needed to understand her partner's work and be able to help him in it. "Oh oh," sang a little warning song in my head. "Looks like this whole alien bunch is not so alien after all. They're as sexist as the earthlings."

So when my turn came to talk to Ann, I asked her if there were any women in the group from outer space. There were. What do they do? They help the men.

213

Worse and worse. Much to my surprise, this made me feel like weeping. I guess I would have liked to believe in the wisdom and power of something outside myself for a change, if just for a while. But I didn't need to believe that sexism was galactic, even universal. It is intractable and discouraging enough on just this one small planet. What can we possibly do about the *universe*! That was just too much.

But I pressed on. Why was I not invited to the summit meeting that afternoon? I had a large network, and was the bearer of messages to many women. Why hadn't a woman been invited in her own right, with the acknowledgment that women are an important and essential constituency to reach with this message? If there was any group in the world that needed to know what to do next, surely it was the female half of the human race.

No answer was forthcoming to these questions. Perhaps Moka was too busy with the men. But just then a woman from another time and place presumably arrived on the invisible scene, calling herself Mary, *the* Mary, and *she* certainly had something to say to me!

And guess what? It was all negative! Hadn't she been listening to Moka and the boys? She criticized me roundly for my position on women. "Come on now, admit it. Wouldn't you *really* rather be inside the cave taking care of the children than out fighting the mastodon?"

"Madam," I answered wearily. "There are no more mastodons. And even given an equivalent danger, staying in the cave is not a choice I — or millions of other women — have anymore. Even if we did, we'd likely choose the mastodon." (Later, of course, I thought of the perfect comeback: "Women are the only ones who *are* fighting the mastodons on this planet!") But "Mary" couldn't take that in, I guess, because she went on for some time tediously out-Jerry-Falwelling Jerry Falwell. It was all pretty depressing.

And, back at home, thinking it over, I was pretty depressed. Not because I believed the "Mary" nonsense. That seemed clearly Ann's own belief system forcing its way through. (This is interesting in itself. Ann could see "them," Moka said, because her spirit was so pure. Just like the patriarchal males of planet Earth, I thought to myself on the drive home, to mistake Ann's lack of any sense of herself as a woman for "spiritual purity," and to reward her for it!) But I was depressed because finally one of my nightmare fears had surfaced and couldn't be squashed back down into the dark sea of my unconscious: what if sexism isn't just a peril peculiar to this planet? What if it's universal? Who wants to "think galactically" if it's just more of the same old Penis Almighty?

Trying to find some comfort, I called a friend of mine who knows about metaphysical things, partly from association with a program called Alpha Awareness. She told me about an experience with parallel realms the man who runs the Alpha Awareness program had had. Skiing down the side of a mountain in Utah, he took a sharp turn and found himself in another dimension. There were many people there, and they communicated with him about inner peace — without words.

In his class the following spring, he said, "In some places the wall between us is very thin. That spot on the hillside is one of those places."

So he took the class there, and three daring students went down the slope to the designated spot. When they returned hours later, they reported that though they had seen no one, they had received very clearly and strongly the message that the basic conflict to be resolved at this time on this plane is the conflict between women and men.

As my friend spoke, I thought again about how non-sexist thinking is an important sign of advanced evolution. Perhaps our poor planet, because it is the "soup pot of negativity in the universe," as Moka called it, is the one on which the great struggle to shift the universal power-over paradigm must take place — here, where it exists in its most acute and virulent form. And perhaps if we can't learn how to cure it here, then its tenuous grasp will become a steely grip on other more "advanced" planets, where, as Moka has it anyway, they need no laws because everyone loves everyone else and communicates spirit to spirit. If this gender-based negativity comes to prevail elsewhere as it has on earth, eventually it will strangle them all as it is strangling us.

It came into my mind and stayed there for long periods in the succeeding days: the idea that planet Earth is not just the test case, but the cosmic hope; that what women are doing here is of utmost significance, not for this world alone, but for all worlds, everywhere.

Nothing like feeling responsible for the entire universe!

This experience helped me to understand better — though not to accept — the New Age Movement's insistence on total positiveness, part of which translates into acceptance of this era of time as "post-feminist."

In July of 1984 in Oakland, California, at the Peoples' Convention — a convention intended as a protest and alternative to the Democratic convention that was being held at the same time in nearby San Francisco — I met and talked with a well-known New Age woman who was also running for office. We discussed the purposes of our campaigns, and though she let me say a little of what I was about, she did not really listen. She kept saying, in one way or another, that we had to be totally positive now.

I told her that being positive and being ignorant were not synonymous, that first we have to know that women are *not* free and why, and what that fact means for everyone, for the whole world. I assured her that despite New Age propaganda this is *not* the post-feminist but rather the feminist age; that we have yet to understand and internalize the feminist world view. I told her that feminism is the bridge between the old and the new worlds, and that it cannot be flown over or wished away. We have to walk across it every step of the way.

But her eyes glazed over and I assumed she was imaging me as a silvery tropical fish or a beautiful flower.

A month or two into the campaign, I stumbled upon a way to get people in my audiences to contradict the feelings of their society-spawned powerlessness. I was spending a morning with a group of women in Vermont. When I suggested to them that they think of themselves as President and feel what happened to them, a woman standing against the wall, who later introduced herself as Batya Weinbaum, spoke up and said, "Why don't you get people in your audiences to do it together? You could say, 'Everybody stand up and shout what you'd do if you were President.'"

So that night in Burlington, I tried it. I told the assembled group that I could prove to them that each of us there could be a fine President. I led them in a visioning exercise: "Close your eyes and see yourself standing in the Oval Office. It's late January 1985. You have just been inaugurated President of the United States of America. Say to yourself silently, with great conviction and solemnity, 'I am President of the United States!'

"You are all alone in the room. Outside the windows, the sun is shining on the snow in the rose garden. It's 8:30 in the morning. By noon, you can change the world. Propaganda to the contrary, the President of the United States alone can, and has, changed the course of world history in a very short time.[3]

"You are relaxed and confident, feeling very strong and able. Now see yourself walking purposefully over to the big desk with the Great Seal behind it, sitting down and beginning work. Think of the first three or four matters you consider most urgent and would address immediately.

"Now stand up and raise your arms high over your heads, shout, "If *I* were President, I'd . . ." and at the top of your lungs call out what you'd do."

Pandemonium reigned for about three minutes. Then, when everyone was back down in their seats, I continued: "You were all so busy—and noisy—being the best President we've ever had that you weren't able to hear what everybody else was doing. And since not hearing what other citizens think needs to be done is one of the major weaknesses of Presidents, you need to hear one another's ideas.

"So I'm going to ask you to do something I saw done in

Nicaragua last New Year's Eve. Tomas Borge, one of the leaders of the country, took our delegation of women to a people's mass. At one point in the service, the priest asked the congregation to call out names of absent persons, living or dead, who they felt were with us there that night. People began to call out names—here, there, randomly around the room. The priest didn't call on anyone. If two people shouted at once, one of them fell silent and tried again later. Let's do that. Call out loudly: what would you do if you were President?"

After that night in Burlington, I included this experiment in almost every campaign speech I made for the next 10 months. Thousands of people imagined themselves President and told one another how they would perform on their first morning in the Oval Office. All over the country, I heard the same responses again and again:

> Call up Chernenko* and make an appointment to
> see him the next day
> Dismantle nuclear weapons
> Slash the military budget
> Shut down nuclear power plants
> Stop U.S. investment in South Africa
> Pull economic "interests" and military out of Cen-
> tral America
> Give farmers a chance
> Eliminate pornography
> Initiate emergency research for safe, reliable
> methods of birth control
> Put abortion rights into the Constitution
> Give their lands and mineral rights back to the
> Indians
> Get the missiles out of Europe
> Scrap plans for Star Wars, MX; discontinue man-
> ufacture of all weapons

---

*The names changed rapidly in the Soviet Union that year.

Strengthen and enforce affirmative action
Subsidize mass transportation
Stop registration for the draft
Stop arms sales to *everyone*

And so on.

One Black woman in New Jersey called out, "Rename the White House!" — indeed an auspicious way to begin any administration.

I didn't always hear everything everyone called out, but most of what I heard belonged in my platform. What is more intriguing, however, is that I never heard anyone call out a suggestion for fundamental change to which either of the two men nominated by the big parties would have agreed. It didn't matter how large the group was that went through this process, or how many ideas they came up with, it was always the same.

What does that mean? What it tells me is that we're witnessing a profound shift among a large and growing population in this country toward values that have for centuries been associated with women. It tells me that that shift in values is not happening among the people in power, and that they are not even aware of it. It tells me that globally we have incompetents making the decisions, and that the people are far, far ahead of those they call "leaders." It reminds me of a cartoon popular a few years ago that showed a group of women and men rushing up the street with purpose and energy. Trailing along behind is this hapless little fellow, waving his arms, and crying, "Hey, wait for me. I'm your leader!"

So I would tell my audiences that the truth is that *we* are the leaders. Leaders are those who know what to do. And what they shouted are among the things that need to be done, that should be done. And some of them *must* be done if we're to survive. Clearly the established order does not allow people to be President who are spiritually healthy and receptive to the messages of their times, the urgent messages pouring in from every direction of the universe telling us that the status quo in all

219

areas of human life must change dramatically and soon. Since the existing order is set up to allow only dinosaurs to wield its brand of power in its name, we must start wielding another kind of power in our own names.

"We are the leaders now," I assured them. "The future of this planet and of all life on it — and perhaps ultimately of all life everywhere — is at this most dangerous and delicate juncture entirely in our hands. This is as it should be, since in the world of which we dream, all are leaders, equally responsible. To bring that world into being, we must begin behaving as if it is already reality, behave in the ways we believe are wiser, more loving, ways that make everyone's lives richer."

Immediately after my announcement back in October, we had begun the campaign. A handful of us ran it for the first six months. A couple from New York, committed, bright members of the Citizens Party, took on the jobs of campaign coordinator and assistant campaign coordinator — the wife was coordinator and the husband was her assistant. Though he had been a primary mover in getting the party to run a Presidential campaign and a woman as candidate, and though she was far more enlightened than most of the other women in the party, from the beginning both of them had difficulty dealing with my unmitigated feminism.

They thought of themselves as "progressives," and like the rest of the Left were non-philosophical "issue" people. They regarded feminism as one among any number of very important issues. I, on the other hand, regarded what they called "issues" as pieces of the over-all feminist agenda.[4]

We struggled with this dissonance constantly, but neither side would budge, and frustration mounted daily. I think they saw early on that they had made a miscalculation in choosing me. What they had really wanted was a "women's rights" feminist; maybe they weren't aware before they came to know me that there was any other variety.

As my campaign materials began to go out, many Citizens Party members were alarmed about their thoroughly femi-

nist—non-Leftist—perspective. I have to hand it to my coordinating team. Even though it made them uncomfortable, they
wanted me to be represented truly, and they defended me to
the rest of the party even when they themselves chafed.

But one day in May when I called home I found that Susan and Julie had been deeply offended by the campaign coordinator and her assistant for "defeminizing" the latest press release. I was scheduled to be in Albany for a press conference
a few days later, my second in that city. The assistant coordinator told me that since I had done my "woman's stuff" in Albany
the last time I was there, this time I had to be serious. One
press conference on inconsequential matters was enough.

My campaign coordinator had explained it to me earlier:
"The press corps in Albany is more sophisticated than in Bing-
hamton (where I was scheduled for a press conference at the
Women's Center after Albany). Therefore, you should talk
about the New Bedford rape trial at the women's center in
Binghamton, and El Salvador in Albany."

There are men's issues—the important, serious, military
matters such as Central America. Then there is the softer, less
"universal," less urgent "women's stuff," such as gang rape—
totally unconnected to events in Central America, of course—
with which you don't want to bore and embarrass "sophisticated" press people.

The situation was very difficult for all of us, but it rapidly
became unbearable for the male assistant coordinator. "There's
no role for men in this campaign," he'd storm, though men
were working in the campaign all over the country. What he
meant was that since there has been only one generally acceptable role for men in relation to women for many millennia—
the leader—when he couldn't be leader, there was no other role
visible to him as a possibility. Though he was actually playing
a very important role in the campaign, since it wasn't *that* role,
he didn't perceive it as a role at all.

Despite our differences over priorities, I had come to love
my wife-husband coordinating team, and suffered when I had

to let them go. But I knew I had done the right thing when, shortly after they left, an entirely new band of spunky and adventurous women, who recognized the campaign as the once-in-a-lifetime chance it was to proclaim feminism nationwide, took leave of jobs, lovers, and family, and gathered themselves in from all over the country to take up the reins.

So began one of the most delightful—and difficult—six months of my life. Imagine trying to run a Presidential campaign by consensus. I'm sure we were the first group ever to try it, and we didn't give up even when we didn't do it perfectly. We never did perfect the process, but despite the difficulty, we never surrendered, never sighed and said, "Okay. We've only got a few months. We haven't got *time* for this!" I'm proud of us that we chose to struggle rather than to revert to old patterns.

Actually, our unconsciously reverting to old patterns was what prevented us most often from being as democratic as we wanted to be. One of these old patterns was assuming that some women had more authority than others, and resenting it. All of us had a hard time saying what needed to be said when it needed to be said in the way it needed to be said. This is hardly surprising. Our acculturation teaches us not to be direct, not to confront problems, but instead to wait and hope they'll change, to approach them in some roundabout manner, to try to get someone else to deal with them, to manipulate the people involved—anything rather than simply to face them, name them, and plunge in and take care of them. We are afraid of hurting others' feelings—they may not love us if we do—and especially afraid of others' hurting *our* feelings. It was very difficult.

Reading Carol Gilligan's book, *In a Different Voice*,[5] helped me understand another phenomenon I witnessed among us at the campaign office. A cycle developed: a few women came into the campaign with glorious preconceptions about what working in it would be like, became disillusioned and unhappy, and left. They told us why they were unhappy just as they were leaving, when it was too late to do anything about it. They neither took responsibility themselves to change it, nor gave us a chance to change. We were all shortchanged of a chance to grow.

Gilligan noticed the quit-the-game phenomenon again and again. Whereas little boys argue, fight it out, and go on from there, little girls on the playground stop the game if anything goes wrong. Since the disillusioned women on the campaign couldn't stop the game, they quit playing and went home.

We haven't been taught that the girls' game must go on, that we must learn to work together, that since there is no getting out of it we may as well figure out how to do it. We've been taught precisely the opposite — that we must *not* work together, and that there shouldn't be a serious girls' game in the first place.

The conditioning is *very* strong. Even some of the women in the campaign who recognized what was happening to them couldn't stop themselves from going through with it to an end they really didn't want.

Despite the persistence of old patterns, we were able to do remarkable things by consensus, the most remarkable being that we allocated all our funds — including the nearly $290,000 in matching funds — using this process. Though this is a minute sum as campaign funds go, winning and spending it by consensus has to be another first in the history of political campaigns, and making the government subsidize my anti-male-supremacist platform a truly spectacular accomplishment. In fact, I often lay awake at night grinning into the darkness at Uncle Sam's paying me to campaign against patriarchy.

As each of the new campaign workers walked into the office on her first day, we tried to match her skills to campaign needs. On the face of it, none had any experience that seemed relevant. But, hoping for the best, they each sat down and simply began doing what had to be done. Amazing things happened.

Julie Ainslie, freshly graduated sociology major, arrived when we needed a treasurer. So with no experience whatever, just intelligence and commitment, she became the treasurer. And was told by the Federal Elections Commission auditors that she had done a much better job than whoever handled the money in the Hart campaign. We are one of the few campaigns in history that ended up without debt, to ourselves or to others.

Liz Seaborn, feminist historian, carpenter, Jill-of-all-trades from Massachusetts, walked in the door when we needed a person to take over ballot access,[6] and Melanie Thompson dropped down from New Jersey for two weeks to "stamp envelopes" and stayed to become, with Liz, one of the very few ballot access experts in the this country.

Another new graduate, Lynn Fontana, walked through the door just as Susan was asking frantically, "Who's not intimidated by governmental rules and regulations?" "I'm not intimidated by anything," Lynn answered coolly, and settled down to making sure we followed, to the comma and semicolon, every small-printed requirement for getting matching funds.

In fact, at one point, the Federal Elections Commission sent back our submission denying the validity of our claim for matching funds, maintaining that we hadn't raised the $5,000 in one state after all. Lynn looked over the returned forms, went to bed, and dreamed. In her dream, she saw one of the sheets from the FEC and realized that they had made an error in their calculations. In the morning, she called and pointed out the error. They spent a couple of hours checking it out, and called back admitting a little shamefacedly that she was absolutely right. Because of Lynn's dream—and the incredible dedication of scores of people—I made history by becoming the first alternative candidate to receive federal primary matching funds.

I was also immeasurably helped in this by a wonderful fundraising letter. It was written by Sheila Roher in New York City and signed by Mary Daly, Barbara Deming, Andrea

Dworkin, Leah Fritz, Robin Morgan, and Gloria Steinem, and began like this:

Dear Friend,

Wouldn't you love to hear—

> Ronald Reagan say: "The oppression of women is the model for all other oppressions. If we can't stop rape in the streets of one U.S. city, we can't hope to stop violence on a global level."

And love to hear—

> Walter Mondale declare: "We will no longer tolerate an economic system based on the exploitation of women's labor, in the workplace or in the home."

And

> Jesse Jackson preach unequivocally: "Reproductive freedom is an essential human right for women. No matter what else they gain, without this they will always be oppressed."

And

> Gary Hart admit: "The issue isn't really old versus new. It's the locker-room macho mentality versus a feminist vision."

Well, don't hold your breath.

None of these guys has said—or is likely to say— these things. And it means something that they're *not*.

Only one candidate has been bringing this message into the campaign debate. Only one candidate has had the courage to tell the truth about violence against women — physical, economic, and psychological — and its relationship to violence against other peoples and nations.

And only one candidate has the radical vision to point us in another direction.

Of course, we mean Sonia Johnson, Presidential candidate for the Citizens Party.

Susan held out for that letter against the original coordinators' stubborn determination to keep the campaign attractive to a larger liberal constituency. That's like Susan, without whom there couldn't have been a campaign at all. A passionately dedicated feminist, she has more courage in her little finger than a hundred large liberal men have together in their whole bodies (which is probably underestimating her). She is absolutely clear about principles and priorities.

Perhaps the best example of this is her organization of the continuing First Amendment case against the Federal Communications Commission, demanding that the Presidential debates be opened to all qualified candidates, not just Democrats and Republicans. The gist of the case is that the Republican and Democratic parties, which jointly control both the Congress and the Federal Communications Commission, have decided that all those who represent different voices in Presidential elections should go to the back of the electronic bus.[7]

What this case is trying to do is to restore to U.S. elections the traditional freedom of competition that characterized them before the turn of the 20th century. And what it seeks to use as the tool to accomplish that result is the plain language of the First Amendment.

On October 5, 1984, the day before the first televised debate, I was guest columnist in *USA Today*. My column was entitled, "Want a Real Debate? Invite me."

When Ronald Reagan reluctantly agreed to debate Walter Mondale, he proved that the debates have become an integral, mandatory part of the election process.

To bar from this electronic ballot any qualified candidate is therefore to violate political freedoms protected by the First Amendment.

Democracy depends upon free and fair competition for all candidates, including their ideas. What finally compelled me to request inclusion in the debates was the realization that the two better-known candidates would neither raise nor discuss ideas upon which life on this planet depends. . . .

Though polls confirm that some of these ideas are favored by more than half the population, neither well-known candidate seems to hear the millions of us who passionately wish our nation to invest in people's lives rather than in planetary annihilation. . . .

I challenge broadcasters, those creators of public opinion and Presidents: take seriously the indispensable, historic contribution to democracy of alternative parties. Surprise the public with thought-provoking, robust, irreverent, genuine debate. Invite me!

If, in 1988, the public has the great good fortune of seeing candidates and hearing messages other than the same old worn-out, dangerous nonsense, they'll have Susan Horwitz to thank.*

---

*Other wonderful people joined us at campaign headquarters in Arlington, Virginia, among them Ann Taylor, Cheryl Newell, Pam Smith, Lynette Cornwall, Joan Boyer, Jackie Wilson, Kathy McCleave, Cecelia Lange, Robin Parks, Martha Ryan, Leslie Reed, Margot Gebhard, and Jeffrey Gale. I was fortunate to have attracted such able, gifted women and men, and I am inexpressibly grateful for their commitment and sacrifice.

The indispensable man in the campaign was my running mate, Richard Walton. Dick, a much-published author on political matters, particularly foreign policy, had been active in the Citizens Party since its early days and was highly respected in progressive circles. Looking—and acting—like a cross between Santa Claus and Ben Franklin, Dick ran almost constant interference between me and the Executive Committee of the Citizens Party. Without him, the chances of my being nominated would have been practically nil by convention time.

And then there was me, an ex-Mormon housewife, running for President of the United States and not making a fool of myself. In fact, making the only thoroughly good sense of any candidate out there, since my platform was feminism, the world's only sensible philosophy. People would actually ask me who I was going to vote for (do you suppose they ever asked Fritz?), and I always replied that for the first time in my life, I was going to be able to vote for someone I knew could do the job.[8]

Though I seldom felt consciously afraid, I realized how terrifying the campaign was on some deeper level when one day in April, as I was resting on a couch in the United Campus Ministries house on the campus in Athens, Ohio, I suddenly found myself feeling solaced by the ordinary, everyday sound of footsteps on the stairs. That sudden awareness of the commonplace around me shook me out of the uncommonness of my position long enough to allow me to recognize my fear.

All along, I had to invent ways to bear the strain. For instance, outside San Luis Obispo, California, earlier that spring at a Peace and Freedom Central Committee meeting, I escaped for a couple of hours into the hills. As I climbed, I sang along with a meadowlark nearby in the grass, "Sonia is a prettylittlegirl," which is what Mother always told me meadowlarks sang. Into my memory sprang images of my simple, peaceful childhood. How had I got myself into this complicated, difficult place from that little rural town in southern Idaho?

The sky was blue blue and blazing with sun, the tall grass lapped like waves of baby hair in the wind. I climbed to a rock near a cluster of oaks and felt free of the campaign for a blessed half hour. Looking out over the wide, still valley, I felt as if I would burst if I didn't shout or sing, or make some inordinately loud noise full out into the wind. So I shouted to my sisters all through the universe, all through history, to all my friends wherever they were, to come to me and help me do the work before me to the end.

When I stopped shouting, I felt them very near, and I climbed back down the mountain lightheaded with relief. I recommend it highly, shouting from mountainsides to those you love.

Every time I faced particularly difficult or frightening tasks on the campaign, which was daily, I called for courage — silently for the most part — to the women who had gone before me and to those who are to come. I'd close my eyes (standing in the stall of the lavatory before a TV program, for instance), and imagine great throngs of women before me in the sky as far as I could see, out past the horizon, on and on forever, thousands, millions of them, young and old, all strong and sure and shining, walking toward me with arms opened wide. I imagined them embracing me, telling me how they understood and appreciated and loved me. I understood them, too, and felt as if I knew their hearts. Reaching out my hands in both directions and touching them — before and behind me in time — always restored my serenity and my faith in myself. It was a good habit, one I decided to keep.

People ask me what I believe; do I, for instance, believe those women are really there? "That's beside the point," I answer them. "What does it matter? And what does 'really' mean? They are there for me. Imagining them refreshes me, makes me feel whole and powerful. That's the reality to me, that and loving them; that and loving myself."

What I saw happen in the campaign convinced me that I had always been right: women can do not only infinitely more than we think we can, we can do anything we need to do. And since right now what we need to do is to save the earth, watching myself and the women working in my campaign all over the country gave me daily draughts of faith that we can and will do it. Obviously, the Goddess (or history, or the universe, or destiny) has chosen the right group for the job.

I can't and won't pretend the campaign was without crushing evidence that internalized oppression is alive and flourishing in the women's movement. Sometimes lying awake at night pondering this, I felt very close to Matilda Joslyn Gage, whom Susan B. Anthony and Elizabeth Cady Stanton so deliberately erased from history in the last century. It was happening to me. Though I cared for my own sake, I suffered mostly from what I knew it meant about the possibility of women's changing the world. If we can't take ourselves seriously *unless the men do*, we shall never take ourselves seriously, and shall never do the work before us of transforming human society.

Because men in power had not approved me, well-known feminists could not recognize or acknowledge me either. Deeply and unconsciously identifying with men and their power, thinking that men's political ways are the only ways, their parties the only significant loci of power, their game the only game in town, these women effectively helped make that the reality. A blind and grievous error.

For an entire year, the best-known national feminist magazine made no mention of me, and did not print one of the letters they received about my campaign. The reason for this, they assured me, was fear of being perceived as endorsing me and thus endangering their tax status. I was embarrassed that they had to make such a transparent excuse—no tax law threatens magazines for mentioning a candidate or for printing a few letters. Mostly I was sorry that they were acting out of fear: fear of losing credibility if they came to be seen as taking me seriously when no one of importance—meaning the men and their media—did, and fear of taking votes away from the Democrats. Watching them subvert their own purposes by not acknowledging the most important message of this age, the message the magazine itself came into being to advocate, was not a spectacle designed to gladden the feminist heart.

Two other examples of erasure are worth mentioning. On one occasion, a group of high-powered, nationally-known Democratic women were on a TV panel discussing women in politics. Although I knew a couple of them personally, my name was not mentioned, even in passing. It could be argued, I suppose, that I was not mentioned because in fact I was not "in politics" in the male-defined sense which those women interpret as being "in politics," and therefore mentioning me would have been an embarrassment.

But if I was not "in politics," what *was* I in?

During the question-and-answer period following a well-known female politico's speech one night, a friend of mine in the audience asked her about my campaign. The speaker addressed the subject carefully for several minutes. Then, a very short time later, while responding to someone else's question, she declared passionately, "If there were a woman running, I'd support her!"

If I was not a "woman running," what *was* I?

What I was was a woman running without the men's approval, which meant I could not be regarded as *really* running. I was an embarrassment because I thought that my own approval was enough; because I was playing the women's game of feminist activism on the men's board. I hadn't been invited, so I was crashing the party.

I wasn't even trying to do it as a female impersonator or a junior man, which would have eased the discomfort a little. I was doing it blatantly and unashamedly as a woman, calling deliberate attention to my woman-identification—calling myself a feminist and proposing a complete feminist agenda, not just for this country, but for the planet. And I was doing this when practically everybody is embarrassed when we become too serious about "women's stuff."

Since politics is quintessential patriarchy, making feminism not just tangential but central is a serious gaffe. So the co-

231

opted averted their eyes, and held their handkerchiefs delicately to their noses, pretending it wasn't really happening, as we do when someone farts in public.

I hadn't been invited, and, worse yet, I was crashing the party in my authentic, and therefore inadmissable, garb: womanliness.

10

Telling the Truth

From the beginning, one of the reasons I wanted to run for President was because it would force me to come up with a feminist perspective on all the issues. Ever since I'd first seen the necessity for doing it during the NOW campaign, I'd been sure there was a way to apply feminist analysis to every problem in the world. But it had seemed such a difficult project that I had let it slide.

However, the need for such an analysis had become increasingly urgent in the world, and therefore in my own life, and it would not let me rest. Already into the campaign, I struggled to make theory practical in some unified, coherent, meaningful way, but month after month, speech after speech, interview after interview, discussion after discussion, the connectedness I first sought, then craved, still eluded me. I began to think I wasn't going to be able to put all the pieces together satisfactorily in the time left, and the thought made me feel ill.

Then one night in late May, seven months into the campaign, I spoke at George Mason University close to my home in Virginia. The speech was the worst I have ever given. A

complete bumble from beginning to end. Even what I *had* together—and I had a great deal together—fell apart. Obviously,
the integrity of the speech—and of the campaign—depended
upon my making some crucial and missing connection. And
fast.

On the way home in the car, Julie and I howled with
laughter over what a debacle the speech had been. "What's
missing must be so obvious!" I said when I caught my breath.
"Why, *why* can't I assemble it in my mind?" I shook my recalcitrant head with both hands. "Come out. I know you're in
there. Give yourself up. I've got you surrounded!"

Then, as we laughed and joked, suddenly I realized how
to do it! The tangle which I had not been able to unravel for
so many months somehow, miraculously, straightened itself
out. All the threads came together into a perfect web. From
then until the end of the campaign, I felt clear and cool as
crystal.

That night, I remembered a story I'd heard once long ago
about an experiment with frogs. There was once an inhumane
but well-intentioned biology teacher who brought two frogs
and two tin cans to class one day. With all eyes upon him, he
filled one can with water, dropped a frog into it, and put the
can on a hot plate. Little by little the water heated up. Little
by little the frog adjusted to the increase in temperature. Adjusted, that is, until the water boiled, at which point it couldn't
adjust any longer and died before the horrified eyes of a room-
ful of teenagers. Then the teacher took the other can, filled it
with water, and put it on the burner. As the water began to
boil, he tossed the other frog into the can. The frog, who was
no fool, instantly leapt out of the can.

We survive day by day on this planet by adjusting down,
adjusting down. Little by little, imperceptibly, we adjust to increasingly deadly conditions, and come to accept them as "natural" or inevitable.

Little by little we adjust to greater and greater violence in
our personal and national lives.

Little by little we adjust to the poisoning of our water, our air, our soil, and our food.

Little by little we adjust to having freedoms stolen away from us, to having fewer and fewer choices, less and less voice in the decisions that affect our lives.

Little by little we adapt to the big corporations and the military establishment of this country making the decisions for all of us — and for most of the rest of the world.

Little by little we adapt to making less and less money for working more and more.

Little by little we adjust to the daily increase of radiation in our environment.

Little by little we adapt to more roads, cars, and parking lots and less open green space.

Little by little we come to believe that money and the things we can buy with it are the most important life goals.

Little by little we adjust to deafening noise, deadening entertainment, lack of conversation, leisure, dreaming, quiet, meditative space, lack of real connection with other people.

Little by little we come to believe we cannot do anything about all this, that this is "progress," natural, inevitable.

Little by little the water heats up, and because we are one of the most adaptable species on earth, we keep adapting to new and ever more dangerous conditions and ideas. What should seem horrendous comes to seem normal. We forget how life once was, how blue the sky was, how good food tasted, how we didn't lock our doors at night, how we had time for one another. We forget because the change is gradual and unannounced. But as with the first frog, the water is heating up around us.

Let's imagine ourselves as people from another planet, where wisdom dictates public policy (and we need to imagine such a place!). Let's pretend that one day we land on planet Earth. Stepping out of our airships, we recoil with horror. "This air is toxic, the soil is contaminated, the water is lethal. Life isn't possible on this planet!" we cry. "Let's get out of here!"

And like the second frog, who was introduced suddenly into a life-threatening situation, we leap to safety.

We are being challenged even now, as the water heats up, not just in our physical environment but in our moral, spiritual, political, and economic environments as well, to make the biggest evolutionary leap in all human history. We are being required to take the leap into feminism, the only positive, generative order of existence posited upon our planet.

What I realized that night in the car was that when I prodded audiences all over the country to stand up and shout what they'd do if they were President, nearly everything they shouted was feminism, based on at least one of three major feminist principles: that violence cannot solve problems, that cooperation is more supportive and life-enhancing than competition, and that life, including the quality of life of all living things, is the foremost consideration in making decisions.

Everyone wanted a non-militaristic world, a world without domination of any group of individuals by any other, a world in which people's lives matter more than making a profit or looking "strong." They wanted a society in which everyone has a part in making the decisions that affect their lives, where diversity is valued, where there are many genuine and positive choices. They wanted a non-materialistic, non-militarized, economically equitable, cooperatively run, non-violent, life-centered world.

When I announced to my audience at the end of the exercise, "The way you think, your values, everything you'd do if you were President—this is feminism," some people were offended and most were skeptical. On the whole they had thought of feminism very much in the same way as the reporters whose first question to me was, "How can you base a national Presidential campaign on a single issue?"

It is discouraging enough that the public views as a "single issue" the concern of half the human race about every aspect of our lives, public and private.[1] It is doubly disheartening that many feminists also equate feminism and "women's rights."

While women's rights are an important aspect of feminism, they *are* only an aspect. Feminism is not about "issues" at all. It is about a totally different human possibility, a non-patriarchal way of being in the world. It is about a new universal habit, a new mind.

That stunning, gorgeous, glorious world view called feminism is what finally persuaded me to run for President. I ran to share it with as many people as I could, and to help them understand that what feminists are saying must be taken very seriously if anyone is to survive. In all those halls, in all those public squares, on all those street-corners, quads, radio shows, and TV programs, and in all those newspaper interviews— again and again I taught Feminism 101.

Feminism, I said, far from being a "single issue," is a perspective, a way of looking at all the issues. It provides a framework for evaluating them. It is a world view, a complete and complex value system, the only alternative to patriarchy. Feminism is, in short, the most inclusive and descriptive analysis of the human situation on earth—at this time or any other, as far as we know.

When socialists among my hearers became ruffled and angry at this heretical assertion (how could *anything* by women be better than the best by men?), I asked them to imagine that instead of a couple of brilliant men analyzing the industrial revolution, and trying to impose their revolutionary urgency upon workers, all the workers in the industrialized world had worked it out together themselves. Imagine the analysis—and the revolution that would have sprung from it—if small groups of workers had sat down together week after week, year after year, and talked about their lives: how they felt about the work they were doing, how their lives were different from those of their parents and grandparents, what accounted for those differences, what those differences meant to their sense of themselves in the world, their personal relationships, their view of the future, of the possible; discussing how it had all come about, who benefited from it, discovering the mechanisms set

237

up to keep them ignorant of their exploitation, and finally translating this understanding into ideas of how they might alter their behavior so that the situation would have to change.

That women did this—and are doing this—is the difference between feminism and all other -isms. What early on was called "consciousness raising" was the genius of the women's movement,* and I do not use genius lightly. Because of it, the depth and scope of our movement has never been equaled, or even approximated, by any movement in history. As Hazel Henderson writes in *The Politics of the Solar Age*:

> It is in this psychological area [that feminists are revealing and explaining] that Marxism has run aground, as has most economic and social theory. French Marxist Roger Garaudy courageously explores this new terrain, and in a recent conversation, told me that the feminist critique of industrialism, socialist and capitalist, was the only fundamentally innovative analysis available.[2]

Feminism is not an analysis thought up by several brilliant women peering in from the outside and then trying to impose their conclusions upon those enmeshed in the actual situation they describe. Though hundreds of women from as many countries may write about it, may work to form the richness and abundance of it into coherent theory, the raw material is provided by the daily epiphanies of half the human race.

Right now, hundreds of women in the United States alone, who never gave feminism a thought before, are having some experience that is causing lights to flash on inside their souls. Some secretary is trying to ward off her boss's advances, some housewife is picking up her husband's dirty underwear or herself off the floor where he knocked her again, some woman

---

*Consciousness raising today, at least as promulgated by the National Organization for Women, is another, and far less revolutionary, process than it was originally.

is training a new male recruit who will soon be her boss. These women will find one another and talk it over; together they will figure out the biggest scam ever pulled off, and they'll never be the same.

As Jan Raymond writes:

> . . . that women be equal to their Selves, equal to the women who have gone before them, and equal to the task of creating a woman-centered existence . . . this is one of the more important distinctions between radical feminism and liberal and Marxist feminisms: their starting points. The former starts "among the women." The latter begins among and with the men, i.e., in tangential relation to men as a group, whether they be men as oppressors or men as oppressed "brothers." Both brands of feminism investigate and locate women mainly in relation to male persons, history, and culture.[3]

One of the basic tenets of radical feminism is that any woman in the world has more in common with any other woman — regardless of class, race, age, ethnic group, nationality — than any woman has with any man. To be female is reason *in itself* to be in servitude, to be hated, wounded, and killed in every country, every culture of the world. As Andrea Dworkin writes in *Right-wing Women*:

> . . . There is no state of being or act of will that protects a woman from the basic crimes against women as women or puts any woman outside the possibility of suffering these crimes. Great wealth does not put a woman outside the circle of crimes; neither does racial supremacy in a racist social system or a good job or a terrific heterosexual relationship with a wonderful man or the most liberated (by any standard) sex life or living with women in a commune in a pasture.[4]

I have lived and traveled widely in five countries and at least five distinct cultures outside the United States in my adult life. Though I was anesthetized by patriarchy at the time, the years I was in Samoa, Nigeria, Malawi, Korea, and Malaysia proved more than ample time for me to identify, often to the point of physical pain, with the women of those countries.

I grew up in the Mormon West—a subculture in the United States—and spoke a sort of English. They grew up in the steamy city streets of Lagos and spoke Yoruba, or on an exhausted quarter acre farm in Limbe and spoke Chichewa, or in a brothel near an army base in Korea, or on the blue-gold shores of Upolu and spoke Samoan, or on a rubber plantation in Port Dickson and spoke Malay. It did not take knowing their language or their culture well to make the connections between the Malawian women carrying burdens on their heads that make them moan and weep as they walk, and the desperate lives of the tens of thousands of prostitutes in Seoul. I may have bought the canard that these were simply "cultural" idiosyncrasies, but I saw that it was always women who were crushed by them, and something as yet unexamined and unnamed responded in me, as if I, too, were somehow being crushed.

I saw that women in all these countries existed for the use of men and were essentially barred from any existence with a purpose other than this, though I didn't understand that the "use" could take far more subtle forms, as it does, sometimes, in this country. (And in Nicaragua, where there has been another patriarchal revolution and women are learning that, though they are "useful" in fighting wars, and in having babies to keep the population stable, they are not "useful" in filling even one of the nine seats of the major power structure.)

It did not require a doctorate in anthropology for me to recognize that women and girl children ate last and starved first in every country.

I ran for President to reach millions of people with the urgent message of radical feminism, the most transformative and dangerous—because the most taboo-defying—philosophy in

240

existence: the message that the oppression of women is the archetypal oppression, the one upon which all others are modeled. Feminism posits that men raped and exploited and enslaved women *before* they went across the river and invaded the neighboring tribe. It posits that men learned the power-over paradigm in their kitchens and bedrooms, their caves and huts, through their most intimate, most formative relationships, which were with mothers, lovers, and wives, and that they subsequently applied it in all areas of their lives, operating within that dominant/submissive, dichotomous mindset in all subsequent affairs. Thus did the sadomasochistic paradigm, which is patriarchy, slouch into the world.

Radical feminism holds that out of their experience in dominating women, men developed, perfected, and established the hierarchical world view which now threatens all life. As Virginia Woolf writes in *Three Guineas*: "The public and the private worlds are inseparably connected; the tyrannies and servilities of the one are the tyrannies and servilities of the other."[5]

Because it attacked their deepest fears and their deepest sources of identity, this was not a welcome idea to most people in my audiences. They squirmed and looked around for a way out. I could almost hear them turning me off with, "I hate it when women get like this. You can't even talk to them!" So I often had to elaborate upon this concept for some time before I saw signs of genuine understanding on most faces.

I would point out that the global mind at the end of the twentieth century is a mind that absolutely and uncritically believes that women are designed and meant to be owned and used and exploited, and that this is true in every race, every culture, every ethnic group, every class, every country in the world, every building, every school, office, church, home, store, every street, on every square inch of planet Earth.

Thus, the mind that thinks the subordinate position of women is "natural," and therefore necessary for order in the universe, and believes, in addition, that God ordained that men rule women — with the most incredible violence and political terrorism imaginable, because there is no other way to keep adult human beings enslaved; the mind, in short, that finds this global massacre of the spirit and body of women legitimate, functions automatically and comfortably *at all times* out of a basic modus operandi of tyranny.

How this translates is that since it is justifiable (in light of the Bible, Koran, other religious documents and teachings — Confucianism, Islam, etc., ad nauseam — which make up venerable tradition) for half the human race to rule the other half, it seems completely "natural" and legitimate for one nation to relate to another nation as the "man" or ruler — reducing the other nation to "woman"; legitimate for people of one color to rule people of another color, the rich to rule the poor, the strong to rule the weak — all as men rule women. Basic to patriarchy is the necessity to reduce as many other groups as possible to "woman" as proof of manhood and hence of Godhood.

(This leap from the bedroom to the international boardroom is made simpler by the fact that all other groups which men in power wish to oppress are smaller in size than half the human race. I am not trying to set up a hierarchy of atrocities: "My oppression is worse than your oppression!" All oppression is equally horrific, ugly, and hurtful, and its rationalization the basic evil. I am only stating the fact, still so invisible and so unacceptable to so many, that no oppression can begin to match the *scale* of woman-hating, or the antiquity. Fifty-two percent of all other oppressed groups are also women. The majority of Blacks, third world people, Native Americans, Jews, Asians, and homosexuals, are women. And these and all other women have been oppressed by men continuously, everywhere, *as women*, for at least 50 centuries.)

Men in power like to say to us, "Now, ladies, we know you have problems, and we want to help you. But can't you see that we have some real *crises* out there right now? The Middle East is on fire, and there's a conflagration in Central America. Terrorists are on the rampage. The tension between the Soviet

Union and the United States escalates by the hour, and the world economy is collapsing. When we get these urgent problems taken care of, then we'll get around to you."

But women, not taken in any more, are saying, "No, you don't understand. The way you treat women is central to all those problems: central to making peace in the Middle East and Central America, central to decreasing tension between the Soviet Union and the U.S., central to eliminating terrorism, central to restructuring world economy." Feminists insist in the face of monumental disbelief and boredom that sexism is the Original Sin, "the fundamental lie that marks all human ideas, customs, and institutions,"[6] and that all the seemingly insurmountable problems in the world are the fallout from this most radical corruption. It is clear, therefore, that the only hope for this planet is in a global transformation in the status of women.

It is also clear that no matter what else men do, there is no shortcut, no way around or over this fact. Many groups in the world are putting their particular pieces into the puzzle of how we are going to survive: the anti-nuclear groups, the environmentalists, the advocates of U.S. divestiture in South Africa, the cooperative movement. But right in the center of this puzzle is a big empty space waiting for the piece that connects and empowers all the other pieces, the piece that awakening women hold. Without it securely in place, none of the other pieces will fit or come to anything. People of good will can work their hearts out, but if they don't understand the centrality to *all* their work of their attitudes toward and their treatment of women and values that are considered "womanly," they will surely fail. Violence against women and violence against the planet and all species—that we see in the form of missiles and bombs and military bases all over the world, overpopulation, toxic wastes, acid rain, desertification—they are all the same violence, and originate in men's domination of women.

This means that if we can't stop rape—just rape, not incest, not battering, not forced sterilization, not pornography, not poverty, not even marital rape, just garden variety, generic rape; if we can't stop rape in one street of one city in this country, if we can't stop rape in one fraternity house on one campus, there is not even a glimmer of hope for global peace.

What radical feminists are saying is that if we can't learn peace in the microcosm, there is no reason whatever to believe we can learn it in the macrocosm. If, in our personal relationships, we can't learn democracy, compassion, and love, there is no possible way we can learn them in some larger arena.

Everywhere I went during my campaign I asked the people of this country to tell me how they think we're going to learn to have peace among nations if we don't learn it first in our own kitchens, our bedrooms, our offices, schools, and churches. I ran for President to ask them to make that simple but profound connection, and to say, unequivocally, that if we don't stop the war that has been raging against women in every sphere of our lives from the moment we're born to the moment we die — if we can't stop *this* war — we can never abolish the *idea* (or the *idealization*) of war, and we are going to destroy ourselves as a species. Soon.[7]

A species that fights one-half of itself with the most vicious spiritual, physical, and emotional cruelty, maims and wounds, humiliates and murders women's hearts and souls and bodies, is a species that is on its way to extinction, that *deserves* extinction. Species survive and evolve because they learn to unite against a common danger. We are in unutterable danger, and patriarchy has divided us to our great peril. We will die unless the world listens to women, takes us very, very seriously.

When I am speaking or being interviewed and I say there is an all-out global war being waged against women, there are always some people who shake their heads and say, "*Really,* Sonia! War is a very big word. Obviously, things aren't good for women, but you mustn't overstate your case. If you exaggerate, nobody's going to believe anything you say. Why not tone it down a little?"

I tell these people how fervently I wish war *were* too big a word for what happens to women in this world every day, how

I can't wait for the day when war *is* too big a word and I *am* overstating my case. But the fact is, war is far too *small* a word. There isn't a word in the men's dictionary monstrous enough for what happens to women on this planet, and has happened unceasingly for thousands of years.

It's no accident that there is no word for it. If there is no word, there is no concept, and if there's no concept, we can't think it, and if we can't think it, we can't do anything about it, and patriarchy is safe. Words do not simply reflect reality; they help create it.

When these people still look askance at me, I give them a few little pieces of evidence that war is too small a word, evidence right out of the culture of their own United States of America. I remind them that today—and I don't care what day it is—men will rape over 2000 women in this country. (That figure is derived from FBI statistics, so it's undoubtedly low.) Two thousand women is a lot of women. When I speak to a group that large, I can hardly see the back of the auditorium. Imagine: two thousand women a day, day after day, week after week, month after month, year after year—and the number increasing. Two thousand rapes a day is too many rapes to lay at the feet of a few freaks and oddballs. This is what is so hard for many people to accept; the implications are too painful to look at squarely and rationally. Their denial is ferocious. For instance, at the end of my campaign speech at a Moorestown, New Jersey, high school one afternoon, a young man raised his hand and said, "It may be true that that many rapes occur, but why are you blaming men? It has nothing to do with men. It's like people get struck by hit-and-run drivers; the sex of the offender and of the victim is accidental."

One day in Dallas during the campaign, my friend Charlotte Taft and I were driving back to her house after a radio show, talking about the way in which our language and syntax so often absolves men from responsibility for their violent behavior toward women. Suddenly I realized that in my campaign speech I had been saying, "Today over 2000 women in this country will be raped." By using the passive voice, I made rape sound as innocuous as "today it will rain," as if rape just falls out of the sky on women, just "happens" to us. As though there were no rapists.

In fact, when I say, "women are raped," the syntax helps convey the impression that *women* do the acting, that *women* are responsible. But when I say instead, "Today, men in this country raped over 2000 women," I lay the responsibility exactly where it belongs. Rape is *not* passive. Women are not raped. *Men rape women.*

My naming men as the rapists is almost always interpreted to mean that I hate men. Because we speak the unspeakable about men, feminists are always accused of viewing men as the enemy. The only response to this absurd reversal is that all evidence supports the reverse: men view women as the enemy.

As unbearable, as unfaceable as it is for so many, the truth is that it is men who hate women, not the other way around. Women do not rape and beat and incestuously violate, and impoverish, and sexually harass, and kill men in vast numbers every year. It is men who do these things to women. Women do nothing hurtful to men with the blessing of the system, with the legal system turning the other way. This is a luxury and privilege for men only. Let us get clear once and for all on this point: in patriarchy everyone is taught to love men and to hate women. This is the definition of patriarchy and its methods of perpetuation. In no other way could male supremacy have survived for such a long time.

That men hate women is a fact so unbearable as to be virtually invisible in general society. My daughter, Kari, is a very bright and gifted young woman, but she thought for several years that my feminism was a bit extreme. Oh, she could see the problem all right, but it didn't seem so central as I painted it. After all, she didn't want to be "narrow."

Then one night a few years ago she called me from Portland, Oregon, where she had moved several months earlier to seek her fortune. I don't know what had happened that made

246

everything come clear; she tells me what she wants me to know. All I know is that after a long pause, she said in an uncharacteristically small voice, an anguished, bewildered, very shaky voice, "Mom, why do men hate us so much?" Oh, my dear, I moaned to myself, so now you know the very hardest truth of them all.

We have been trained to believe that telling the truth about men means we don't love them anymore. On the contrary, telling the truth is the only redemptive act of love left between the sexes.

We are also taught that telling the truth is a very dangerous business. But how could it be any more dangerous than not telling the truth has been? Our silence has not spared us one of countless daily humiliations and the most grisly atrocities.

Nevertheless, women are certainly aware that to tell the truth about men's behavior toward us is not the way to keep out of immediate trouble. We know that to tell the truth is the most revolutionary act available to us, because in doing so we repudiate our deepest acculturation, which is to be loyal to and to protect our oppressors. For a very long time we have had to buy our lives with silence and with loyalty to men, and in this way collaborated in our own oppression. Now we realize that we can save all life *only* with our loyalty to ourselves and other women.

The truth is that men rape women. Daily, brutally, and in large numbers. And though, as Alix Dobkin points out, it's not all men, it's always men. Rape is never accidental, never arbitrary. It is an *institution* of patriarchy, absolutely necessary for maintaining male privilege and power. Women are strong adult human beings. There must be daily reminders, daily terrors to keep us in our place.

For this reason, rape is not only encouraged, it is insisted upon; not just condoned, but blessed. (Any who think this is an overstatement need watch only one week of network television — never mind movies and videos and magazines and popular music and fiction, and especially never mind pornography in all its malevolent ubiquity.) For this reason, also, the overwhelming majority of "good" men, who claim to be appalled at its viciousness, do nothing to stop rape. *All* men, whether they physically rape women or not, participate in the benefits of rape, just as *all* women, whether they are physically raped or not, are kept enslaved by it. The cessation of rape would herald loss of privilege for men, would usher in an entirely new order of things, would radically realign power.

On some level, all men know and fear this. So while they may consciously deplore rape, their unconscious knowledge keeps them silent accessories. As does their far more conscious and often articulated fear that if women ever attained sufficient power we would repay them in kind for all male hatred and violence toward us over the centuries. It is impossible for many men, thoroughly acculturated in the dominant male value system, to comprehend a value system in which vengeance is not only *not* a foremost consideration, but not a consideration at all. Feminists understand that to the extent that we are motivated by revenge, we will inadvertently reproduce the old implacable world view and order of things that has so trapped and crushed us. Like Mary Wollstonecraft, we "do not wish women to have power over men, but over themselves."[8]

Rape is a paradigm for all male behavior toward women, and by extension toward all groups in "woman" position. All other assaults, all other unholy violations of women — physical, economic, emotional, spiritual — are simply variations on the theme of rape.

I am still surprised by the rapist mentality of the men in the Left. In the 1985 Four Days in April march in Washington, D.C., a group of young men with anti-war banners chanted as they walked along, "Rape Nancy Reagan!" And "Ronald Reagan should screw Nancy instead of us!" The women near them in the march were furious and shouted, "This is a march against violence. Stop that!" But the men didn't back off easily. It took a long fierce shouting match to get them to quit. Interestingly, no men joined in the criticism against the chants.

Then Jesse Jackson spoke, and totally alienated women by calling all people "men"—i.e., "men are marching for justice"—
and always referring to God as "he." By the time it was all over,
the women felt completely excluded, invisible, and battered.

If rape is not enough proof that war is raging against
women, we only need remember that women are the poor of
the world. According to United Nations statistics, though
women do two-thirds of the world's work, we make only one-
tenth of the world's money and own only one-hundredth of the
world's property. (I wish more Socialists realized what sex their
beloved "workers" really are! But would they view this, as the
high school boy viewed rape, as accidental, incidental, or coin-
cidental?) This is undeniable evidence of profound and systemic exploitation. It is slavery, pure and simple.

Economic slavery is an ever-present and painful reality in
most women's lives, but especially in the lives of women of
color. In the United States, the prognosis is that by the year
2000, the entire poverty population will be women and our
children, including women of color out of all proportion to
their numbers in society. Viewing us as their rightful economic
resources, men daily violate and exploit women. This sentence
explains and sums up global economy. Poverty is total war.

Incest is another piece of evidence I offer those ignorant
enough to consider war too big a term for women's lives. A few
years ago when I first began mentioning sexual abuse in my
speeches, the number of girls and young women victimized
was one in every four. Lately, in various publications, I see the
body count being tallied as one in every three, 38 percent, a
dramatic increase. And it is an actual increase, not a mere
matter of better research and reporting. History and common
sense combine to tell us that when the slaves begin to rise, the
masters redouble the violence and terrorism and propaganda
ordinarily needed to keep them under control. It is certainly no
accident that as women wake out of our long brainwashed
sleep, all the brutal institutions of patriarchy increase in
strength.[9]

One out of every three females in this country, before she reaches age 18, will be sexually assaulted, incest accounting for nearly half the assaults.[10] Maybe she will be violated once, maybe hundreds of times. Maybe by only one male relative (much of the time it's Daddy), or family friend, maybe by several. As one woman wrote to me: "Believe me, once is enough to make you afraid of it forever after and enough for all the self-loathing and not-trusting syndrome to become well established."

Incest, the most profound betrayal of trust possible between human beings, is so devastating to the heart, such a murder of the spirit, that many women struggle all their lives to recover from it. Nothing nearly so damaging to people's feelings of worth, to their sense of wholeness and identity, happens to men in those wars men *call* wars. In fact, the rape and violation and murder of women is as common and necessary an ingredient in men's wars as the shooting of enemy soldiers, often more common, because, though there is not always "action" in a war, and all soldiers are not on the "front," there are always women to hurt and the war against them to fight while waiting for the "real" war.

Those who become annoyed or even angry when I use the word "war," maintaining that it misrepresents the issue, are, in a sense, more accurate than they know. Incest is on another level altogether, a level totally out of the range of our vocabulary. Worse than war, worse than political terrorism, worse than these combined.

Incest means that those on whom we are totally dependent, those who have complete authority over us and from whom we have no recourse, whose approval we desperately fear to lose, those whom society assures us care most about our happiness and welfare — *those who say they love us* — destroy the inner core of our lives, our wills, our sense of dignity and justice, our feeling that there is meaning and decency in human relationships and safety in the world. We have not been warned that Daddy is our enemy, or Grandpa, or Uncle Steve,

250

or brother Harvey. We have been lied to about the meaning —
for females — of "family." How do women ever unsnarl the confusion of such betrayal in their psyches?

Incest is all this. And though it seems to be a raging epi-
demic, it is actually *endemic* to patriarchy. It is not the perver-
sity of a few bad men in a few squalid households, or even in
hundreds of thousands. It is a way of life for millions of families, a corruption that pervades our society and all this patriarchal planet. Men who sexually "use" their daughters and nieces
and granddaughters and sisters are everywhere. They are our
doctors, our school superintendents, our ministers, our lawyers. Incest is distributed equally over class, race, national ori-
gin, occupational category. It is a great leveler.

Like rape, incest is not accidental. It is an *institution* of patriarchy — like the church, like the law: absolutely necessary to
maintaining male privilege and power.[11] If we were not so
maimed, so confused and hurt, so wounded in our spirits, we
could not be kept enslaved. Like rape, despite rhetoric to the
contrary, incest is not only encouraged, it is insisted upon; not
just condoned, but blessed. It must be in place or women would
be whole and strong and rise up in that power that comes from
deep within, from knowing who and why we are, and say, con-
clusively, "Stop this wickedness at once. We will not stand for it
one more second." And *not* stand for it one more second.

Or for battering, another of patriarchy's institutionalized
gynocidal games. Fifty percent of us in relationships with men
experience violence at their hands, everything from a slap in
the face to murder. Over 4000 of us are murdered every year
in this country by men who say they love us (and this is an FBI
figure again so we know it's low), not to mention the huge
numbers of women who are permanently disfigured and incapacitated. And only the tiniest percentage of the murderers
of women are even charged, let alone brought to justice, because women are the enemy in patriarchy. As Lenore Walker
puts it, "Rapists are the shock troops to keep women in their
place; batterers are the home guard."[12]

Men have been encouraged with every scrap of invidious propaganda at the system's command to assault and hurt and kill us. That is the reason murderers and rapists and batterers and incestors and sexual harassers and economic exploiters and pornographers are so infrequently prosecuted. They only do that which is required of them, behave as they have been taught and are expected to behave, as they *must* behave, since the system depends upon this behavior. They deserve medals and pensions from the patriarchal state, and candle-lit marches honoring them such as the New Bedford rape gang inspired, not jail sentences. It wouldn't make much sense for the men in power to prosecute consistently and assiduously for such acts, since if they did they could not be sure that enough men would kill and rape and beat and exploit and humiliate women for male supremacy to reign unabated.

This raises the question of how the system could successfully prosecute pornographers and stay intact. The answer is that at this time of the world it couldn't, and therefore doesn't. And won't, without a unity of consciousness and will among women which seems far distant at this moment.[13]

The eight-billion-dollar-a-year pornography industry functions, as Andrea Dworkin makes very clear, as the nerve center for all the other male institutions of violence and control. It is the central office, the Central Intelligence Agency, upon whose efficiency the rest now depend. Pornographic magazines and movies are the guerrilla manuals from which men learn the methods for debasing women, for physically and emotionally dominating them, and from which they get society's "go ahead" signal. Another absolutely necessary institution of patriarchy.

So we send our kids to the local convenience store for milk and bread and apples and they can't help seeing the other staple of our times. There we are, our beautiful, powerful, mysterious bodies tied and bound and gagged in degrading positions, helpless, being sodomized, gang-raped, raped by animals, hanging from meat hooks, machetes or rifles or broomsticks bristling with razor blades being rammed up our vaginas, pincers tearing the flesh of our nipples.

Our wonderful bodies going through meat grinders and coming out hamburger (*Hustler's* idea of humor*) is just one of the countless messages to us that women are only meat:

> . . . Women who have walked by a construction site, given birth in a hospital, strutted down a runway in a beauty contest, lined up for customers in a brothel, applied for a job as a television news reporter — these women know. The connection is already there for us: in the photograph in the pornography magazine showing nude women hung from meat hooks; in the restaurant advertisement showing a photograph of a woman's nude torso on which is written, "Best Ribs in Town"; in the chart demonstrating cuts of meat using a drawing of a woman's body; in the term used for new women in the pornography film industry — "fresh meat"; in the uniform a restaurant tried to force its waitresses to wear: red hot pants with a cattle brand on the left buttock.[14]

The cover of one porn magazine sums up women's situation in patriarchy: a man kisses a woman in what appears to be a tender embrace — while savagely stabbing her in the back. Too many women — feminists among them — are looking at the tender eyes, the loving kiss, and failing to perceive the knife, ignoring the hatred that drives it into our bodies.

The claim that pornography is harmless, since there is no "hard data" (an interesting phallic term Pauline Bart pointed out to me) to prove that men imitate what they see in pictures, is manifestly absurd. Such an assertion could only be taken seriously in a society where the mechanisms of women's oppression must be hidden at all costs, often at the cost of reason,

---

*When we protested, *Hustler* spokesmen said, "You see? Feminists have no sense of humor!"

common sense, and all that is philosophically and scientifically understood about what causes people to think and act as they do. The basic message of most religions and schools of ethical thought — except for feminism, all one hundred percent andro-centric — is that "as a man thinketh in his heart, so is he." But it is typical of patriarchy to disconnect the important terminals of cause and effect when it serves its purposes.

The argument that, though pornography is everywhere, commonly seen and purchased and perused in its many mani-festations, it has no effect upon attitudes toward women, or toward sexuality, or upon behavior, would make Pavlov fall down laughing. This disregard of the massive evidence of con-ditioning is so foolish that we know it is calculated. Our rulers capitalize upon their knowledge that they have us so thor-oughly conditioned to believe sick is well and pain is pleasure that when it comes to anything concerning women they can feed us the most transparent balderdash and we will just nod our heads and say, "Yes, Master."

Even if all else we know about human behavior did not ar-gue for the harmfulness of pornography, the actual lives and many testimonies of women who have been directly and deliber-ately hurt by pornography — the making of it and the use of it as a do-it-yourself manual for rapists, husbands, boyfriends, fa-thers, ad infinitum — should at least begin to persuade us. And it would, if we had not all been taught *not* to listen to or believe women, or only to believe women who have achieved some cred-ibility with men, which by definition means who have seriously compromised themselves and betrayed the rest of us.

The fact that pornography is inundating our society, that it is a vast and rapidly expanding industry, that it is protected by the Constitution of "the greatest democracy in the world,"[15] that even the "liberal" (save me from liberals!) ACLU — per-haps because they are lawyers to *Playboy*? — laugh at women's legitimate desire for protection from the violence it spawns and the caste system it perpetuates; the fact that there is no recourse for women against men who force or trick them into the making of it (and proceed to make fortunes from it, none of which the women share), that snuff films — so called because women are actually killed in sadistic ways in front of the camera — don't even raise eyebrows in our legal system let alone investigations, arrests, and prison terms, that no state or serious federally-sponsored research is being conducted into the effects of it — all this shouts a loud and unmistakable message to men:

"The degradation, wounding, and killing of women is fine with us. We know it's just good healthy sex. Don't listen to those puritanical fanatics who don't want you to have any fun. Whatever feels good to you is right. And women *love* to be hurt; the more you hurt them, the better they like it. They can only be sexually aroused if they're dominated by a big, strong, virile man who isn't afraid to show who's boss. Besides, we know you have to make her scream to have an erection. That's good. That's normal."

The message to women is equally clear: "We hate you. We have complete control over you; we can do whatever we want to you and there's nothing you can do about it — we'll kill you if you try. We can kill you on a whim if we want, just for fun. So *fear* us! And be very very nice to us, placate us, lick our boots, go along with our sexual politics. Grovel!"

That sex and violence, "love" and violence, have become so intertwined for millions of people in our society that they are nearly inseparable and indistinguishable is a sign of the decadence of patriarchy — patriarchy being so completely, so unmitigatedly itself that it doesn't even try to pretend anymore; patriarchy so ripe it is rotting.

All institutions of patriarchy participate in connecting sex and violence, "love" and violence. All institutions are pornographic. Remember the teacher telling a little girl on the playground who was being hit by a boy: "Don't be upset, dear. Don't you know that when boys hit you (or tease you or chase you) it means they like you?"

Listen to our language. A slap is a "love tap"; we sing, "You always hurt the one you love"; parents say when they

255

physically punish their children, "This hurts me more than it does you. I'm doing it for your own good, because I love you."

Total reversal holds sway in the world: pain is pleasure, hate is love, war is peace, authoritarianism is democracy, insanity is lucidity, cowardice is courage. And men are playing around with the ultimate topsy-turvy: death is life. And not playing around very gingerly.

Pornography is the most blatant political terrorism on earth. Although this fact seems lost on all but a few feminists, it wouldn't be lost on anybody if it were primarily directed against any group but women.[16] For instance, if this country were suddenly flooded with billions of magazines and books and movies and videos, 98 percent of which portrayed graphically and in detail pleasure and power gained by the debasement, humiliation, and physical maiming—to the point of dismembering and killing—of Black South African males, or Sandinista males, or Jewish males, a hue and cry would arise in the liberal community such as would put all former human rights outcries to shame. Masses of outraged people would rampage through the streets of every city and town. Something would be done *immediately* to stop it, and the ACLU would be there, leading the pack. An interesting phenomenon would occur. Liberals would suddenly recognize pornography as the deadly political weapon, as the potent forger of societal attitudes, and as the powerfully persuasive legitimator of oppression that it is and is intended to be. They would know it for the ultimate terrorist tactic.

But pornography is not primarily designed to reduce men to meat, to objects, to bloody pulp. It concentrates on reducing women to meat, to objects, to bloody pulp. When it does this to women, it's suddenly, magically, not political at all. It's erotic! It's being really sexually "free." It's sexual hi-jinks, and lots of fun! Surprise, everyone!

This is the truth of women's lives: that we live in a world where invisible institutions with inaudible voices command men to do everything possible to stop us from being fully human, fully ourselves; to hunt us down, and, if necessary, to slaughter us, emotionally and physically. We live in a world where the strongest women are deliberately and subtly co-opted into leading the cheers in the woman-hating contests. Nothing like this systematic breaking of the heart and spirit of half of humanity happens in the wars men call wars. There is no battlefield so strewn with broken bodies and lives as the sexual battlefields which constitute the foundation of every "civilized" society in the world.

Men speak humorously, or so they say, of "the war between the sexes" — a transparent and guileful attempt to mislead us into thinking that there is a natural enmity between women and men, and that the "sides" are evenly matched. Nothing could be further from the truth on both counts. The "war between the sexes" is man made, and it is not *between* anybody. It is *against* women.

We know what it means to be born female when we hear doctors admit that they often treat three-month-old, two-year-old baby girls for gonorrhea of the throat. We know that this — and more, oh, so much more — has to be in place in our society, and must function daily with great efficiency. How else can we be kept lying flat on our bellies with our faces in the mud at men's boot tips?

We know that to be born female in patriarchy is to be born behind enemy lines.

During the question and answer period after one of my campaign speeches in Delaware, a man rose at the back of the hall with a pencil and paper in his hand. "You say that over 2000 women are raped every day in this country. I did some quick figuring. That makes about 40,000 a day worldwide." Significant pause. Then he exploded: "*That's* the number of children who starve to death every day! Think about *that!*" And he plopped down in his seat with a smug, duty-done look on his face.

At that point, another man, encouraged by his colleague's outspokenness and impeccable logic, arose and pointed out that no matter how bad incest is (he called it "child abuse" since he was apparently unable to face the implications of "incest"), he was furious at my saying that what happens to females in incest is far worse than anything that happens to men in wars. How could I be so *insensitive*? How do I think he'd felt, leaving the blasted bodies of his buddies strewn all over Vietnam's battlefields? Didn't I have any conception that men were being tortured even as we sat there, in El Salvador, for instance?

What they were saying to me was very clear. As long as *any male, anywhere* is suffering, women are selfish to mention that they are suffering, too. I'm sure neither of those men realized the woman-hatred behind their feeling that everything and everyone should come before women.

I pointed out quietly that in every country where children are starving, women are starving also. In every country where men are being tortured, women are being tortured also. I was insensitive enough to point out that Vietnam is also strewn with the blasted bodies of women, and that many, many of those bodies were not simply blown up, but were also sexually abused — raped, gang raped, used up in prostitution, tortured (cutting fetuses out of living bellies and beheading them in front of women's eyes before they died themselves was a favorite sport. My Lai was not an isolated incident.) No matter when or where or what men suffer, women's suffering is on some totally different, more exquisite, plane.

No one wants to hear that women are suffering.

I told them that I did not intend to belittle anyone's suffering, only to put women's in perspective. I pointed out that all the one man said about men and war has been glaringly visible for thousands of years. Men's ordeals are recounted and described and depicted in every conceivable way in every medium on earth, and have been from earliest history. We are always asked and expected to look at and listen to and understand and sympathize with men's pain and suffering, and we have always done it, all of us, men and women.

I told them that it seemed only fair to ask that the capacity to acknowledge and understand and deplore another's pain be extended to the other half of the human race, though I knew that for obvious reasons, this had always been and was still forbidden. Women's agony at the hands of men must never be revealed. If women steadfastly and courageously began to tell the truth and would not stop, would not be co-opted, would not become afraid, the truth of our enslavement would be undeniable, and the jig would be up. That this might indeed happen is terrifying to most people. It would stand the whole world on its head. This is why any time women say, "Look at what is happening to us!" someone invariably rises up on the spot—as patriarchy has trained us all so well to do—and shouts, in order to divert us, to frighten us, to remind us of our vulnerability and danger: "But what about *men*?"[17]

"This is what you are doing for this group," I explained to the distraught man whose buddies lie in fragments all over the corpse of Vietnam. "You are performing this function here tonight. May I interrupt this well-rehearsed performance to point out that we have given men 5000 years of undivided attention." (Is it any wonder they have remained spoiled little boys?) As Pauline Bart points out: "We are not allowed, even now, to speak of women's suffering without someone saying, 'and men, too,' although we have always spoken of men's suffering without adding 'and women, too!'"[18]

Patriarchy has worked hard to make women's experience appear so trivial and so invisible that it is inconceivable to most people that we warrant any attention at all. Otherwise, it would not be so maddening to them to have to listen for a whole hour to a speech about women, though they listen willingly day after day, year after year, to talk by and about men. For many hundreds of years they have heard about nothing *but* men—their wars, their ideas, their art, their politics, their science, their blah, blah, blah, ad nauseam.

Because everything associated with women is degraded by that association, something subversive happens to the glorious male vision of war when we insist on calling women's lives with men on this earth "war." War, to the patriarchal mind, is heroic, grand, full of magnificent courage and color, camara-

259

derie, idealism, moral and physical strength—the whole shot through with religious fervor: God is always on our side because we are right and good and noble. The Old Testament is all the proof one needs that war in patriarchy is the holiest of holies.

Then feminists come along and sully that splendid word. What could be less noble and heroic and grand and magnificent than the furtive ugly sneaking weak and cowardly acts of rape and battering and incest and pornography-inspired sadism, and sexual harassment and pauperizing and sterilizing and obligatory motherhood—to name just a few of the less heroic aspects of this most invisible and vicious and widespread and prolonged and prototypical of all wars in human history.

No wonder people become alarmed, even outraged, when the holy word "war" is used for the disgustingly two-bit work of bullying and brutalizing women into submission. Even to use the words "war" and "women" in the same sentence makes a mockery of all they reverence.

Yet, the screams of women, their moaning, the crying of the women of the world, past and present, echo through the chambers of the unconscious in every human being alive. On some level, each of us knows what is going on, but it is as if we have signed a pact not to let on that we know, have sworn to keep it secret. What else can account for the public aghast when one minute fragment of the hidden hoard of evidence escapes into public awareness? Why the haste to cover the New Bedford rapists with glory, if not to deny the representativeness of what happened there?

Sister Rosalie Bertell provides a useful model for thinking about violence and women's silence. Violence is a social addiction, she says, and those addicted, like alcoholics, must have enablers in order to maintain their addiction. As is almost always the case with practicing alcoholics, those around them seem to be in a conspiracy not to see what is going on and never to talk about it, a conspiracy of denial.

In the world today, women are the enablers of men's addiction to violence. Too many of us fear to face it down and so have silently contracted not to see it for what it is, to deny it, and thus to enable it. As alcoholism cannot be maintained when the co-alcoholic refuses to play the destructive game, violence cannot continue when enough co-violents decide to break the unspoken contract that permits violence to continue.[19]

Sometimes I wonder how we have survived so long, this species, in the nightmare the men are dreaming. I wonder why we have been allowed to continue by whatever it is in the universe that wishes us well? Something in me at these times says with great authority: "It can't go on any longer. Because I say so. Because women say so. We are at the end of the possibility of survival in this kind of hatred and violence." This is why the women's movement has arisen, to make this clear, to announce once and for all that we cannot wage this bigger-word-than-war against half our kind and hope — somehow, miraculously — for peace, for life.

I ran for President to say that we haven't seen peace on this planet for 5000 years. Not one second of it. Not since the men came out of those long-ago kitchens and bedrooms with the greatest evil — which is the idea of owning and enslaving other humans — in their hearts. We wouldn't recognize peace if it came leaping into our midst this moment and shook our hands. We haven't a clue what it feels like, what it takes to have it, how the world would look if we *did* have it.

The word "peace" itself is part of the problem. It is a military term, meaning "the time between declared wars." (Charlton Heston told a *Washington Post* reporter that he couldn't see what anti-nuclear, anti-intervention activists were making such a fuss about; we'd had peace for 40 years!) There is no way to talk about peace without positing war. Peace is the opposite of war in men's language and thought, the other end of the dichotomy: war/peace. It's what they do when they're not fighting and killing other men, and it includes terrorizing and killing women, starving millions of people, poisoning the planet, paying other men to kill other men, and frightening everyone with extinction. That's peace? Some word!

Sonia Johnson

We need a whole new vocabulary that doesn't dichotomize all conditions, a word for peace which means abundance and happiness and health and wholeness for everyone while not positing the imminence or even the existence of an opposite. Part of building a new world will be going out of our old minds into a new mind from which we can speak with an authentic tongue.

Though I believe—despite Moka and his cohorts from the other planet—that tearing the scrims away from our eyes is necessary, that it is essential to look clearly at women's lives, and without flinching to see the truth about men and women, I do not believe it is necessary for anyone to feel guilty about what we see there. Enlightened, yes, and even sorry. Definitely outraged and "had" and ready to do something about it.

But not guilty. Guilt is not a useful emotion,* as women know better than anyone, having been manipulated and incapacitated by it for so many centuries. We have learned another natural law from our painful experiences in the world and that is that negative motivation, such as guilt or fear, cannot prompt or support sustained positive action.

By calling out "Why are you blaming men?" the young man in the New Jersey high school auditorium enabled me to leap inside his world view again for a moment—I'd been going further and further out of that mind for years. I could hear the unspoken but obvious continuation of his question: ". . . instead of women?" What he was protesting, in fact, was my breaking of the unwritten contract women made to buy life: to remain silent about men's behavior, or, if to speak, to speak the party line, which is to blame the victim. Blaming the victim is one of the most venerable and popular of all the party games at the Old Boys' Club (where God is president). Nothing has more decidedly obfuscated and turned actuality upside down.

---

*Perhaps guilt is not an emotion at all, but, as Emily Culpepper suggests, a societal construct designed specifically to keep women in line.

My young listener's question lays bare another habit of the masculine mind: if something is wrong, the first thing to do is find someone to blame. Blame is absolutely necessary to maintain tyranny, as we all should have learned from Hitler, but only so long as it's never placed on the right person or group. It must be laid, and preferably at once, and no matter the cost to reason, upon the enemy.*

But blame has no part in the agenda of the women's movement. What *does* is having the courage to face the truth and taking responsibility to do something about it. Though men regard and treat us as their deadliest enemy, men are not *our* enemy. Feminism, as the biophilic philosophy and world view that it is, has no place for the concept of "enemy." Feminism is about cutting away the arras of deception and treachery of centuries with the swift sharp merciful blade of truth. Because it is negative, blame is counterproductive in building a positive new order.

Telling the truth is not blaming. It is telling the truth.

---

*Mary Ann told me a fascinating insight she'd had. "The right-to-lifers are cases of classical displacement. Listening to the preachers on the radio agonize about the pain and suffering of the unborn during abortion, I realized that they were talking about themselves and the bomb. Because their ideology forbids acknowledgment that we are on the brink of destruction, but because somewhere in themselves they know it full well, they must come to grips with their terror by displacing it upon fetuses and putting the blame, not on their system, but on women, who are the historic scapegoats for the patriarchy." Linda Barufaldi adds, "I have noticed that all fetuses are male to them."

11

Listen to Women for a Change

"What makes you think a feminist President would act differently from a man, or from a woman like Margaret Thatcher who imitates men?" members of my audience always wanted to know during the campaign. "What do you think she'd *do*?"

I was glad they asked because it gave me the chance to remind them that in every society there are at least two separate cultures — male culture and female culture — each with its own very distinct set of values and code of behavior. The first question at all our births was, "Is it a boy or a girl?" and to answer it everyone present peered anxiously at our miniature sexual apparatus. Depending upon their findings, we plunged irrevocably at that moment into one or the other of these cultures, embarked immediately upon a course as different from that of our cohorts of the other sex, received as disparate a view of the world and how to function in it, as if one or the other of us had fallen from the moon.

When we remember that in patriarchy the male is God (because God is male), we aren't surprised that one's gender is far and away the most significant fact of life for any human being, the most portentous, and most fraught with consequences. It determines, after all, whether one will be master or slave.

Crucial to keeping men masters and women slaves is the belief that male and female are opposites, polarities; that there are "male" traits and "female" traits that are as different as night and day, that are genetic, unchangeable, god-given, and non-overlapping — the dangerous yin/yang justification for tyranny: since men are "naturally" leaders, authoritative and decisive, and women are "naturally" submissive and passive, it follows that men's ruling women is "natural." People must believe that there are eternally unbridgeable differences between the powerful and the powerless for domination as a way of life to be internalized as "natural" and "right."

This is why the concept of "unisex" so unnerves the New Right. Heaven forbid that we should discover somewhere along the line between male and female a huge overlapping in both directions of character traits presumed to belong exclusively to one sex or the other. Heaven forbid that we should find out the truth that there is no characteristic that is *only* male or *only* female. Patriarchy couldn't survive it. The fiction that males are *this* way — which fits them for ascendancy and domination, and females are *that* way — which fits them for servitude, must be vigilantly, solemnly, religiously maintained at all costs.

The patriarchal revolution of some 5000 years ago depended upon the definition of "man" becoming increasingly and fervently "not a woman." To consolidate and maintain male power, all evidences of womanliness had to be meticulously excised from male culture. So those values most clearly associated with women were debased and dropped from the moral repertoire of the true loyalists and heroes: "manly" men.

And what of the values that triumphed? Chief among them is "face" — the imperative always to be in the strong, on-top male position. Face in turn gives rise to the other major masculine values, all of which are interdependent and synergistic: competition, linear dichotomization (us/them, good guys/ bad guys), domination by force, violence as the prime problem solver, materialism, efficiency, objectivity (meaning, in this context, not influenced by feelings such as compassion, acting out of "reason"). These major masculine life-hating values developed in reaction to women's life-loving culture, which had prevailed worldwide for most of human history. And all masculine values have since been in the service of the power-over patriarchal paradigm that had its beginnings with men's domination of women.

One by one values perceived as "womanly" were weeded out of the male code of behavior until today, though the yawning moral chasms are glossed over with rhetoric, there is almost nothing positive, humane, or life-enhancing left in male culture. And so no reason not to reject it totally and immediately.

Any people who rule unchecked become tyrants. Still holding on, by hook and by crook, to our own cultural perspective, some women continued down the centuries to critique this steady dehumanization and narrowing of the dominant culture's moral range. But the iron heel upon our necks, the fire at our feet, and finally the terror in our hearts prevented us from checking the men's headlong rush to extinction.

This does not mean that all men are monsters, though all of them participate in and collude with a monstrous culture. It is true — and hopeful — that some men reject aspects of male culture. Every woman, of course, wishes to believe that the man in *her* life is an exceptional man, a man in a million, and that therefore she is the exceptional woman. But the odds are 99.9 to 0.1 against her (and .1 is probably a high estimate), because almost no man, no matter how gentle, no matter how liberal, could bear to reject the innumerable privileges — operant in very subtle as well as blatant ways in every sphere of his life — of being male,* even if it were possible (which by and large it isn't).

---

*A friend once wrote to me, "For me, the bottom line now with men is that *any* man (my brother, too, whom I love dearly) will sell me out if it's a choice between me and patriarchy, me and his male privilege."

What this means is that the only place in society where the female values, discredited and cast aside by patriarchy, values deemed trivial and demeaning, could and did survive was in women's culture—the "other" culture. That's why, despite obvious and inevitable infusions of patriarchal values, women's culture is without question superior to men's. Within it are preserved all the discarded "womanly" values, those which, ironically—and fortunately, since they have not been lost—are the very ones we must all now internalize and act out of if we wish to survive and evolve. Though they have been named "womanly," the goal of the women's movement is to un-dichotomize them, to make them universal, to extend and expand—and radically edit—the definition of what it means to be human.

Just as when I speak of male culture I do not include every individual man to the same degree, when I speak of women's culture I do not include every woman equally. Many women, in trying to establish themselves as credible in the male world have rejected their own cultural heritage to a greater or lesser degree. All women do it to some extent. It makes sense that far more women adopt male culture than vice versa simply because male values and modes of behavior are the ones with status. On the other hand, female values, having for millennia been laughed and sneered at and at best treated as "frills," are quick to be abandoned by most women who wish to be "successful."

And slow to be picked up even by well-meaning men who are hungry for them. They know very well the high cost in patriarchy of appearing "womanly."

Feminism is the articulation of the ancient, underground culture and philosophy based on the values that patriarchy has labeled "womanly," but which are necessary for full humanity. Among the principles and values of feminism that are most distinct from those of patriarchy are universal equality, non-violent problem-solving, and cooperation with nature, one another, and other species. Feminists place great value on non-hierarchical social, political, economic, and emotional or psychic relationships. Prizing compassion and genuine hearing of others' words and feelings, we put human needs and the quality of life at the top of our list of priorities. Our women's culture teaches us to respect intuition and the non-rational creative deep mind more than, but not exclusive of, the capacities of the brain. Because feminism affirms the connectedness of all life, among our principle values are holism, universalism, democracy, abundance, diffusion of wealth/resources/power and information, decentralization, and social responsibility. Feminism is a celebration of spirit, of the life in all things, an attitude of empathy, openness, and respect for feeling and emotion as essential and major parts of intellect.* And this just begins to describe it.

One of the reasons I ran for President was to translate into concrete terms what feminism could mean to the world, how it could shatter the us/them dichotomy most essential to patriarchy. I campaigned to begin to build the vision — and thus to create the possibility — of women's operating out of the power of our own value system, out of our integrity as women, out of feminist principles. I wanted to expand the narrow and commonly held view of feminism, and to awaken people to how much they were already accepting and acting out of feminist principles.

I was always aware, however, that if a woman who was a feminist *were* elected President, it would mean that patriarchy was over and that we were living in an altogether new world. And though I understood that there was no way we could know

---

*Several men called in to various radio talk shows during the campaign to tell me they'd never vote for a woman because women are too emotional. "Fortunately, men in power aren't emotional," I agreed with them, tongue in cheek, "because if they were they'd storm out of arms talks in Geneva, storm out of talks in Stockholm, storm out of talks in Vienna, fail to communicate because of hurt feelings and high dudgeon, hate and constantly plan to destroy one another. Think of the mess the world would be in if men operated out of their emotions!"

in any detail what that world would be like, almost certainly a position such as President would not even exist. The best I could do, trapped in the necessity of "making sense" in a Presidential campaign, was publicly to ignore this paradox and demonstrate how feminist principles could be applied to problems in this world at its current patriarchal worst.

I began by talking about violence. Women on the whole do not value—and for obvious reasons have not been acculturated by patriarchy to value—violence as a method of solving problems. I like to believe that women have never valued it in all of history, even before our enslavement. At least as a cultural entity we have not valued it or sanctioned its use, though individual women may have done so. In fact, it is part of women's underground cultural heritage to understand, sometimes very dimly, as if in memory, but nevertheless to understand that violence is the ultimate resort of weakness.

In fact, one of the most compelling arguments that patriarchy is dying—becoming weaker and weaker every day—is the incredible burgeoning, worldwide, of all varieties of violence.

We know that the bully on the playground smashes the other kids in the nose because he has no creativity, no new ideas.[1] He has no talent for interpersonal relationships. He doesn't know what to do to get respect and friends. He feels lost, so he strikes out. It is weakness, not strength, that motivates him to smash other kids in the face, and women know that. We know we're looking at an impoverished kid.

So when we see the men in power in every nation acting like that kid, we realize we're observing cases of severe arrested development. But we only realize this for a moment, because we can't believe our own judgment. After all, who are *we*? Just mothers and secretaries, just women. So we go on avidly listening to the news, go on with the habit of believing men are doing something significant in all this mayhem. We ought, of course, to follow our first impression and laugh uproariously at the idiocy that passes for pomp and circumstance among men.

269

Women also know a great deal about the nature of violence from having been on the receiving end of so much of it for so long, and from a wisdom deep inside ourselves from ancient, ancient times. We know that violence breeds violence, that it can never solve a problem — because it *is* a problem. Because violence carries the seeds of more violence in itself, solving problems by using it is metaphysically impossible.

So if men think violence has ever solved a problem, they are deluded. Those problems they think they solved by violence may seem to have disappeared, but in fact they have expanded, and have been entering the fray in other guises. All those old problems have just piled up unsolved behind us, and they are overtaking and about to overwhelm us. We haven't solved an important problem for the past 5000 years; we've just put them off. They're all still here, and they've combined to destroy the planet — that massive violence that's been building up and with which we have never dealt.

Even those who teach other women always to fight back during rape never suggest that as a group women should attempt to overthrow patriarchy by force. Everyone knows that is an absurd idea; men have all the weapons and the superior physical strength. But more important — though less often and less clearly understood — it is an absurd idea because we cannot use the methods that spawned the problem in the first place to solve it. We can't put a whole new philosophy of non-domination into the old mold of domination. Because the means are the ends, stopping violence with violence is epistemologically impossible.

The understanding that the means are the ends applies equally to sadomasochism, every act of which reproduces, reinforces, deepens, and prolongs what Cheri Lesh calls "the basic perversion of patriarchy":

It is time to stop pointing fingers and making scapegoats. Time to look at something very hard and real. We are all crazy and weird about sex. Heirs to

270

thousands of years of degradation and torture, of man as S and woman as M, of white as S and non-white as M, of God as S and human as M, of civilization as S and nature as M—who among us can claim immunity, who among us has not tasted the whip sting of poison in the honey, has not confused the slap with the caress? Sadomasochism is the basic sexual perversion of patriarchy.[2]

So in arguments for sadomasochism as a way of relating to others sexually, we must be aware that we each bear responsibility for creating an alternative to patriarchy that *is* an alternative. Hurting others/asking to be hurt, dominating others/asking to be dominated, humiliating others/asking to be humiliated— feeding the basic patriarchal addiction— is *not* finding an alternative. Instead, it is rationalizing and succumbing to the patriarchal imperatives most deeply imprinted on our psyches. It is fiercely seductive — as all addictions are — and it is lethal.

After the election that November, I sat in the middle of what is left of an ancient Minoan palace in Crete and thought about the women who lived at that time and those who lived during the earlier Cycladic times in that place and in Anatolia thousands of years before them, cultures in which women apparently enjoyed high status. I conjectured about their method of protecting themselves from male assault. I wondered if perhaps they had such a strong sense of their own worth, such a firm core of personal power, such an unshakable sense of their immense significance and *divinity*, that they moved in auras of proportions and intensities that made even the idea of attacking them unthinkable. Did their sense of themselves and their power create an impenetrable bubble of light around them in which they walked in perfect safety and freedom?

Sitting there surrounded by Goddess culture, I remembered that most articles written these days that deal with how to ward off assault suggest that women walk with confidence, firmly, surely, head up, back erect, arms swinging, feet hitting

271

the pavement with purpose, not mincing (as one must in high heels—imagine what the Goddess women would think of *them* in these dangerous times!) but striding—in every way giving off messages of fearlessness, inviolability, courage, and power. Since it is apparent that ultimately we cannot use force to stop force, using the powers of spirit and deep mind, which are women's terrain anyway, seems the obvious next step.*

For my campaign audiences, I painted in very broad strokes a fantasy of how a feminist President would think and act in the crises of these times. Operating out of the value system of women's culture, which recognizes violence as addictive, self-propagating, and always futile, she would know that either war is finished or we are; so that sending in the Marines, selling armaments, making and testing weapons, using and even having weapons, have now altogether ceased to be options. Since we wish to live, the first value that would have to change is that of power over others through violence, and the first things to go would be all institutions and engines of war.

Feminism is fundamentally anti-militaristic; Ms. President would immediately begin to demilitarize the world, and to take the initiative in engaging other nations, notably the U.S.S.R., in this effort. At 8:30 on the first morning of her administration, she would call the Soviet leader and tell him she was leaving for Moscow on the next plane and would be in to see him the next day.

This move would be facilitated by her inability to think in terms of losing face. Women do not value face. Perhaps because we have never had any face to lose—but more likely be-

---

*Obviously, until we learn to create these bubbles of psychic power around us, we must defend ourselves from assault in any way we can. But if we'd spend as much time developing our psychic offensive as we do learning karate and other defensive skills, we would be well out of masculine reality and reach. A friend wrote, "My karate teacher said, 'The first weapon on your body is your eyes.' And once, many years later, I actually knocked a man back away from me, as he approached me in a dark deserted parking lot, with the strength of my eyes focused on him. Knocked him *back*! Then, you see, since I didn't *need* to, I didn't hit him.

cause we see it for the immature reaction it is — we aren't handicapped by fear of losing it. It is hard to believe, though we know it is true, that saving face is the highest value in male culture. In all male interactions, the one-up/one-down configuration must be quite clear from the outset. This figures mightily in the mystery of why neither superpower leader visits the other; why the one who leaves his own turf and goes onto the other's turf loses face and becomes one-down, or in the dreaded "woman" position.

So neither of them is going to make the first move, and certainly neither is going to visit the other one because they must at all costs retain their identity as men and masters. They must always be one-up. Face is *always* more important than integrity or principle in male culture. These latter values are only rhetorical in the Old Boys' Club, and transfer readily to behavior only when they are commensurate with preserving face. (We witness examples of this almost weekly. I remember when Congress voted down Reagan's bill for Contra aid. To prove his strength and to save face, he immediately slapped Nicaragua with an embargo.) This intractable situation is what spawned diplomacy: how to get around this impasse? Obviously, both parties cannot be one-up.

Only now is there unfolding on this planet for the first time in written history the concept of win/win as opposed to win/lose. This is a feminist concept, a mode of being that comes from women's more cooperative culture. But the male "leaders" of our countries are dinosaurs, centuries from this level of moral development.

Anyway, Ms. President wouldn't bother with win/lose nonsense. Off she'd go to see the head of state in Moscow and say, "Friend, tomorrow, as President of the United States, I will announce to the entire world that the United States is going to dismantle its nuclear arsenal immediately by one-third. We hope you'll join us. It would be wonderful if the two biggest bullies on the global playground finally had the courage to be "womanly" and did what must be done to save all life on the planet. But if you don't join us, we'll do it anyway, because otherwise we will all surely die."

He would listen politely and disbelievingly and make non-committal grunts, thinking all the while that such an idea was naive and simple-minded and idealistic. Just like a woman. But he might remember late at night as he lay awake in his bed that the heroes of history and those men most revered in all cultures were men considered at first to be naive, simple-minded, and idealistic: Gandhi, Jesus, Lenin. . . .

In the morning, the United States would begin reversing the doomsday scenario.

What's the worst that could happen? Many fear and predict that the Soviet leaders would say, "Heh, heh, heh," in their evil-empirish way, "What a perfect opportunity to build up our arsenals and take over the United States!"

But Ms. President would go to Moscow again. "Friend," she would say, "We dismantled a third of our nuclear armaments and made the world that much safer. But there is so much more that needs to be done. The people of the world are waiting in a kind of wondering, hopeful hush to see if we've got the courage and wisdom to do it, and tomorrow the United States will show them that we have: we will begin dismantling the next third of our nuclear arsenal. All those people in our country who were using their brilliant, creative minds for purposes of destruction, are now busy designing and carrying out plans to convert our military economy to a life-centered one. As a nation, we are full of excitement and hope. Will you and the Soviet people follow suit? If you don't join us, we're going to do it anyway, because there is nothing to lose, only everything to gain."

And then she'd go and do it. Because even if the United States disarmed two-thirds of our nuclear warheads, we'd still have more than enough to destroy the Soviet Union—that is, if we wanted to extinguish all life on planet earth by firing them off. Pentagon officials tell us we have enough nuclear material ready right now to destroy the Soviet Union twelve times over.

That seems a bit excessive, even for rank militarists. People can only die once.

The rigid patriarchal minds among us would then say, "Yeah, well, that's all very well for you to say, but what evidence do we have that the Russians will disarm if we do? You must trust them an awful lot more than I do."

"Wrong," Ms. President would reply. "I don't trust the Russians any more than I trust the men who used to be in power in this country, which is not at all. That isn't the point."

When I was on a very conservative radio talk show in Providence, Rhode Island, early in the campaign, outraged listeners, mostly men, responded to my argument for disarmament by shouting: "Why don't you go back to Russia where you belong, then!" and sneering, "You have to be the most *naive* lady alive to trust Russia the way you do!"

When we were off the air during commercials, the host continued the argument. He insisted on comparing the righteousness of the United States with that of the Soviet Union (what he thought *that* proved, besides his dichotomous, competitive mentality, heaven knows). finally, during one commercial break, he leaned intently across the table and said, "You must admit that at least *we* have never done anything really *evil!*" So saying, he sat back, self-satisfied.

I was too stunned to speak. What country was he talking about? Across my mind wove the long weary lines of Native Americans being driven from their homelands, in a country that had belonged to them and their ancestors for hundreds of thousands of years. I saw their families slaughtered, their villages laid waste, their cultures destroyed. I saw ships setting sail from the shores of Africa with steaming holds so full of black bodies there was no room even to sit, no water, no food, no toilets. I saw how those who survived were starved, beaten, humiliated, raped. I looked in my memory at the slums of every city in the United States where their descendants are still riddled with poverty and all its pernicious attendants. I remembered that our founders were slaveholders, that this coun-

275

try was *born* in evil, and that the men who had led it ever since have never stopped doing evil. I thought how blind and hypocritical, ridiculous and dangerous we are when we point at any other country in the world and yell, "Evil!"

No, it is not a matter of trust; it is a matter of playing the odds. Scientists and military experts (the latter mostly retired; they wanted to be sure to get their pensions before they spoke out — such admirable courage!) from many countries tell us unequivocally that if we continue to build up arms, we will surely blow ourselves up. Either by accident, which Alva Myrdal and other disarmament experts consider most likely, . . .

Or by design. The lesson history teaches us is that men have never made weapons they haven't used. It is unthinkable, a loss of face in patriarchal culture *not* to put machines to their intended use. "Everything that is possible must be done" is a motto that reflects basic rigid patriarchal thought. (As the bumper sticker has it, THE ONE THAT DIES WITH THE MOST TOYS WINS.)

In addition, simple knowledge of how we create reality tells us that we are doomed if we continue to think and plan war. Recalling Elie Wiesel's "whatever is imaginable is possible," we know that if we spend all our time and energy and resources preparing and thinking and imagining — concentrating upon — war, war is the reality we create. Our every decision, large and small, moves us in that direction. Why is it such a hard concept to grasp, that if we prepare for war, we have war? Because the fundamental reversal mechanism of patriarchal thought turns everything upside down and tells us that only if we prepare for war can we have peace; if we dare give ourselves over to peace, we'll surely have war.

That we create what we focus on is not a hard concept for feminists. I was not surprised to read Sidney Lens' article in *The New York Times* reporting a 1960 study on deterrence done by the Canadian Army. The method used was to look back through history at all the recorded instances of the stockpiling of arms as a strategy to prevent war, and to see how often it had succeeded. Of the 1600-odd times documented, in all but ten war had occurred. The patriarchal mind never learns from experience. (As someone once said to me, amassing a mammoth arsenal of weapons to prevent war is like stockpiling condoms to prevent intercourse.)

"What would our feminist President do about Nicaragua, and the Philippines, and South America, and Korea?" someone in the audience always asked.

The answer always was that she would behave again as feminist theory and principles dictated. Paramount in women's culture, as we are beginning to grasp and crystallize it, is the value of horizontally shared power. Despite the allegations of our detractors, this concept of equality doesn't imply a desire to be the "same" as men or the same as one another. (The *last* thing radical feminists want is a 53-percent-share of patriarchy!)

Another sane and lovely concept in women's culture is that difference is desirable, the antithesis of the demand for conformity in male culture. In actual practice among us, this tolerance is still largely potential, but it shines as steadily as Venus over the wilderness of change, guiding and heartening us.

As feminists we have understood that what we are talking about when we talk about equality is an end of the sexual caste system and all the resultant oppressive hierarchies of class, race, and age. We are talking about an end to the global one-up (male)/one-down (female) mentality of male supremacist culture, and the beginning of side-by-side, shoulder-to-shoulder participation of all human beings in the affairs of the world. All this applies to countries as well as to individuals.

Though we know what kind of power we don't want to see in the world any more, we haven't yet arrived at the perfect cooperative model. This doesn't mean we can't imagine, up to a point, what national and international policies would arise out of the feminist values of cooperation versus competition, equality versus domination by force, variety versus homogeneity. But we can say that at least a feminist President certainly would never think of dictating to any other country who their leaders had to be, or what kind of political or economic system they had to have for us not to kill them; she would never uphold despots in poorer, darker-skinned countries so that our multinational corporations could exploit the people with impunity, never have a CIA to police, interfere, undermine, and foment, never use economic or physical strength to force other countries into the mold that most benefits the United States. She would design a new role for this country's relations with other countries, a role consistent with the same principles of self-determination and sovereignty we demand for ourselves.

Feminists see this time in the history of our species more clearly now than people have for centuries. We see that we live in the end-time of the bitter tyranny of the fathers. The wretched of the earth are rising everywhere out of enslavement to the male/female — the over/under, superior/inferior, ruler/slave — model of human interaction, and nothing can stop us; it is now that time of the world. Instead of battling the inevitable — and in doing so, destroying everything — our challenge is to midwife the new humanness in ourselves and the new order struggling to be born.

The same "womanly" principles that apply to foreign policy apply, of course, to domestic issues, the environment, and the economy: the principles of non-violence and cooperation and — that habit of mind central to feminist philosophy — caring about people's lives above all else.

A feminist President's environmental policy is instantly clear. An end, and at once, to all violence against the great Goddess, Gaea, our mother the earth. Because she is "womanly" — life-giving and nurturing, life-loving, bountiful, fecund, gorgeous, resilient, and patient, because she is wild and free, and because women have identified with her intimately for ages — our bodies and our spirits dancing to her rhythms — she has suffered our common woman's fate: rape, brutalization, exploitation, domination. Like us, she is regarded by men as put here by God for their use, which gives them a right, a special dispensation, if you will, to dominate and exploit her.

278

The innumerable and immutable connections between the health of all plant and animal life and the health of the earth are short-circuited in the splintered male consciousness. Even a casual stroll through the typical patriarchal brain would reveal that "health issues" are filed in the AMA cabinet, dozens of corridors away from the "nuclear energy" file, and even more corridors away from the "industrial waste" and "automobile emissions" files, which are widely distanced from each other. None of these files is cross-referenced to any of the others. "Cuts in aid to families with dependent children" is probably not in this brain at all, but far away in someone else's brain. And so on and on, drearily, predictably, disastrously.

The knowledge that all living things are as dependent upon the earth as if they were babies in their mother's wombs is unacceptable to the dis-integrated patriarchal mind. Since to be independent is "male" and to be dependent is "female," to be incontrovertibly masculine, men must reject and deny their dependence upon Mother Earth just as they must deny their dependence upon women. In just such a way they have rejected — en masse — the reality of the interdependence of all life.

But as women know, men are on the whole immensely dependent beings, dependent in a far more basic way upon women than women are upon them. Masters are always more dependent on slaves than vice versa, not only for the daily smoothing out of the wrinkles of life, but also for the constant reassurance that they are superior beings, the only framework within which life makes sense and is desirable for them.

Since the deepest well of patriarchal power is the belief that because of men's natural superiority, the earth and all that is on it was made expressly for their use, an awareness of their profound dependence would be excruciatingly dissonant and anxiety-producing. It would also be intolerably humiliating, striking at their always precarious illusion of god-like immunity to cause and effect. It is a desperate bravado, a pathetic attempt to prove they are above the natural laws (or habits) that govern the rest of us, that causes men more and more

279

madly to irradiate and destroy and poison their own and their children's amniotic fluid—the air and water and soil of the earth.

A feminist President, knowing that either we learn peaceful, cooperative ways of living with the earth or we die, would quickly make liberated military money available for massive research into ways to harness the rich treasures of healthful energy the earth so freely offers—sun, wind, tides, biomass. During her administration, nuclear energy would be abandoned as an non-viable alternative. Life and health come first in feminism, and a basic axiom of feminist thought is that we can make choices. We are not bound to do anything simply because it is possible. Everything that is possible to be done does *not* have to be done. In fact, being human means not only being able to choose, but also that we *must* choose. It means that we are required to use wisdom in the service of life. Clean air, pure water, rich, uncontaminated soil—these are the rightful legacy of every person, every plant, every animal born. A feminist President would stop the human fathers from squandering this inheritance of health and joy.

A new value system would automatically restructure the economy. As Hazel Henderson so brilliantly insists, there is really no such separate discipline as "economics." So-called economists, anxious to have a "science" of their own, have merely invented and ghettoized it. What we are really talking about when we talk about economics is values. The economic system will change, she assures us, when we change our ideas of what is important, when we realign our priorities.[3] Whereas the patriarchal economists want to impose an artificial separation between money matters and societal attitudes, feminists understand fully their intimate connection.

Think, for instance, how international banking, how industry, how everything concerned with money would change if, as a society, we really *did* put people's lives first—everywhere, and not at the expense of animals or any living thing. No more military budget, no more capital flight, no more International Monetary Fund abuses of power, no more workers and consumers without control over working conditions, wages, and products, no more inflexible work schedules for parents and others who wish to enrich their lives and the lives of those they love by doing something other than the traditional nine-to-five, 40- to 50-year job, no more nuclear weapons tests, no more resources drained into nuclear power plants, no more pollution.

When we care about people's lives, we care about everyone's participation and opinion. Hazel Henderson suggests that we talk about what work we consider essential, what work should entitle one to be paid and what work — which everyone would share — should not. A basic feminist value is that we participate in making the decisions and agree on the basic structures of our lives, instead of having them thrust upon us without recourse for someone else's benefit. As far back in time as we can see with any clarity, women have been excluded from these decisions.

In the world feminists build, inequities in privilege and abundance will not exist because of the honor and respect we have for one another. In order to begin evolution in this direction, we must finally see the divine in every woman's face.

If one accepts the assumption that movement in nature is always toward growth, toward survival and therefore toward greater adaptability, toward evolution to higher forms, it is not hard to understand why some people — women *and* men — speculate that men are genetically defective. Something, they say, must have gone awry in nature for this subspecies to have developed that did not only *not* advance, but that degenerated; that became, instead of more and more adaptable, less and less so, until they not only threaten their own existence, but imperil the existence of all life forms on the planet they control.

This point of view is extremely difficult to counter. Even a cursory look at the world men took over some 5000 years ago argues powerfully against men's having the simplest, most common wisdom, compassion, sense of justice, or morality. If

that is true, then women's task is well-nigh hopeless—not completely, of course, because testosterone can be controlled; not
hopeless, but very nearly so.

My arguments against the theory of men's genetic defec-
tiveness are philosophical and personal, not scientific. I argue
the "nurture" side of the "nature or nurture" debate for two
reasons.

First, to assume that men and women have totally different, even opposing, natures, thus fitting them for altogether
different ways of being in the world, is to accept patriarchy's
most basic rationale: biology is destiny. Many people do not
like how men think and behave, but to lay this solely at the feet
of their gender is profoundly patriarchal; to see half the human
race as "other" is the imperative of that old, deadly mind. Philosophically, we have no choice but to refuse this view, like it or
not. If feminism does not eradicate the fundamental sexual dichotomization upon which patriarchy depends, then it cannot
fulfill its destiny of transforming global society. Feminists must
persist, therefore, even in the face of terrific masculine pathology, in seeing all creation whole, all life connected, each as part
of the other.

Second, I have three sons whom I love as much as if they
were daughters. When they were little people, really small—
maybe a year and a half or two, up to about age three—they
were as "womanly" as any woman I ever knew. As intuitive, as
empathetic, as aware of their feelings and able to express them,
as tender and compassionate and nurturing. They made me
realize that these characteristics must therefore be neither exclusively male nor female, but human.

I remember sitting on the couch many times with a baby
nursing at the breast, milk running out of the corner of its
mouth down its neck, eyes rolling back in its head—all sticky
and gooey and warm. (No drug known offers more apparent
bliss than nursing gives babies.) I remember sitting on the
couch with both the older boys at different times, snuggled up
close, talking and patting, one of us holding the baby's foot,

and having them say to me, when they were just old enough to frame the thought, "Oh, Mommy, I can't wait until I grow up and can nurse the baby!"

I had to be the heavy. I had to tell them, "Well, honey, chances are that you're going to grow up to be a daddy instead!" Anyone who has ever tried to sell that alternative to a little boy at such a moment has discovered that daddyhood in this culture has precious little to recommend it.

Both boys were crushed, and both grieved. But my oldest son wouldn't take no for an answer. He followed me around the house for a couple of days, every once in a while saying something like, "Are you sure?" One time he intimated that he was thinking of being the first.

Then one evening he thought he had me. He came rushing into the kitchen where I was getting dinner and shrieked in triumph, "Daddy's doing it *right now*!" We flew out to the living room at once. And sure enough, there was Rick in nursing configuration — baby in the crook of one arm and book in the other hand. My children had seen me sit like that for hours, holding the book and the nursing baby. Eric simply assumed that since Rick was sitting in nursing position, he must *be* nursing. He hadn't wanted to investigate too closely; he'd just wanted to believe.

What my little boys loved about nursing is what nursing has so richly to offer, and what every human craves: intimacy, closeness, affection. But most important, irrefutable evidence of connectedness. Here the milk comes out of Mommy's breast and is avidly sucked in and swallowed by baby. In that process, one person's body literally becomes part of another person's body. Nothing could illustrate more clearly that we are all part of one another; we must therefore be far more alike than different. And nothing could reassure us more that we are all in this business of life together, that we are not alone.

So, because of my sons and my daughter, it seems to me that what all human beings long for ultimately — men as much as women — is intimacy, closeness, the feeling of being part of a larger life, part of a wider flow and more universal rhythm, a feeling of being connected and important to it all. Although they were acculturated differently from the outset, my sons and daughter demonstrated no significant early difference in this, in how they related to other people, in what they needed from them and gave to them.

Then my little boys trotted off excitedly, in all innocence, neither decidedly male nor female—just small malleable humans—to nursery school. I actually took them there myself day after day. But how could I have known? Everyone told me they needed "stimulation" (which means mother's company is stultifying), social interaction, experience on their own. Who was I to quarrel with the experts? I was just a mother, than which in patriarchy there is nothing dumber or less expert. So I took my little sons to nursery school.

And I never saw them again. They toddled out of my presence and my female culture into male culture, where their most desirable traits—to my way of thinking—were suddenly very off limits. I miss those little boys of mine very much. Their absence is one of the sources of deepest grief in my life.

Anyone who could see my sons now would wonder why I can't speak of them without sorrow. They are handsome and intelligent, witty, irreverent, and they love me; they never give up trying to understand me, though it's often rough going. They're not without their problems, but they are good men. I'm proud of them and love them inordinately.

But I remember how they once were. I know how they might have been. And it's one of the tragedies of my life that they were not allowed to be what they began to be—neither masculine nor feminine, just themselves. Being "good men" is not an acceptable substitute.

I cannot speak for them. Women cannot speak for men's experience any more than men can speak for women's. But I know how it seemed to me, and I can speak of my own perceptions. Year after year I watched in pain as they struggled to fit the narrow, pinching, sterile, and boring masculine mold. I watched them cordon their feelings off little by little into smaller and smaller, more and more peripheral areas, until they had shut down a large part of themselves, abandoned and denied all that the "real" world called in disgust "womanly."

The difficulty inherent in this separation from femaleness cannot be overstated. After all, all of us began as female in our mothers' wombs, and only later did half of us become male: we were all female first.[4] In addition, it is believed that for the first six months or so after we are born, we cannot distinguish between our "primary caretaker" — who is almost always female — and ourselves. This means that for much of our most impressionable early lives, we not only identify with our mothers, we think we *are* our mothers, that when we are smelling and touching and tasting her, we are touching and tasting ourselves, that her breast and arms are parts of our own bodies. To try to undo this powerful female identification must be very painful on some level. From my own observation, I believe it is damaging to the heart and to the character.

Finally, as my sons became older adolescents, it was demanded of them that they hate in themselves those womanly ways, that they rip them out of themselves and kill them.

All this time I saw they were afraid, afraid perhaps that if they weren't very cautious they would inadvertently expose themselves in some small but damning way as not "regular guys" after all. The beatings after school and at church, and the taunts, and the cruelty of the constant popularity contest at school, helped them discipline themselves into zombiehood. They became strong and silent (about certain things), wary and numb. To the degree that they have been successful in their required self-mutilation, they have become separated from themselves, their core consciousness has been split.

And underneath it all — according to my interpretation of what I witnessed at very close range over many years — they felt a growing rage and grief. If this is true, and if it is true for men in general, the most obvious place to project all that fury is, of course, upon girls and women. There, right before their eyes, are people who exhibit all the characteristics they have been taught to loathe and fear, to ridicule and beat out of others and to kill in themselves.

Is it any wonder then that men hate women so? Is it any wonder that they beat us and tear us apart and stomp us to death? They so hate the "womanly" in themselves, so fear it.

And, I believe, so miss it and love it and grieve for it, which is another reason to hate us. We are allowed to be women, to exhibit those characteristics openly and publicly, everywhere, all the time, a constant reminder of their lost identity.

But also, a constant reminder of their unkindness to us. I suspect that they cannot forgive us for reminding them, by our stubborn survival, how they have raped and beaten and cheated and deceived and maimed and killed us for 5000 years. We always hate those we hurt, and then it becomes circular: we hurt those we hate.

Many people have difficulty facing the inevitable and consuming hatred that those who mistreat others have for those they mistreat. One reason is that the injured stand as a reminder that the assumed superiority of the oppressors must constantly be proved, constantly be re-established, which means it is really very tenuous — and therefore not inevitable and "natural." Most of all, the unconscious knowledge that someone who mistreats others is not superior, but is really inferior, prevents people from looking at how men treat women.

I don't intend this to mitigate the reality of male violence against women or to exonerate men in any way. But I have lived closely with males most of my life (three brothers, a father, three sons and, for 20 years, a husband), and I have needed to try to understand. As I have pondered this the last few years, the thought has occurred to me more than once that on some level men know that our coddling of them has not been truly compassionate, that it has not been loving of us to allow them to become monsters, unwittingly to have facilitated the maiming of their characters. Perhaps men cannot forgive us for never having made them stop hurting us. Having been a

mother most of my adult life, I know well that children want
to be stopped before they go too far, and they become terrified
and enraged when they are not. Men are our children in far
more ways than one; in far too many ways, in fact, and in far
too few of the innocent, good-hearted ways of real children.
For thousands of years they have been going too far, much,
much too far. They are frightening themselves badly. Though
it is irrational — or maybe *because* it is irrational — they may hate
us because we have not stopped them. They may want us, their
mothers, to take responsibility for setting limits for them in
their dealings with us and all others.

But women know men cannot be useful in the evolution
of the species until they find their own internal controls and
learn to control *themselves*, grow up and learn to set their own
limits; mature, that is, in "womanly" ways. We can do much
as women, but we cannot do that for men. And must not even
if we could. The most loving and compassionate act that
women can perform for men is to stop feeling responsible for
them, for their feelings, for their happiness, to disengage and
let men do it themselves.

Fortunately, there are *men* in the world to help men, men
who rebel against their conditioning, men who have somehow
escaped with only relatively minor damage. And though they
are ultimately irrelevant to women's work, that they exist at all
bodes well.

That some of these men sit through my speeches and rise
to their feet applauding when I finish demonstrates to me that
for purposes of education they can be made — at least for a moment — honorary women. Though this is, I admit, perhaps too
facile a closure, it is also an honest attempt — how controversial
an attempt I am well aware — to break down the dichotomous
patriarchal paradigm chiseled into each of our brains, that to
be a man is *not* to be a woman. It is an attempt to demonstrate
that the habit of masculinity is just that — a *habit*, not an eternal
verity. Habits can be broken, new morphogenetic fields are
possible. I make men honorary women to reinforce the prime

idea of all my life and work which is that to survive, and to flourish, *all* human beings must begin to act like women at our best. The entire human race now needs to think and feel like women, live out of women's value system (minus the patriarchal smog with which it is overlaid).

I do not make men honorary women to teach *them*, though their responses assure me that it affects them powerfully in various ways. I do it to teach *women*, to teach us how important our womanliness is, that it is so important that men, who have been believed and felt to be the "real," the significant, ultimately the *only* humans, must listen to and learn from *us* for a change, must model themselves upon *us* for a change, must cease being "manly," and humble themselves enough to rise to being "womanly." It is to affirm women as the only experts on life on earth.

The stipulation always to the men so honored is to do something about male violence, personally and publicly. I warn them they will be worse off morally than they were before they were so honored if they ever again laugh at an off-color joke, or buy *Hustler* or *Playboy*, or strike or humiliate a woman, or pay their female employees too little or not pave their way to advancement, or sit and read the newspaper while their wives or women friends clear up after dinner, or have sexual intercourse without arousing their partner, or think that organizing men against rape or starting a counseling center for batterers and incestors is too much trouble. Enormous and weighty responsibility is upon men of more enlightened mind to reach and teach their brothers.

For men to act womanly takes a kind of courage that women despair of finding in them, the courage to work against their own ostensible and concrete interests on behalf of what will bring them only some abstract characterological or spiritual benefit. How can you stack "righteousness" up against money and power and opportunity and respect and honor and privilege of all kinds, not to mention ego gratification? How can you stack being a better person up against playing God?

Many liberal males believe that women's liberation is a cause to be struggled and suffered for—by women. It is our problem, and they wish us well with it—or so they say. I suspect that what they really believe is that we can't do it without them, so leaving it to us protects their privilege forever. In the most important way, however, they are quite right. It is a historical truth that the oppressed must rise and free both themselves and their oppressors;* that the oppressors never, of their own accord, curtail their violence or relinquish the privilege it buys them, though individual members of the powerful group may wish for an end to it and work toward that goal. The burden, unjust as it may seem, is upon the victims to refuse to accept further victimization, and to rise out of it in strength and unity. Though this may smack of patriarchy's favorite pastime of blaming the victim, in fact women must face the truth: if we can render patriarchy impotent *now*—and we *can*—women *always* had it in our power to do so. Patriarchy cannot flourish, and never did, without our collaboration.

People often argue that men are also oppressed. Although it is true that patriarchy will not let them be fully human, men cannot be said to be "oppressed" as males in the same sense as women are oppressed as females. The experiences that most men interpret as "bad" in their everyday lives are truly random. They are not systemic, not woven inextricably into the fabric of society.

This does not mean, of course, that certain groups of men are not oppressed. As Marilyn Frye points out,[5] oppression occurs, unlike random "bad" things, absolutely and nonrandomly to people because they belong to a particular group, a group from which they can never escape. Women are oppressed *as women*, Blacks *as Blacks*, Jews *as Jews*. But men are never oppressed *as men*.

---

*I suspect that this means that the most oppressed—women of color in third-world countries—must rise fastest, farthest, and most powerfully of all women. And this, in fact, seems to be what we are witnessing.

Therefore, if we use the word "oppression" to describe all harmful situations and conditions that affect people, the word soon becomes so stretched out of shape as to be useless. In addition, if we use it to describe the destructiveness to men of their dominant role, we disguise the fact that the experiences of men and women in this relationship are wildly different in every way. We hide the fact that under patriarchy being male is *always* rewarded according to male cultural values: with money, status, and opportunity; that, in fact, male *privilege*, the opposite of oppression, is institutionalized, systematized, utterly pervasive in society.

But if we cannot use the word "oppression" to describe men's plight, how can we speak of it? That, of course, is the point: we cannot. Because patriarchy does not recognize the ultimate destructiveness of tyranny to tyrants, the fathers have no word — and therefore no concept — for the kind of dehumanization, the severe characterological damage, done to men by their use of violence of all kinds to dominate women and all "others." Men who are becoming conscious must find their own language for their experience.

Without adequate language for it, I can only say that the masculinization — the dehumanization — of men in patriarchy is unacceptable to me. I am not willing to have spent most of my life rearing sons who are simultaneously trained by society to turn upon me and upon the world I love. Though women won't, we should simply not agree to have any more children until patriarchy is gone from the earth. And though I cannot yet forgive what has happened, what is happening, to my beautiful children — my daughter, my sons — I live to find a way for us all out of its horror.

And I'm hopeful. Redefinitions of power are basic to the shift of consciousness I witnessed everywhere in this country (and several others) during that long election year of 1984. The embryo of a profound and final rejection of power as it has been defined by thousands of years of male rule and culture is apparent everywhere.

Everywhere the legitimacy of rule by force, by superior size and strength—physical, economic, military—is being questioned. Everywhere patriarchy's basic assumption that vertical stratification of society is inevitable and "natural" because God confers favors of wealth, influence, and the right to rule upon those who most deserve it—everywhere this absurd assumption is being discredited.

Everywhere the shift is away from the masculine value system— based upon power over others, achieved and maintained by violence for the benefit of a very few—and toward values and behaviors that have always been associated with women.

All this is very good. But I closed my campaign speech with a specific suggestion about how to hasten it along. It has to do with courage.

Courage is the agenda of the women's movement. It applies across the board to all people alive on the planet at this time, because we are all up against incredibly desperate odds. Being up against such odds as these, we know that the courage we need is greater than we ever dreamed possible for anyone to have. What the women's movement has come upon the world to tell us, just now, just in the nick of time, is that we must have the courage to face, to think, and to say—women and men, shoulder to shoulder—the unfaceable, the unthinkable, the unbearable, and the unspeakable: that men control women with the most implacable, grinding, merciless violence imaginable. We must first have the courage to look squarely into the truth of our lives, without blame, without guilt, with love, and to say, "This is how it is. This is why we are on the verge of destruction. We can and will do something about it."

We begin by performing the most difficult, the most seditious, the most risky, frightening, revolutionary, transformative act possible in patriarchy. Something we have never seen done. Something we have been taught in thousands of ways every day since we were born *not* to do. Something so courageous, so audacious, that it is finally the only meaningful response left to our imminent and deadly danger:

In a global society *based* on the hatred of women, and dying of that hatred, the most redemptive act possible is to love women. The universe is therefore challenging us—all of us—either to learn to love women or to die. It is challenging us to love ourselves as women, to deeply honor and respect ourselves and all other women, to *listen* to and trust—and be trustworthy to—and to take women and our culture very, very seriously. If we do not do this, nothing else we do matters. If we do not do this, all is lost.

The universe is challenging men to love that which is womanly in themselves and in all things, and to honor and respect women everywhere all the time. It is challenging all of us to transcend patriarchy by internalizing those traits it denigrates as "womanly," and to base our behavior on the principles of women's culture—starting right now and not stopping until feminism has replaced patriarchy as the global paradigm.

Women have the saving gift to give earth's people, the only alternative to the male model that imperils us all: how we think, how we perceive the world, what we value, how we *are* in the world. This is our genius. Our mission is to map out ever more clearly what it means to be female at its best, and then, undeviatingly, steadfastly, to be in all circumstances, at all times, the North Star to a race in desperate search for itself.

> Shall there be womanly times
> Or shall we die?

> There will be womanly times.
> We will not die![6]

12

Leaping Over the Barriers

The campaign was over, and for the first time in two years I looked forward to time to be still, time for reflection. But first there was a meeting in Rome of the international feminist group Susan and I had founded during the campaign, and Susan was determined that we use some of the Gathering processes there for brainstorming.

Thinking about how to do this during the long flight to Italy, I reasoned that the short visioning process I sometimes incorporated into my public speeches and workshops hadn't been as effective as I would have liked because the instructions were diffuse and overwhelming: "If you could step outside the door right now, snap your fingers, and have the world *exactly* as you want it, how would it be—in detail?" So I revised them in my mind, narrowing them down in a way I hoped would encourage participants to begin on a smaller, more personal scale.

A couple of days later in Rome, I tried out the new version with a small group: "If you were to wake up in a perfect feminist world tomorrow morning, what would you be looking forward to doing that day? How would you dress? Who would be at breakfast — how many, what ages, what relationships? What would they be eating? What would they be talking about? What would they all be planning to do that day? Would the kids go to school? If not, how would they be 'educated?' Where would the adults work? Doing what? How would they feel about it? Would the television or radio be on? If so, what would you be hearing and seeing? How would you govern yourselves in your household? In your community? How would communities relate?" And so on.

Although this seemed a little more useful in helping women project themselves into the future, what I sensed should and could happen out of the right theory simply didn't. Something still felt wrong about the whole thing. As usual with me, this manifested itself as blankness, as a kind of deadness of thought and feeling when I thought about the process further. So I did what I do when I come to a dead end: I put the problem on my mind's back burner to simmer.

I know now that in structuring the experience so that it encouraged us to look at change closer to home, in a more personal way, I was moving one foot in the right direction. But the other foot was still stuck in the future-orientedness of the patriarchal mind. Over the next months, the straddle occurring out there on the periphery of consciousness became increasingly uncomfortable.

During that time, nearly bursting with information I hadn't yet had time to examine, I began to write this book. I knew that reflecting on my experience would help me realize what I had learned, where I had arrived in my thinking and feeling, and how I had got there. I wrote out of an urgency to organize this new knowledge, to make it more accessible to me in my search for what to do next.

I wrote furiously nearly all that year, and almost from the first, the Gathering was central to my thinking. Not because I felt any more enthusiasm about most of it than before, but because I still thought the theories were correct and therefore very significant. And also because I wasn't listening to my intuition faithfully, or I would have known that my feelings of boredom and dullness were messages that something was awry.

As the book neared completion, Susan and I argued regularly about a second, large Gathering chapter. I told her I wanted to edit it down drastically; she thought it should remain in all its detail. Since my dissatisfaction was only a vague feeling for which I had no explanation, I kept the chapter as it was simply out of inertia, a feeling of, "Why not? It's good stuff. It can't hurt anything."

(But I was wrong. It wasn't harmless. And when I suddenly realized why, I discarded the whole chapter and replaced it with this one.)

A year later the book was finished — or so I thought. And I began my search for a publisher. From the moment I had sat down to write it, I had felt certain that the book would be published by the right publisher at the right time, and that I didn't need to worry. Even through the long months when it looked as if this would never happen, through all the rejections, I remained sure. But I must admit that I found myself asking the universe why *now* apparently wasn't the right time.

And I also must admit that I felt something lacking in the book. My mind told me it was full and rich. But the feeling persisted on a very deep level, rumbling along just out of earshot on the cusp of my consciousness.

I think now that in some part of myself I was waiting for the idea that was to complete this book. Futuring theory — that we must be able to imagine the change we want before it can come about, that the imagining itself in some powerful way *causes* the change — was a necessary step in my journey out of my patriarchal mind. Although it was only a step rather than the transformative concept I'd hoped it was, I'm glad for it. Struggling with it has launched me into the full tide of revolution.

In August 1986, Susan and Mary Ann and I drove up to New York City to participate in the Women Take Liberty action our friends from the Midwest had organized around the Statue of Liberty's centenary. I was troubled about the event and about having agreed many months before to speak at it. By this time I was absolutely certain that reaction was the most potent variety of collusion, and I wished fervently that I could wriggle out of this commitment. But I had promised, and I loved the organizers, so I rationalized and temporized and turned up and did my bit.

The three of us and a friend from England, Fran Willard, stayed that night at the Dobbs Ferry home of a member of the original Group of Women, Mary Wood. The next morning at breakfast, we began talking about the action, struggling again with our limited knowledge of why and how resistance operates to shore up the system. By this time, the question of what to do instead had been simmering on the back burners of our thought for nearly four years, as had our dissatisfaction with the Gathering as an answer. Much unconscious disentangling had been going on inside us and we were finally ready to leap over the barriers our old minds had set so firmly in our way. Thanks to Fran, who had her tape recorder on in the middle of the table, I can trace our mindsteps as we ran:

Mary Ann: It's amazing how well we're programmed to believe that if something we've organized doesn't go as well as we want it to, if not enough people show up, it's because we didn't do it well enough. We don't think to ask ourselves if there is something basically wrong with the action itself.*

Sonia: And if we're not berating ourselves, we're blaming women's passivity, or the paralysis that comes from their despair. And that passivity and despair are real enough. But they don't explain all of it. I think we can trust women. When a whole nation full of women simply cannot get excited about protests, or about civil disobedience, we've got to take that judgment seriously. Because that's what it is, a judgment

---

*The organizers had worked on this action for at least a year, creatively getting the word out nationwide. They expected thousands of women to join them at the Statue of Liberty. But despite diligent planning and preparation, no more than five or six hundred women turned up throughout the day. The organizers were disappointed and puzzled.

against reaction. Women don't want to do it, and they don't want to do it because their internal voices are telling them not to. It seems to me that those out there who are determined to get women demonstrating and protesting and resisting have got to think hard about how much they trust other women's intuition.

Mary Ann: With me it's more than just knowing not to react. It's knowing that all these centuries we've identified patriarchy solely as what the guys do and seldom as what we do to help the guys do it. When we say women have collaborated, we're not blaming women. The truth isn't blaming.

Sonia: The truth is always liberating. If the truth is unfortunate, that's just the way it is. And the truth is that patriarchy exists because we allow it. All oppressed people collaborate. Oppression is an unwritten but very clear contract between the rulers and the ruled. Both have to agree to it and abide by it in order for it to continue.

Fran: Does it make any difference that patriarchy began and continued because men used force against us, because they killed us if we didn't comply?

Mary Ann: No, it doesn't matter what happened before. What matters is now. We can change it now. They're killing us now, too. The only way they can keep on killing us is if we allow it, if we engage with them.

Sonia: When we react, when we resist injustice, we are not free, we are bound to the perpetrators, dependent upon their every move, attached to them as if with puppeteers' strings: they pull our strings and we dance. It's as if there's a silent agreement, a contract. But if we refuse the contract, if we refuse the reciprocity — in our attitudes, in our feelings — if we disengage from their strings, no amount of pulling can make us dance. We're free.

Mary Ann: It's so simple, if we could figure out what it means. It reminds me of something. . . . Christianity before Constantine was a religion of slaves, the most powerless people of the Roman Empire. Between 32 and about 120 B.C., there went from being *no* Christians to being one out of five — 20 percent of the Roman Empire. It was a silent movement, no propaganda, no public oratory. One of the hardest tasks of Christian scholars is to try to find out how it happened, the tremendous social change that took place. Look at the messages: turn the other cheek; leave your father and your mother and the whole social system and follow me; resist not evil. We're talking about a successful revolution, at least early on. Look at the early church and how it grew — silently, with no notice from the Roman Empire, something that took up a tremendous amount of space. This resist not evil, turn the other cheek . . . . And the business of leaving the whole social system behind, of stepping out of it entirely, not carrying any of it. I think those principles are the real principles for overturning a social system. What are *our* messages?

Sonia: You talk about disassociating from the social system. Unfortunately, what "the personal is political" has most often caused women to do is to associate ourselves always with, see ourselves always *in the context of*, a particular political system, to define ourselves always in relation to it. And about turning the other cheek, certainly that can't be one of *our* messages. Turning the other cheek is a philosophy for men. For 5000 years women have turned the other cheek, and every time we do, it gets slapped harder. Sometimes it gets slapped so hard we die. Only rulers can afford to turn the other cheek, not slaves.

Mary Ann: But we're taking it one step further.

Sonia: We're saying, "Get your cheek out of there altogether!"

Mary Ann: It's important to talk about resistance as a necessary part of the war model, the other half of the war dyad: attack/resist, attack/react.

Sonia: I've come to dislike the term "Woman Warrior" for that reason. We reinforce the war model when we use that language and those concepts to define ourselves. There can't be war without reaction, without resistance, without reciprocity.

Susan: It's like you're out on the balcony and someone lunges toward you and you move and he plunges over the railing. There hasn't been a war; there hasn't even been an attack. There's been a *suicide*.

Mary Ann: Thinking that we must react to the system, that we must fight it, prevents us from understanding what we learned from Aikido, which is how to let the violence carry itself to its own conclusion in those who are violent, letting the cycle complete itself in them . . .

Sonia: . . . as we stand aside in our own peaceful place. Our conditioning prevents us from learning how to refuse the violence when it's handed to us—like a hand grenade. We're trained not to realize that if we don't take it when someone hands it to us, it will explode in *their* hands, not ours.

Mary Ann: Even passive resistance and non-violent action is collaborative because as we engage in it we receive the violence of others, reinforcing the war model.

Fran: That slogan, "What if somebody gave a war and nobody came." Well, there *is* a war against women, and if we don't come, this war can't go on.

Sonia: But how can we stop arriving at the battlefront every day, bright and eager, faces all washed, ready? The one thing that's hardest for me to do is to have to say to women who want me to tell them what to do, "I don't know what to do. We each have to figure it out for ourselves, in our own lives." Women want to be led in battle, that's the model, and there's no leading in a no-battle model. I know that disengagement, non-reaction, non-resistance is a correct anti-patriarchal, feminist principle because there *can't* be any leaders. Every woman *has* to do it for herself. Another thing that tells us it's revolutionary behavior is that it is an example of the means being the ends—how we are now is the future. So if we want a non-hierarchical future, we have to be non-hierarchical now. And having to have faith in our own personal voice *now* is the only way we'll have it in the future. The new world we want is the world in which everyone listens to their own hearts. So if we want it *then*, we have to have it *now*. There's no way to get there except to *be* there. As Mary said last night, there's no way to have

299

peace except to be peaceful. How we know it's right not to be able to see the next step is that it forces us to be the way we want to be *now*. There is no future. The future is born every moment. We are birthing it this second. It doesn't matter where it's going to lead. All that matters is that right now I am this way. That's all I have, this second. Right now is the only time I will *ever* have. The only power is in the present and in how I *am* in the present. How do I learn to live that, how can I live in that consciousness? It's a kind of meditation. A concentration on the spirit. That's how feminism is the greatest spiritual revolution on earth.

Mary Ann: One of the ways patriarchy traps us in the future is by making us live in fear.

Fran: That's right. We worry about what's going to happen to us, so we plan. And planning is always for the future.

Mary Ann: It's almost as if we must not know what the future holds.

Sonia: It doesn't matter whether we worry and plan or not because worrying, and thinking and planning ahead, can't insure the future, anyway. But if we remember that the future is *now*, then we know full well what is going to happen because it *is* happening. This *is* the future. We can predict the future by looking at our feelings in the present.

Fran: That's how we make our own reality, with that consciousness.

Mary Ann: When we plan we relinquish our own reality.

Sonia: We've got to learn to live completely in the present. Nothing is too much to bear for this one second. For this one second I can be fully myself, powerfully authentic, any way I choose to be. And since that's all I've got to live anyway, this moment, for the present — *which is the future* — I am any way I *can* be for this one second. I must learn to live from second to second, not merely to *anticipate* living . . .

Mary Ann: Which makes you hostage to the future . . .

Sonia: Or only to remember living — which, by catapulting me back into the past, robs me of my access to my only life time, which is right now. Patriarchy conditions us never really to live, never really to be present in the present. Living, totally conscious people are dangerous.

Mary Ann: The patriarchy always aims us toward the future this way because it takes us out of the power of the present. In the Zen monasteries, that's the purpose of the koans, the stories; the paradoxes force us unequivocally into the present, into total consciousness.

Fran: Sonia, when you talked at the table last night about living in community and couldn't figure out how you could do it, this is the answer. You were anticipating, you were looking at the future and saying, "I can't live with other women so closely" — foreseeing difficulty. Since you've foreseen it, difficulty *is* the future: you've created it that way already. But if you are living *moment by moment by moment* in peace and harmony with yourself, and everyone else is, too, there is no future, there is only now, and now there is no difficulty, so there is no difficulty in the future. That's the secret!

Sonia: So the practice is to live in community *in this way*.

Fran: That's right!

Mary W.: And the future is the present which is to come.

Mary Ann: And the more consciously this is done, the more it changes the morphogenetic field.

Sonia: *So the question "What shall we do?" is the wrong question.*

Mary Ann: That's the door right back into the patriarchy.

Sonia: *The question, then, is "how shall we be?"*

Fran: "How shall we be with one another?"

Mary W.: That's the exact opposite of existentialism.

Sonia: The opposite of patriarchy.

Mary Ann: Patriarchy focuses us outside our center. We must get beyond the concept of controlling *anything*.

Sonia: Anything outside ourselves. And we don't need to worry about what to do. What to do is not the question. How to *be* is the question, and if we *be* right with ourselves, we will do the powerful, meaning the totally disengaged, non-collaborative thing. The feeling will lead us. We don't have to think about action that proceeds out of true and positive feelings about ourselves, because we automatically respond appropriately, correctly. We've got to stop *feeling* patriarchy, then we'll stop *acting* it. We've got to start *feeling* free and we'll start *acting* free. Feeling an authentic and direct, not a relational or conditioned, feeling, automatically disengages us from patriarchy.

Susan: So it's a radical action to live in the present. It's a radical action to change feeling in the present.

Sonia: It's the most radical, apatriarchal act possible. *Feeling,* not doing, makes a movement. Our feeling at this moment is everything. The future lives in it. It is the *source* of the future. I said to the Gathering that we can't move into any space we can't envision, but this is not true. The truth is that we can't move into any space we can't *feel.* We can only change patriarchy by changing our feelings, but we don't change for that reason. We change because we want to be our own genuine selves. It's not a process. It's *being* there.

Mary Ann: Process *is* product, it is what we are doing right now or not at all. The only truth is the present, and when we say, "I'm going to do this tomorrow," we're not doing it now. Either we feel and do it now or it won't happen at all.

Susan: That's the answer to those people who despair that there isn't going to be any future. Since the present — being all time, being the *only* time — *is* the future, as long as we are really present in the present, we have a future.

Fran: Whee! Look what we've been doing here this morning! It's gorgeous, like a spiral!

We were so excited we could barely contain ourselves, whooping and interrupting and hugging one another. My mind felt spacious and radiant. My body, too — buoyant and pulsing with energy — was telling me we were on to something really significant. Convinced by the total joyous involvement of body, mind, and spirit, I knew we were moving quickly and brilliantly toward making connections we hadn't seen before, connections with world-changing potential.

I was also aware that there was really nothing new to me in what we were discovering that morning, that I had already said each bit of it in some speech or somewhere in this book. But it had been like having all the notes for a piece of music without the rhythm.

At the 1984 Women Gathering in St. Louis, Missouri, for instance, though I clearly hadn't made all the connections, I told the assembled women:

"We know there is neither time nor space on the thought plane, on the level of mind and spirit. Nor is there past or future. There is only this moment. Everything is right here, right now.

"We also know that how we're behaving at any given moment is the end, that means don't exist separate from ends, as patriarchy would have us believe. The truth is that we form reality as we go along, according to how we choose to feel and behave at the moment. This is why 'tough politics,' 'tough money,' and 'hardball politics,' are not going to change the world. All that can possibly come from them are more tough politics, more hardball, more back-room deals, more sleaze.

"*This* is the future, right now, right here. It's not going to happen tomorrow. We're living in it. We must transcend all the patriarchal linearity, the lies that there's distance and difference between present and future, between means and ends.

"Since the means are the end, and the world we want is a world in which spirit is recognized in all things and governs the brain, we can only bring such a world about by living that way now. Our tools are going to have to be metaphysical tools.

"We've got to start thinking in daring, breathtaking ways, regardless of how others view us. And begin to get cosmic with this stuff!"

I only dimly grasped the implications of all this then because I was still convinced that visioning the future was the path to the new world. It took me two more years to realize that I had fallen into a carefully laid trap. Focusing on the future is precisely what patriarchy wishes us to do because it robs us of our greatest asset and ally, the present. Since it is the only time we're alive and therefore the only time we can act, the present is the only time we can change anything, the only time we have real power.

On the way home in the car after the initial breakthrough in Mary's kitchen, we returned immediately to the work of pushing out the boundaries. I was particularly interested in figuring out what our insight about *being* not *doing* meant to the Gathering, how it changed the theory and practice. Right away it was clear, of course, that it not only changed everything, but changed it at root level. For one thing, it meant that we would have to discard both intentioning and visioning the future because through them we forfeit the present and our power. I had thought that women's problem, like that of all oppressed people, was that we dream too small. But I saw that at the root of that small dream lay small feelings, that feelings precede and dictate the vision of any people, not vice versa, as we had thought. Being all too familiar with my patriarchal habits of mind, I wasn't surprised to find that I had originally had everything almost exactly backwards.

As we talked about this, we were struck by how insidious the messages to us had been that had initially persuaded us to believe that what are actually patriarchal processes were *not*, and could somehow liberate us from patriarchy. We were sobered at how readily we had succumbed and how long it took us to recognize what we had done. The whole experience is a perfect model of the traps patriarchy sets for us and into which we all too frequently fall. For instance, when the Gathering didn't become the self-sustaining process in women's lives that we'd meant it to be, we thought, as we've been indoctrinated to think, that we simply hadn't done it well enough. So instead of asking ourselves if perhaps something was basically wrong with the idea, we tried to fix it. How could something be seriously wrong with the idea of visioning the future? Highly respected people were advocating and doing it. And it made sense to our old non-sensical patriarchal minds.

As we talked it over, we realized that another fundamental fault in futuring is that it doesn't address the central issue of power at all, it doesn't specify where the change potential *is*. Since the present is the only fulcrum for changing basic power equations, futuring is, at best, a method of making minor reforms in situations that don't involve any genuinely fundamental change. My friends and I had often used visualization, for example, to reach in-system goals: to get matching funds, to sell a house, to pass tests, to get jobs. But getting ourselves out of patriarchy is a different matter, one that involves total redefinition and realignment of power. When we envision the future without first changing our present feelings, without undoing our indoctrination, we project all our unexamined assumptions into the future, recreating the old reality, making it inevitable. Anything we try to do without grounding ourselves in new and powerful present feelings and perceptions will be compromised from the outset, hopelessly contaminated, simple tinkering at best, perilously complicit at worst.

An examination of my experience with the more concrete, personal version of the visioning process that I'd used in Rome taught me other reasons for the futility — and more than that — the *complicity*, of this process. When we try to imagine even a specific experience in a perfect future world, we plunge instantly into our reservoir of ideology and come up with the stock answer, the politically correct response. For instance, at the breakfast table that morning in the future world, obviously we will be eating natural, organic whole foods, raised communally. It is impossible to extrapolate from one reality to another.

In addition, when we imagine what we will be *doing*, we reinforce our patriarchal patterns of thought in two ways: by projecting ourselves out of our present-power into the future, and by concentrating on acting instead of on the feelings or states of being out of which all action naturally and automatically arises.

Perhaps the most serious defect in this theory, however, is that in imagining how we want the world to be we shore up the patriarchal habit of thinking and living from the outside in, which is an exact reversal of the true path of power: from the inside out. We are taught to think in this backward, powerless, relational, and derivative manner because as long as we do, the status quo is perfectly secure. To make sure that nothing ever changes in any important way, all we have to do is keep on believing that if somehow the external world, or our external circumstances, changed for the better, we would feel better, instead of the truth, which is that if we feel better, if we change internally, the external world has no choice but to change, and no choice but to change *in* the direction and *at* the direction of our internal state. So we reinforce the system every time we think, "If I had more money, I'd feel more secure." "If this street were better lighted, I'd feel safer." "If my parents had loved me, I'd feel more lovable." "If people praised me more, I'd feel more competent." "If the mushroom cloud weren't hanging over me, I'd feel more hopeful." "If the men in power weren't so sexist, I'd feel more powerful."

Believing in this reversed cause-and-effect, we rush about to make more money, lobby to get the streets lighted, brood about how our parents mistreated us when we were young, do our work always with an eye to praise, try to change U.S. military and foreign policy in the dozens of totally collaborative ways we've been indoctrinated to do it, lobby the men for more equitable laws, and so on. And in doing all this we keep ourselves always far, far from the locus of change, running pell mell in the opposite direction, convinced that the ideal state or condition depends on a change in someone or something outside us.

The truth is that we can only change ourselves, nothing or nobody else. This is not a bleak view, however, but quite the contrary, because the change in ourselves not only *can* but always *does* change something or somebody else, and it is the only thing that can. This means that our feelings about ourselves *in the present moment* are the sole source of change, and that they are therefore our only source of power. Like gravity, this seems to be a habit of nature.

306

During the drive from New York to Virginia that day we pondered how to unhook ourselves from patriarchy by both changing our disempowering feelings and feeling the positive enabling ones in situations where we need them most.

"Does our Gathering affirmation process do that at all?" I asked. As we thought back through it carefully, we agreed that it did. We still believed, perhaps even more passionately than we had three years before, that changing our feelings about ourselves as women, as the primary aim of the women's movement, is the most important work on earth and that affirmation was central to it. But all of us felt now that the theory of affirmation we'd used since 1983 contained some serious metaphysical defect. Days later, Mary Ann finally figured out what it was:

"It works all right, and sometimes seems to work well, you know — saying a high-powered affirmation over and over until we feel it. But I think it can't create permanent change because when we try to *convince* ourselves that we aren't the way the tapes in our heads insist we are, when we struggle against those old feelings, we are still in the old patriarchal war paradigm."

The more we thought about it the more we understood how having to convince ourselves, to fight our feelings, to contradict them, hooks us back into them, re-engaging us with patriarchy and keeping us in the resistance mode — our old feelings resisting our new feelings, our new feelings warring against our old feelings. I saw that our new perspective makes my earlier tape metaphor totally inaccurate. We don't tape *over* anything, contradict anything, discharge anything, shovel out anything. We have to think of some way — and if the theory is right, there *is* a way — to leap over all that destructive nonsense, right into the present, right into the new feeling. We have simply to *be* there.

As we thought more about it, we understood, too, that thinking of affirmation as a way of *getting* there defeats its whole purpose by pitching us into the future and out of our change potential.

So if we refuse to engage with our chronic negative feelings or to try to counter them in any way, we reasoned, it should be enough merely to say, for instance, "I'm smart," and to *feel* that way as if we had never felt otherwise — feel that way right now, in the present.

Understanding these dynamics, how struggling against old feelings keeps us engaged with patriarchy and powerlessly focused on the future or the past, we realized, once and for all, that any truly transformational theory *must* locate the power for change in present feeling. We looked at one another and said, "Well, then, what about inventing a process that brings together everything we know now and call it 'present-ing!'"

There were, we knew, probably dozens of ways of doing this. Following just one idea, however, we decided to take a conundrum in our lives, a pattern of experiences that we can't seem to break out of, close our eyes and imagine, *feel*, ourselves in a situation of this sort at this very moment, ask ourselves, "How would I have to feel for this situation to change?", from that formulate an affirmation, say it over and over until it begins to feel true, then take that feeling back into the situation and watch the situation change: "Because I feel fearless, how is the situation now different?"

"Let's try it!" Fran suggested eagerly, so we started with her.

I facilitated. "Think of a hard situation, one you find yourself in a lot and in which you never feel as if you act the way you want to. Have you thought of one?"

"Sure, that's easy," she said. "I just happen to be living every day in the kind of situation I never feel I handle well. I bought half a house from a woman who had lived in it quite a while by herself. Since she had been living in the whole house before, naturally when I moved in the place was filled with her furniture and possessions. She asked me if the two upstairs rooms were all right for me, and they were so much better than where I'd moved from that I said yes.

"Well," she went on, "I soon began to feel like a boarder, not a part owner. I had to go into what felt like 'her' space every time I used the kitchen or the living room, and the closets were full of her things. Resentment against her began building up in my heart, and has been growing steadily now for months. I keep thinking, 'Can't she see how impossible this situation is for me? Why should I have to be the one to bring this up?'"

"Close your eyes and be in this situation right now, Fran," I directed. "How do you feel?"

"I feel worthless, as if I don't count. I'm resentful, and I'm angry. Hey, wait a minute! I thought I was angry at her, but I realize now that I'm angry at myself for not valuing myself enough to stand up for my rights."

"Standing in your house right now feeling this way, how will you have to change for the situation to change?"

"I'll have to feel as if I'm worthy, as if I deserve to have my needs met."

"Okay, then," I said, "make an affirmation out of that. And to be sure it makes *you* responsible, makes you, not something or someone outside you the agent of change, put it in active rather than passive voice."

"I'll try." Pause. "How's this? 'I'm a completely worthy person and deserve to satisfy my own needs.'"

"Good. Say it several times very firmly, with total conviction, but without trying to convince yourself, as if it's simply true and you never felt otherwise." I further instructed her. "Then take that affirmation and that feeling back into the situation you're experiencing at this moment in your imagination and see if anything changes. It may help to remember a time when you *did* feel deserving and to take the feeling from there with you into this situation."

Almost immediately she exclaimed, "Wow! *Everything's* different. The whole house is different!"

"In what way?"

"I can't explain it. It just all looks different, it all feels as if I own it. I'm not angry any more. I'm going to tell her to move her things out of the hall closet so I can move my things in. But I don't feel belligerent about it, or confrontational. It just feels like the natural thing to do. Whee!" she whooped.

"Everything's going to be different!"

I was excited, too. "Everything's going to be different, because it *is* different right now, and now is the future!" There was a thoughtful pause, and then she demanded, "Ask me what happens in my body when I face the old situation with a new feeling."

"What happens in your body, Fran?"

"I feel terrifically energized, full of zest and happiness. Very light and buoyant, weightless. Wonderful! I'm sure that's an important clue, how our bodies feel. We have to take their messages seriously."

The rest of us, remembering how we felt during our kitchen-table talk, agreed with her that our bodies can be trusted to give us accurate information about the goodness and usefulness to us, the "life-ness," of any idea or practice. Perhaps the most important reason for this is that the body is always in the present, never in the past or future. It is a conduit to the present, and therefore to our power. And since patriarchy views the body as gross and obscene, as merely the defiled casing for the spirit, and worthy of only the most grudging attention, the understanding that the body speaks the truth as clearly as the spirit, that, in fact, it *is* spirit — permeated with spirit, indivisible from spirit — and is to be reverently attended to always, is a profoundly anti-patriarchal understanding, one that propels us out to the farthest margins of our old minds.

When we got home, the other three of us had a turn at it, and in each case, taking the most unpleasant repetitive situation we find ourselves in, we watched miraculous changes *in every aspect* of the situation as a result of our new, positive, powerful way of being in it. Not being in it *in the future*. Being in it in imagination *right now*. We felt elated, and to our delight, our bodies rejoiced with us.

There were some glitches. We discovered during Susan's turn that ideology can stand very solidly in the way of change. One of Susan's most painful recurrent experiences is being in a group (like ours, unfortunately) where everyone talks fast

and hard and (alas, I must admit it) often still with much interruption.

"Put yourself in that situation now," I suggested to her,
and we all burst into laughter because she *was* in that situation
at that very moment. "You've got it easy," I chuckled, "not having to use your imagination to get here and into the feeling.
Now, how do you feel?"

"I feel as if you women are rude and thoughtless, and in
this respect at least, not feminist. You don't even let one another finish a sentence! What does that say about how much
you value one another's ideas?"

"Wait!" I cried. "Try telling us how you feel without saying, 'as if.' It looks as if 'as if' is going to lead us into ideology,
not into feelings. I think that defending cherished beliefs may
be a way to avoid taking a hard look at our own contribution
to a situation."

"Okay. When I'm in this situation, I feel small and stupid
and unimportant. Also self-righteous and angry."

"How would you have to feel for the situation to change?"

"I don't think it's up to *me* to change the situation. I'm not
the one doing it. *You* have to do something about your competitive talking. *You* have to care enough about other women to
change your habits."

She was soon persuaded to put her convictions aside, to
see them as barricades behind which she was hiding. Her affirmation was, "What I have to say is critically important," and
she's persuaded that if she keeps that feeling with her all the
time she's with us, we'll soon see the dynamics change in our
small group.

At this point, thinking aloud, I said, "You know, don't
you, that we're going to be accused of concentrating on the personal to the exclusion and detriment of 'larger, global issues.'"

"Well, you've been talking about the theory of morphogenesis tonight," Susan reminded me. "That's the answer to
that accusation. And holographic theory is another one. Sub-
atomic physics says that there is no past and no future, that all

time is right here right now — like a globe, not a line. It teaches us that there isn't any distance, either, and that space and time are not discrete dimensions but inseparable."

"The dichotomization of space — far/near, personal/global, inside/outside — is another of patriarchy's little hatchet jobs on our integrity," I interjected.

"That's right, because, like time, all space is right here right now," Susan continued. "That puts the whole world in the circle of our arms. So when we change our feelings we change the world. Simple, isn't it. But then the truth *is* simple."

Fran was shaking her head as if she were trying to regain her old, non-sensical perspective. "It's simple, all right. Maybe *too* simple. Who's going to take it seriously? Who can believe that they have so much power that if they feel whole and strong this very moment, everything must change to accommodate that feeling?"

"And that that's a law," Susan added.

I took up the thought. "We're saying that external events or situations can't change our internal reality if we don't let them. That if we are happy, the happiness is *in* us and inviolable. Happiness is the reality. But even more amazingly, we're saying that when we *feel* powerful, right now, this moment, we *have* tipped over the patriarchy! It's not something we're going to figure out how to *do* in the future. It's feeling worthy and wonderful and lovable and competent and confident in our own right, right now, not tomorrow. And not in relation to someone else or because we've been praised or loved, but because we simply *are* that way, which doesn't depend on anyone else's behavior or on the state of the world. We're also saying that that wonderful feeling in our hearts all the time, *moment to moment to moment*, is what causes everything to change, *not* that everything has to change so that we can have that wonderful feeling."

"Wow!" Fran gasped. "It turns your head inside out!"

With our heads turned inside out, we asked ourselves how we could keep and reinforce this feeling once we felt it. Having disposed of visioning, and of hearing into being—except for limited purposes, such as brainstorming—because it can't be made to focus on feeling in the present, we needed a way, perhaps a kind of meditation, that would "fix" the feeling and make it always available for immediate use. We thought of self-hypnosis, and the next day, began working on a relaxation process to take us deeply enough inside ourselves that we can program our unconscious to produce that feeling—at first on demand, but ultimately, all the time.

"Holding on to this feeling is pretty easy when you're surrounded by supportive women who understand the theory and are all trying to do the same thing," Susan pointed out. "But how are we going to keep hold of it when we're out there knee deep in patriarchy?"

She had a point, of course, so we tried a little simulation exercise. I centered in my affirmed feeling (which was that I am very important) and Susan and Fran began dis-affirming me, trying to engage me, to get me to be defensive and off-center so I'd lose my power.

"You important? What a laugh!" Fran scoffed. "No one knows or cares about you. You're just a used-up, middle-aged woman trying to get attention."

Susan sneered, "You just sit here and diddle with your typewriter. Nothing you do makes any difference. If you died today only a handful of people would even notice."

And Fran pushed the red button: "You can't even get your book published!"

And so on. Through all of it my object was not to react, not to be engaged; but instead—steadily, calmly, and powerfully—to affirm myself. I was not to raise my voice as I did this, but to become quieter as they grew more strident. I was not to try to prove, explain, or defend myself, but to stand emotionally *outside* this, in my own place of power, keeping my feeling of being important through it all, refusing to get hooked back into the attack/react war model, refusing to play patriarchy. Remaining disengaged and calm, firm in my feeling of importance in the face of their shaking heads and disgusted looks, was difficult. But I felt that with another practice or two I could become quite good at it. The little rush of personal power I felt even doing it clumsily gave me a taste of its terrific potential, and I was jubilant.

Obviously, all of this raises many questions that can only be answered by trying many different approaches with many different women. For instance, since we're trying *not* to engage with our old feelings of inadequacy, which are patriarchy internalized, and trying to stay in present time, we should probably not repeat our affirmation again and again as if to convince ourselves. But if not, how are we, suddenly, seemingly out of thin air, to feel the new feeling? In the case of the process we experimented with, perhaps we'll have to do the self-hypnosis to find and fix the feeling at the point where we have formulated our affirmation, *before* we bring it with us into the difficult situation.

Another almost intractable problem is language. What is a genuine feeling and what is a social construct? Can we really say we *feel* intelligent or beautiful or lovable or worthy or competent? Our language has painfully few words for genuine emotions: happy, sad, angry, loving — to name a few major ones — and their synonyms: joyous, elated, miserable. How then can we even phrase an affirmation that doesn't inadvertently energize the value system we're trying to let atrophy?

And all the while we're trying to figure out these two problems, we're up against the slipperiest one of all: time. We know we're still viewing time through our old glasses, and that its apparent linearity is probably not our only hang-up. We have the feeling that some missing piece is right before our noses, perfectly obvious, but that we can't get far enough out of our minds yet to see it.

We also know that other groups and individuals are grappling with similar concepts all over the world, as wildly different in their approaches as neurolinguistic programmers and Buddhist Vipassana meditators. Though what they are about seems to be to help people cope better within the system, we must, of course, borrow from them anything that will help us feel in the present as we must feel for the global patriarchal situation to change. From ideas and methods from any sources we need to do what no one else seems to be doing: we must find a system-shaking process, a simple way of disengaging from patriarchy and remaining disengaged, a way of feeling so worthy and powerful right now that we cannot be hooked back into slavery, a way to be free. Not sometime in the future, but right now. My inner voice assures me that this is possible. And everything in me shouts that it is necessary for the survival of life on this planet. This is the most important work going on in the world and only women can do it.

The theory and how we can make it work in our lives and in the world — all is only beginning to open up to me. But this book waited for just this much; clearly, then, this is enough. And clearly, anyone can go on from here. My hope is that many women have already been thinking similar thoughts, that they are daily experimenting with this incredible, most unexpected source of pure well-being and strength, and that soon enough of us live free from fear and guilt and destructive feelings about ourselves and one another — *moment by moment by moment* — to quickly create a new morphogenetic field, the feminist paradigm, the world we have loved for so long with such tenderness, such patient desire.

13
Going Out of Our Minds

A woman in Missouri told me this dream. She was in a city, standing on top of a tall building, looking out upon other buildings as far as she could see. She was a country woman, uneasy amid all the concrete and steel, and longing for home.

Gradually she became aware that to get home she would have to leap off the edge of the building. Looking down at the miniature cars creeping along the miniature street far, far below, she said to herself, "But that's ridiculous! I'll kill myself if I jump off here!" Still, the feeling persisted that if she didn't jump, she would never get home again. And the grief that overwhelmed her at the thought of being exiled forever from the grass and trees and fields of home became so much stronger than her fear of dying that she leapt.

As she began to fall, a rope appeared before her; she reached out, grabbed it, and swung way out over the street. At the end of its arc, she knew that if she didn't let go, she would swing back to where she had been before and not be any closer to home. So she let go. As she began to fall again, another rope appeared. Grabbing it, she swung out to the end of its arc, and let go again.

Trusting herself, letting go, reaching out, swinging out over the abyss, trusting, letting go, reaching out, she found her way home.

She told me she knew her dream was a message from herself, from the wise old woman who lives deep within her—showing her how, step by step, rope by rope, women are leading the species home.

Although all people long for home, perhaps women's longing is keenest and most poignant. For a very long time we have been regarded as squatters at best, at worst as trespassers on our own land. We have been colonized not only in our own homelands, but also in the territory that is our own bodies. So going home means more to us than creating a new, safe order; it means being reunited with our mother, the earth, and with our own bodies.*

For years the belief that I was at least headed in the direction of home, though I had no idea where it was, loosened my grip on the rope every time. But as each rope has carried me deeper inside myself, I've learned that the joy and serenity I've felt all along *are* home; that home isn't some place outside us, or some utopian place in the future; that home is wherever and whenever we feel most truly and strongly ourselves.

Only by trusting ourselves, letting go of the familiar, the sacrosanct, reaching into ourselves—which is out into the universe—and swinging fearlessly out over the abyss, will women lead everyone to that home.

The leap off the doomed building of patriarchal anti-civilization is more than believing, it is *really feeling*, in every cell of our bodies, that women are now the critical people on earth, that each one of us is absolutely essential, a leader; it is *really* taking ourselves that seriously, *really* understanding that everything depends on us. Though that may be a little frightening,

---

*As kids, playing games of tag, softball, hide-and-seek, we called the "safe" place "home," a sad irony—especially for girls and women—since home in our present society is perhaps the one most dangerous place.

317

it is more freeing than frightening because it means we can stop wasting our time and energy trying to get men to change and to make the changes, we can stop concentrating on their hideous "reality," and begin changing our feelings about ourselves immediately and directly. And in doing so get on with the creative work of building the new world right here, right now.

This is women's time in history. *Only* women can make a difference now. Part of the reason for this is that we are, as Virginia Woolf names us, the Society of the Outsiders.[1] The insiders, the rulers — and all over the world, in every class, every race, every nation, men rule women, always with violence — the rulers are always caught tighter in the teeth of their system, are more bound, less intellectually and spiritually free, than those they oppress, which is the basic paradox of tyranny.

Men's lives (in relation to the women's of their group) are so saturated with privilege, in fact, that even if a well-meaning man should wish to, he could not divest himself of it, not even of one evidence of it. For instance, one of the basic entitlements of maleness is to be listened to, to be taken seriously. This privilege seems "natural" to most men; they take it so for granted that they are nearly oblivious to it. Though study after study verifies it, men often laugh at the suggestion that it exists. But women don't need studies to know it does because we always have the opposite experience, and every time we do we know that it would be different if we were male.

How could even the best-intentioned man free himself of this one of the many hundreds of privileges that come to him effortlessly because he has a penis? Could he perhaps wear a large sign on his chest that says, "When I speak, don't listen. Nothing I say is important. Don't take anything I say seriously"? If people then *didn't* listen, wouldn't that be evidence that they had still "heard" him and were taking his message seriously? What if he said to his boss, "Pay me less, don't promote me, give me repetitive, low-status tasks, harass me for sexual favors, interrupt me constantly, always condescend, invade my personal space, make lewd and belittling remarks about me"?

He might get demoted or fired, of course, and he could drop out of the conventional scene, become a street person or a hobo, in his attempt to escape automatic respect. But even this would fail because as a *male* street person or a *male* hobo, he would always have advantages over *female* street people, *female* hoboes, and there is no way on earth that he can change that. This is how men have gotten themselves stuck in the tarpits and why they cannot change their system.

But women can, and that we and *only* we can is partially explainable by an important law of cybernetics. This law holds that in any system the controlling element is that which is the most flexible. In order to survive at all, women have had to become almost preternaturally flexible. Our outsider status also gives us flexibility. Being by definition outside the system, no matter how inside it we may wish or perceive ourselves to be, and having no genuine stake in it, gives us very real freedoms of intellect and spirit. The oppressed, always most outside the system and always most flexible, are therefore always the controlling elements in any system. Women, as the most oppressed people in every category — race, class, age, nation, ethnic group, religion, job — are now the controlling elements on this planet; our feelings about ourselves, which shape all our behavior, will determine its future.

Believing in our historical significance is only one part of leaping off the building. Another is letting go of our thoroughly conditioned view of reality, our deep, numbing, disempowering feeling that patriarchy is very strong, almost invincible, nearly inevitable, *the* reality. As a woman put it at the San Jose think tank:

> But what must we do? That's where I get stuck. I know there are people who own this planet, and it's not us. There are people who own so much of it that it's obscene. It's almost hard to think about. And I don't see why they're going to give it up. So that's the point at which I get stuck. How can we convince

those people that they can't own this planet anymore? Frankly, short of taking them out and shooting them (and we don't even know who they are, at least I don't), I don't know how to change them. Unless we can make them give up their ownership, we're not going to be able to change patriarchy. And I don't know how to do that.

The way *not* to do it is to focus on what seems an overwhelming "reality," but to remember how non-objective any "reality" really is; to remember that though the men own the outer world, that world is merely a reflection of their totally reversed inner reality. Their having persuaded us to internalize this chimera, to let them dominate our inner as well as our outer world, is the triumph of a mirage, of a sleight-of-spirit. Because of the inherent topsy-turvy nature of patriarchal ideology, men's fervent and relentless insistence that their present *external* power is the ultimate reality alerts us that the only genuine power must be *internal*. It tells us that men know they have power over our inner lives, over our feelings, only insofar as we allow it, as we give it to them. They know that so long as we accept the pernicious nonsense that the patriarchal world is all that is possible — with, perhaps, some minor alterations here and there — we will be constantly engaged with it, resisting it, placating it. And they know that in doing so we energize it, give it credence, co-create it as "real." The men understand on some elemental survival level that what we resist persists. Their prime goal therefore is to keep *us* from learning what a powerful and essential form of collaboration resistance is to the system.

A corollary to this, and another truth that is strenuously kept from us, is that since reality is only what we give the energy of our belief to, what we feel as real, all systems are *internal* systems: patriarchy does not have a separate existence outside us; it exists only inside us and we project it onto our external screen. It follows, then, that the instant patriarchy ceases to exist inside our hearts and minds, it dies everywhere.

The greatest fear of all dictators is that the conditioning that obscures such transformative truths will break down, exposing their subjects to the formidable heresy of the inner voice. Knowing this, we know that the way to change patriarchal "reality," is—stubbornly, resolutely, against all odds—to obey the revolutionary commands of our own spirits, trusting them to reveal a new reality to us that we can begin substituting internally at once. When we seize power in our inner world, the outer world will have to change.

Since all systems are internal systems, all genuine revolutions are internal revolutions, revolutions first and foremost of feelings, which translate inevitably into revolutions of values, of beliefs, and of behavior. All bona fide revolutions are of necessity revolutions of the spirit.

Our believing in the old reactive ways is not only futile but dangerous because it wastes our precious time and keeps us— the critical people, the only people who can change and make change—from seeing and acting on alternatives.

One of the first alternatives, one of the first ropes we must grab as we leap off the patriarchy, is the knowledge that we can't trust *any* voices, any feelings, but our own. Only our own inner women's hearts and voices are telling the truth now on this planet. The revolution consists in our hearing and trusting them for the first time in more than 50 centuries. Since slaves are the most other-directed, most outer-directed people in any system, for women to stop being motivated by our need for approval, by our need to be regarded as politically sophisticated, in the know, credible (who *wants* credibility in this system?), freeing ourselves from this need is the revolution, complete and entire. Turning a deaf ear to all the nonsense around us about how change is made, not being afraid to look foolish or to make mistakes, and trusting our own spirits for the answers, the voices of our own wise women inside—THIS IS THE REVOLUTION. Not listening to our junior-men-conditioned voices, which we all have, not listening to our co-opted female-impersonator voices, which tell us that patriarchy is real and impor-

Sonia Johnson

tant and urge us to join the respectable and deadly liberal boys' club. But listening to our own outcast, exiled women's voices that are struggling desperately now within each of us to be heard above the din of our internalized oppression.

We have to remind ourselves constantly, in the face of terrific propaganda to the contrary, that men can never be trusted, that as a class they always lie to us, *always*. Those in power always lie to the powerless; otherwise they would lose control. Because the entire present social/political/economic system is founded on a lie—that women are inferior and meant to be ruled by men—no message it gives us can be trusted *ever* to be the truth. Therefore, those ideas that nearly everyone accepts as "the truth" in patriarchy will never be true. What nearly everyone believes will always be what the system encourages us to believe, will always further *its* ends. Since nearly everyone believes that external "doing"—working for candidates, running for office, working for more and better laws, demonstrating, voting—are the ways to make change, we can be *absolutely certain* that this is not the case; that it is, in fact, a reversal of the truth. We can be *absolutely certain* that those in power have assiduously conditioned us to believe in these methods precisely *because* these methods can't change the system at all; precisely *because* they bolster and strengthen it instead.

But how can we be sure we are hearing our own authentic voices? We can be sure because everything these long and deeply buried voices tell us seems like nonsense, is *called* nonsense by society; everything they tell us sounds wrong, the reverse of what we have always heard, contradicts the lying "truths" of patriarchy, and scares us badly. My voice tells me, for instance, not to give any of the men's old stuff the time of day. It tells me loudly that what Reagan and the other madmen of the world are doing is simply not important, not even dangerous except insofar as it distracts us from our work, keeps us locked in fear and despair, unable to believe in ourselves as the paradigm-changers of the world. It assures me that the actions of the world's "leaders" are important only if they make us un-

322

able to believe that we can turn everything around very
quickly—within the next decade—by concentrating upon
changing our own hearts and minds, if they destroy our faith
that this is not only possible but far simpler than we dream.

We don't need to listen to men's voices any more in any
context, on any subject. Women's are the only voices that need
to be heard, the only new voices in the world, but they will be
lost if we try to use the megaphone of the system to get them
heard. This is women's time on planet earth. Society needs us
desperately but not in any of the ways we have been accustomed to believing it needed us. The world is dying for women
to be *women*, for us to be present to ourselves totally, taking responsibility to speak the new and difficult and healing truths
out of our experience and out of respect for what is best in our
own female value system. Even as embryonic as our understanding of our culture is, it is where we have our only integrity
and authentic power as a group, as a movement.

We must figure out what being a woman means, how we
need to feel in order to live as we wish and deserve to live. We
will have to discover and value, trust and teach, our women's
wisdom as distinct from men's. We will have to figure out what
women's culture *is* and what we want it to be, what and where
our powers are, the tools specifically suited to our hands, what
our particular contributions to the creation of a feminist world
can and must be, what treasures, precious and saving, we have
within ourselves and our culture that we can now lavish upon
ourselves as we live a new way in the old world. We will have
to learn how to feel brave and free and worthy of our total love,
our total commitment.

Once at a "Wise Women's Council," I talked about letting
go, detaching ourselves from patriarchy, cutting the umbilical
cords of belief and feeling. To illustrate what I meant, at least
in part, I quoted something my friend Sheila Feiger had said
in San Jose:

> I'm not interested in doing less than changing
> the world. But I've been in the movement—in

NOW — for 12 years. I've carried the picket signs and gone to the conferences, been in the demonstrations, and spoken, and written letters, and watched Congress, and worked for candidates, and done all the things we thought would change the world. And I know that that is not the way to change the world and I'm not going to do those things anymore.

"And neither am I," I said to the Wise Women.

"But that's just not *practical*" one of them broke in impatiently.* "None of us likes this system, but it's what we have to work with until a better alternative presents itself. I'll be the first to let go when that happens. But in the meantime, we have to deal with the world we have, not the one we wish we had!"

All around us in the movement we hear that we must deal with male "reality" whether we want to or not. This is hard conditioning to overcome, a hard lie to resist, partly because the truth seems quixotic: we can't find alternatives to our present system until we let go of it altogether. Like babies learning to walk by holding on to the furniture, we're never going to be able to explore further until we let go of the table. Or until, like the Missouri woman, we step off the building.

As long as we think we can change the situation sufficiently through electoral politics, lobbying, demonstrating, letter writing, working for more and better legislation, by some sort of external action, we're not going to be able to feel or think our way out of patriarchy or to imagine the new ways; we have to let go *before* there's an alternative to hold on to. This is what takes courage and faith. Even if an alternative should

---

*The ingrained idea that feeling and imagination are not "practical" is strong evidence of patriarchal reversal hard at its brainwashing work again. What we have all been doing for the past 5000 years to change things has not only not been successful but has infinitely exacerbated the problem. Yet it is called "practical," whereas the only work which *will* change things, the only truly practical work — feeling powerful, feeling genuinely detached and free of men's madness and turning our attention to other possibilities — is that which is disparaged as the ultimate impracticality, as "idealistic," "visionary," "romantic."

appear right beneath our noses, so long as we're holding on, our minds and hands will be so full of patriarchy that we will be incapable of grasping it. It's only when we have nothing else to hold on to that we're willing to try something very audacious and scary; only when we're free of the allure, the enticements, the familiar and comfortable lies of patriarchy will we be able to alter our perspective enough, change our feelings enough, gather enough courage to see and grab the next rope and continue our journey home.

As a character in one of Suzette Elgin's short stories says to her issue-oriented feminist friends:

> I tell you you're wrong, with that laundry list of yours. I tell you there've been laws written down since first men could record their wickedness and pride—and there has always been a way to make those laws no more than chicken scratches. Laws are like wars—of their making there is no end, and they're not worth warm spit. I tell you, what we need is a *miracle*.[2]

It will be a miracle when we finally and unalterably know that we cannot change the minds of the men in power, at least not in the ways we are presently trying. The dinosaurs we call "leaders" may die and take us all with them, but they will not change their minds. Taking them on *in any way* is not only futile but dangerous. We face certain death if we work and wait for them to change, if we spend our precious energy and time "lobbying" them to be men of a new age. They will not change. They will not do what must be done. And while we fight them, *we* will not change, either. To change ourselves so that everything else has to change, we are going to have to do what must be done ourselves.

This is a good thing, of course, because it will force us—finally!—out of our power-over-paradigmatic minds, which will be all the miracle we need. We can only change ourselves, we can only change our *own* feelings that keep us slaves, we can only change our *own* minds about what is important and possible. And since what is possible is whatever we can feel as fully as if it already exists, what we have most to fear is failure of the heart.

The Wise Woman didn't agree with any of this. "I believe," she countered, "that work inside and outside the system needs to be going on at the same time, with all of us working on different levels, different aspects of the problem."

Once I believed that, too, but I don't any more, and I told her so. I know that her view is the popular view, and it's popular because it's so easy, so undemanding. Waiting for someone else to take the responsibility to come up with an idea takes no courage, seems to involve no risk. The belief that we must work within the system to save ourselves is so commonly held that it should set off a jangle of warning bells in our psyches. Its very universality tells us that such a belief is necessary for the perpetuation of the status quo.

What would happen, alarmed people protest, if *everyone* thought like you do? I assure them that they don't need to worry about there being enough people to do the old things; there will always be enough of them. But if those of us who have a different awareness, who see a different necessity, if we believe that work inside the system is as valuable as work inside ourselves — which is the only place at present where it is possible to exist outside the system — we, too, are going to use all our energy doing the old wrong things. The old things are so easy, so comfortable; they are, after all, what we know; we can get hold of them with our minds, they affirm our slave emotions; while we can't even imagine how it would feel to live entirely within a new consciousness, disengaged from present society. And they're also acceptable, considered "politically mature" by those we respect — who are almost without exception deeply ensconced within the system. (Though they occasionally dart out of it to say and do a daring thing or two, they always dart right back in again, ironically enough for "shelter.")

These wafflers assure us that the old methods work, that they're tried and true. On the contrary, there is massive evidence that they have never brought about any fundamental change whatever. If they are tried and true, it is in bringing about the most minute and superficial reforms.

When two ways of thinking and behaving are contradictory and come into open conflict, we can't hold on to both of them without sharing the dual-mind, the shattered consciousness, the paralysis, of the fathers. Sheila summed it up in San Jose: "The reformist things we do, by making us think we've accomplished something, lull us into complacency even as they direct our energy and attention away from where the radical change has to be and into the immediately satisfying and socially acceptable but eventually counterproductive kinds of activities."

The point of view of the Wise Woman I argued with at the Council is very typical. Many feminists still think they can have their cake and eat it too, refusing to see that working in the old, "safe" ways is not only ineffectual, but dangerous. It is a constant theme, one I hear all the time: "PAC's [political action committees] are the only way to go, Sonia. Let's face it. Though we may not like it, money is power. That's just where it's at."

That's certainly where it's at for patriarchy, which is the very reason it must *not* be where it's at for those who wish to help patriarchy die a much-deserved death. *Because the means are the ends*, the problems caused by patriarchy cannot be solved through the patriarchal system with the tools that system hands us. The blood dripping from them will corrupt everything they touch.

For this reason, "it" is really "at" someplace else altogether for women. We cannot *be* what is necessary now and at the same time be "safe" in the old roles that were dictated by the system's propaganda about how to make change. (Patriarchy's "safe" is women's ultimate danger. Since in patriarchy, not one of us has been safe for one second of her life, we have no "safety" to lose.) Paradoxically, we are safe only when we learn to feel real self-esteem; "real" meaning based on feminist, not

327

societal, values. For men to rule, women must consent to be ruled. If we withdraw our consent, along with our attention and interest, men cannot rule us, and we are safe.

Nothing important was ever accomplished without courage and risk. In fact, that's one true criterion for all effective thinking and action now: does it take courage? Does it seem incredibly risky on many fronts—to my personal life, my professional life? Other useful questions are: will I be laughed at? Will I be misunderstood? Does it require that I trust my feelings? Does it require that I use faculties that have lain dormant for the most part in humans for millennia: spirit, intuition, imagination, independence of judgment, love of women? If so, it is very promisingly "womanly" and therefore powerful and I should seriously consider it.

Nothing—no course taken by any woman or any groups of women proceeding on feminist principles with courage and integrity and intelligence—can possibly hurt anything now. The prognosis for all living things could hardly be worse. There is no place to go but up.

The most risky thing to do now, in these conservative— meaning profoundly male supremacist—times, is to let go of our belief in and our collusion with patriarchy. Going out of our minds means emotionally, spiritually, and intellectually boycotting patriarchy. Boycotting it where it has deepest hold, in our viscera, almost in our genes and chromosomes.

What I see that frightens me is that many feminists who seemed once to let go, who in the early seventies were magnificently valiant—swinging out over the abyss without nets—failed to let go at the end of the arc and swung back to the "safety" of the rooftop. In the women's movement we like to say, and believe, "Once women have seen, there is no turning back." How I wish this were true! The truth is that there is almost always retrenchment after one has been brave; old slave feelings reassert themselves under pressure. There is almost inevitable panic at seeing how far out above the dangerous void we have swung, how far below the traffic is, how inviting the rooftop looks.

I know it is hard to hold on to the truths we are learning daily, especially when we have only glimpsed them through countless scrims and smokescreens, and when women's feelings have been so ridiculed and women so debased as "feeling creatures" (like the lower animals, non-thinking) that we haven't fully understood or appreciated the importance of how we feel about ourselves, at least not since women's times, over 5000 years ago.

Having to keep cleaning up the bloody mess patriarchy makes of our lives further entrenches us and makes being able to feel and live in our own, positive, life-full, reality hard to do. It's hard to hold on to slippery unaccustomed feelings of well-being and power when the system is frantically and deviously throwing us just enough sops to make us decide, with great relief, that the rooftop is better than we thought and enough after all. But if we don't keep on with our trapeze act, looking neither down nor back, but always up and out (which is in, because to look out of patriarchy is of necessity to look within), no one is going to reach home, that place of personal power and joy—none of the men, none of the children, none of the women; no animals, no trees or flowers, no streams, no birds.

A feminist world is worth anything and everything. I am becoming angry at women who are playing it "safe" and who should know better. Women who should know and once *did* know that "safe" is not *safe*—either for them or for other women or for any life on the planet. Paradoxically, leaping off the rooftop is the only safe act left.

Genuine safety lies in turning our faces from patriarchy and all its familiar cliches and habits, and walking into the unknown with our minds and hands free of its claptrap and full of our own riches, open to the voice of the next human epoch, which is leaping and singing in our own bellies, desperate to be born.

Where does this model of non-hierarchy, individual responsibility, daring, and boundless flexibility locate "organized" feminists? NOW and the League of Women Voters and

the National Women's Political Caucus—all the women's organizations working for the Democrats and Republicans,
working for the men in all the acceptable male ways, are collaborative in precisely the same ways as are the churchwomen
they often scorn for working for the men in the churches. All
of them believe the reversal that they are working to make
change for themselves and other women. The dedicated
women of the Democratic Party and the nuns of the Catholic
Church—even the dissidents in both groups—perpetuate their
own and their sisters' oppression by giving energy to the institutions of patriarchy.

Sometimes when I feel discouraged, I indulge in a most
restorative fantasy. I imagine that the next Sunday or Holy
Day, in every church, synagogue, and mosque, every religious
gathering place in the world, the men in charge, the ministers,
priests, rabbis, imams, look out upon their congregations and
see (oh unspeakable wonder!) . . . *no women!* No women at all!
Neither that holy day nor the holy day following nor the holy
day after that. No women, ever again.

And I imagine that during the next election year, no
women organize, raise money, stump, stamp, campaign, or
come to the polls, no women attend political meetings, put out
newsletters, organize demonstrations.

I see the men crying in terror: Where are the slaves? Their
whole ugly edifice in danger of collapse. *Because they can't do patriarchy without us!*

And us, where are we? Have we just crept back into our
holes? Not on your life! We're where our feelings of wholeness,
strength, and joy are guiding us, doing our own work, taking
responsibility in the new world we're building, letting the old
one disintegrate, as it most surely would without our energy,
our attention, and our faith.

Though I know how unlikely that scenario is (though
Goddess knows it *shouldn't* be—and *wouldn't* be if we had half the
gumption we were born with), it is an immensely cheering
prospect, and puts me in excellent humor for days.

It is true that of the many women I know in the political parties and in the churches, a few have no illusions about what they are doing. They remain in the foyers of the Old Boys' Club because they see no better front on which to fight. "Better to stay and fight where there is an opening," they say, "than leave and wonder what to do with ourselves instead."

But I say no, it is never better to fight. It is always better to leave, and to have to search within yourself for your part in this drama we are improvising. Better to leap off and reach for the rope. Because we're at the end of the reactive phase of the women's movement. We're at the end of *that* rope. That's what this pause, this hiatus in the women's movement, is all about. For us to try to continue in reaction (which, though veiled, is a powerful variety of complicity), goes stubbornly against the current of change. To continue to react is to trap ourselves in our patriarchal minds; it is to prevent our going positively out of those minds — out of the familiarity of our oppression — into the risks and dangers, the responsibilities and ecstasies of freedom.

To continue to put our faith in these comfortable activities is a self-indulgent, short-sighted, and dangerous choice. It is not worthy of us.

Where the women's movement needs to move, and is beginning to move, is into its positive building phase. The third phase of the women's movement consists of each of us revolutionizing our internal worlds in the knowledge that this alone can change the external world. If this new phase is to take hold, enough women must refuse utterly all the emotional sops, all the lures that bind us to men's reality. What would happen if we said no to voting, no to registering voters, no to working in campaigns, no to raising and giving money to candidates, no to lobbying, no to demonstrations — no to organizing in any of the old complicit ways?[3] To the degree that we can stop worshipping these idols, we say yes to new possibilities, we open and go out the doors to a new reality. But rejection is only the beginning. Having said no, we must reach out for the next rope. And that next rope will always be a positive, strong feeling about ourselves.

331

If this sounds too outrageous, perhaps we should ask ourselves why. What have these activities done to stem the patriarchal stampede to extinction? Why are we who stand on the very brink of doom willing to continue to put our faith in them when they have never succeeded in any significant way, and when the minuscule ways in which they have succeeded took massive, arduous effort and sacrifice over decades, and can be undone in a moment? Especially when those meager successes deceived us into believing we were making headway, totally co-opted us and destroyed any genuinely radical vision?

We do not have decades (and even if we did, we would need to rethink the whole scheme, not just blunder on with it like lemmings), and we cannot afford any more self-delusion. The planet will be a little radioactive ember blowing about in the void eons before we can begin to make the necessary transformations using the old anachronistic and corrupt tools.

In my experience, the ideas and ways of coping that we most venerate are always those that need our hardest, most courageous analysis. Laws, for example.

Friends often remind me of *Roe vs. Wade*, the Supreme Court decision that guarantees the right to legal abortion. "You see?" they say, "It proves that change can come from within the system." I remind them that it took half a century and millions of deaths among members of the Society of the Outsiders to bring that about.

Or did we really buy it with our living blood? What if those deaths were actually meaningless, what if they didn't accomplish anything at all? The possibility that this is true is almost too awful to contemplate. But it has often occurred to me that the real reason abortion was legalized was to give men more access to women's bodies, to give impetus to the "sexual revolution," which has been another revolution for men only. By relieving women of the burdens of pregnancy from increased and indiscriminate intercourse, men encouraged us to feel as if we should "put out" more often. The Supreme Court decision, insofar as it helped make us more available as sexual objects for men, was very much *against* us, not *for* us.

Evidence for this point of view is that now that cultural mores have changed and women are expected, and conditioned, to be sexually available to men all the time under all circumstances, the right to abortion is being seriously threatened. In the long haul, patriarchy wants all women to be mother-slaves, far off center stage, producing the other slaves and the cannon fodder and the heroes necessary for its continuation. All around us in the women's movement even ardent feminists are having babies with a zeal unequaled for decades. And each of them is perfectly convinced that hers was a choice uninfluenced by the system's brilliant and truly *massive* "biological time clock" campaign of the past dozen years.

Roe vs. Wade has won another victory for patriarchy: it has kept women focused upon and deeply emotionally invested in the system. Since the moment the decision was handed down, men have forced feminists in dozens of states to spend among them millions of hours trying desperately not to lose it piece by piece. Now, regardless of which party is in power, the groundwork has been laid: the most radical women are being subsumed into and consumed by the state function of motherhood, and their hopes for help are bound firmly once more to the state. The Supreme Court will continue, now that the decision has accomplished its purposes, to gut *Roe vs. Wade*, perhaps retaining as much as is necessary to keep feminists still trusting the system, still under control.

Ultimately, where will all this trusting have got us? A dozen years further away from trusting ourselves and from finding a lasting, non-male-approval-based solution to the problem of our physical colonization.

When will we learn that, since they depend for their very existence upon keeping us colonized, we cannot depend on patriarchal institutions to give us self rule? When will we learn that as long as men have privilege at our expense — and every man alive does — we cannot trust them? (This doesn't mean we can hate them, or that we can wish or do them harm without damaging our own spirits and defeating our cause. Nor does it mean that we can't love them, since many of us can't help loving them, regardless of their corruption. It simply means that we cannot and must not *trust* them.) When will we learn that we must take our bodies back completely, get them out of men's laws and hands altogether, back into our own hands and those of our sisters?

The women's health movement has taught us, if we dare look at the implications, that almost any one of us can learn to perform a simple abortion. Trusting ourselves, trusting other women, feeling sure of ourselves and understanding how critical it is to be independent of men's medical control, we must all learn to do it. Those among us who are trained to perform more complicated abortions, must teach the others of us.

Then no matter what laws men make to try to control our bodies, those laws will be, quite simply, unenforceable. The question of abortion must become moot. Not just for a dozen years. Forever.

I ask those women who blanch when I suggest this how much worse off we would be than we are now if we spent our prodigious effort, instead of trying to change men's hearts, changing our own, believing in and trusting ourselves and making sure that at least one out of every hundred of us knew how to perform abortions — and were willing to do it in a work-exchange program, if necessary? If, one of these days, the men pull the always very dubious and already threadbare carpet of *Roe vs. Wade* out from under our feet, where are we going to land? In the back alleys with ignorant, greedy, misogynist goons? Or in the bright kitchens of our neighbors' homes, with our women friends around us, under the care of a woman like ourselves who has learned how to do the job with care and skill? Even if *Roe vs. Wade* stays put, it is a patriarchal ploy, and we must rescue our deadly belief, and our bodies, from physicians steeped in murderous patriarchal medical ideology and practices.

By this time, we should have no illusions left about male physicians in this country or about traditional medicine as practiced by them, particularly as practiced upon us. We have been their guinea pigs for far too long. With them as the alternative, the only reason we would fear women's doing the job would be our deep-seated feelings that men know how to do everything better and that women are not to be trusted. Until we discard those feelings, until we truly sister one another, we will be in bondage to men and their horrific system, in bondage to the butchers of our minds and spirits, as well as of our bodies.

Another activity our new feelings of worth and love for ourselves might be spurring us to do instead of going to church and to the polls, and instead of spending millions of hours organizing to keep abortion legal and at least partially subsidized for poor women, is to make abortion even more thoroughly a non-issue by developing birth control methods that are safe and sure. Becoming medically independent from the men in as many ways as we possibly can.

These, of course, would be merely interim measures. Ultimately, feeling the swell of strength, the full tide of our power sweep us farther and farther out from the shores of patriarchy, we will train our minds to control conception or to abort unhealthy or unwanted embryos. The necessity for us to do this in order to be free and whole will hasten the time when mind and body become so attuned to one another, so intimately, consciously connected, so unseparate and integrated, that all healing, all physical processes will be under conscious control. We are capable of this as human beings, and we are only as far from it as our expectations, our belief. We must feel as if it is possible—which will real-ize it—and begin living in this reality.

At a Take Back the Night march a few years ago, a woman walking next to me quipped: "Every year we take back the night, but somehow it slips away from us and we have to take it back again the next year. I guess they haven't heard us

Sonia Johnson

yet." "Who's 'they?'" I asked. "You don't mean the *men*, do you? *We're* the ones who have to listen to us. Surely you know the men are not going to hear us until we hear *ourselves*."

Or *see* ourselves. Since a large part of our oppression is that we do not believe in ourselves enough to be *visible* to ourselves, it would be eminently wise if, instead of watching the men so obsessively, we focused our eyes and our attention upon ourselves, if we finally felt real to ourselves. Though we might, before we forget them entirely, stop and look back at the men just long enough to laugh. Not in derision, but as an exorcism of their authority over us. That would do us good; to shake free of our terror and join in the cosmic joke. To hold our bellies, throw back our heads, and howl and shake and gasp and double over with laughter. And after that, every time they pop into our minds, put them out by seeing them as beautiful flowers or tropical fish.

Our conviction that if we stop fearing and monitoring the men in power and their latest crazinesses, that if we abandon our terrified clawing and kicking interspersed with sniveling and clutching—our whole sick sadomasochistic relationship with the masters—they will go berserk and kill us, this is purest superstition. With our eyes fully upon them they go berserk anyway; with our eyes riveted upon them they kill us daily.

We don't need to learn anything more about them or their deadly toys and games (e.g., the difference between the cruise and all previous missiles). We know them through and through, if not the details, the principles upon which they function. They are always the same; thinking we have to re-learn them each time is one of our many methods of denial, another way of being complicit, another way of refusing to face the problem.[4]

The problem is that we don't know what to do about *them* because we hardly know who *we* are. We have been mere reflections in men's eyes for dozens of centuries. We need to concentrate now upon learning about ourselves and the powers of our spirits. We need to concentrate upon changing our internal reality, knowing that as the foundations of oppression inside us crumble, external patriarchal reality must give way. Since men cannot *do* patriarchy without our collaboration, by changing our reality, by refusing to allow them, or the feelings that have bound us to their world view, to continue to be central in our lives, we automatically — without having to give it a thought — change *their* reality. When we refuse to be slaves *in our hearts, in our minds,* men can no longer be masters, and the sadomasochistic habit of mind called patriarchy will cease to exist as the paradigm of this planet.

Suzette Haden Elgin has written a delightful book, entitled *Native Tongue*, that elaborates upon this thesis. Set in a future United States in which women have lost all human rights, at the risk of their lives, they secretly invent their own language. As soon as they begin thinking in it and speaking it among themselves — and even in the presence of unsuspecting males (Láadan can be spoken with the minutest of body signals as well), their feelings of powerlessness disappear and they unconsciously change in their relationship with the men. Without their knowing why, the men begin to find life intolerable. So they meet to find a solution:

> It used to be that a man could do something he was *ashamed* of, too, and then go home and talk to his women about it and be able to count on them to nag him and harangue him and carry on hysterically at him until he felt he'd paid in full for what he'd done. And then a man could count on the women to go right on past that point with their nonsense until he actually felt he'd been justified in what he'd done. *That* had been important, too — and it never happened anymore. Never. No matter what you did, it would be met in just the same way. With respectful courtesy. With a total absence of complaint. . . .[5]

Not being able to bear living on the periphery of women's consciousness, without women's attention and energy, the men decide to build separate residences for the women. The women, who had feared that discovery would mean they would have to flee to the woods with their babies on their backs, or dig themselves forts in the desert, or be shut up in attics, meet to discuss this totally unforeseen development:

> When the announcement was made, the women first sat shocked into total silence, staring at one another. And then their eyes began dancing, and they smiled, and then they laughed until they had no strength left to laugh any more.[6]

They demand of Nazareth, the woman who always predicted that it would work out all right, how she had known.

> "Perceive this . . . there was only one reason for the Encoding Project, really, other than just the joy of it. The hypothesis was that if we put the project into effect it would *change reality*. . . you weren't taking that hypothesis seriously. I was."
>
> "We were."
>
> "No. No you weren't. Because all your plans were based on the *old* reality. The one *before* the change."
>
> "But Nazareth, how can you plan for a new reality when you don't have the remotest idea what it would be like?" Aquina demanded indignantly. "That's not possible."
>
> "Precisely," said Nazareth. "We have no science for that. We have pseudo-sciences, in which we extrapolate for a reality that would be nothing more than a minor variation on the one we have . . . but the science of actual reality change has not yet been even proposed, much less formalized. . . ."
>
> "What did *you* do, then, Nazareth," Grace asked her in a strange voice, "while we made fools of ourselves?"
>
> I had faith? Could she say that? Faith, that

338

dreadful word with its centuries of contamination hiding all the light of it.[7]

For thousands of years, patriarchy has sent us the message in every imaginable way that we can save ourselves by concentrating on the men and their reality. It is not only grossest superstition, and a lie, but it is in fact a complete reversal. As they well know, the truth is that our concentrating upon them gives them the power to destroy us. Our attention, our energy, our fear *feed* their madness. It is true that we inadvertently but powerfully help bring about that which we most fear, which is why fear must be such a huge part of tyranny.

The death of patriarchy depends upon our ability to stop doing all we do in *reference* to men — stop letting our fear of how they'll feel, what they'll think, what they'll do, determine our behavior. Patriarchy's death depends on our ability to turn our emotional backs on it and to decide how *we* want to feel, and to begin feeling that way immediately, which means living in a new world, without asking the men, without their permission, ignoring their opinion. Certainly without informing them of our jail break!

I swear that what we need to do most is that which scares us most and seems to be just the opposite of what we should do: **WE MUST TAKE OUR EYES OFF THE GUYS!**

As soon as we change our feeling that the men and what they are doing is what is important in the world — that it is important *at all*, as soon as we take our eyes off the guys, and *only* when we do, we will see a new reality opening before us. Until then, we will be stuck fast in the patriarchal mind, wasting our energies, trapped and despairing.

So we must trust ourselves that, though everything in our culture screams that we're wrong to stop being "activist" in the conventional and deeply collaborative ways, we have never been more right; trust that we are not "dropping out," as accused, but instead finally "dropping *in*" to the revolution. Since in patriarchy all is reversed, patriarchy's "out" is women's "in," its "wrong" our truest "right." Trust mightily that, having let go of our belief in patriarchy's judgments and lies and methods, believing in women's voices and world, the rope will appear in our hands and out of our sure, strong feeling of ourselves, we will swing free and joyous out of the violent planetary mind into our own reality, into a new mind — or into a very, very ancient, truly archaic,* mind.

What if all this is nonsense? Even then we will have lost nothing by trying it. Whereas in the way we are now headed, just around the next bend lies annihilation. So once again there is nothing to lose and everything to gain by going against our deepest taboos, against what seems to be our very grain. Nothing to lose by forgetting the men's reality, forgetting to be afraid. There is everything to gain by having as our only motivations those that are harmonious with the values of our own culture. Not with fear and dread, but with hope and love, we can leap out of our minds, free of patriarchy, into a celebration of life. I believe there is no other way.

After one of my speeches, a man rose in the audience and said, "That's all very well, you know, but what's your program?" I answered him that I knew that to be credible in patriarchy, one had to present at least a five-year plan. And that for this very reason, pioneers have never been credible. What I didn't tell him is that feminists don't have even a five-*minute* plan of the type he asked for, because we're the first genuine pioneers the world has seen. And pioneers travel a step at a time, a rope at a time, guided not by maps and programs, but by principles, by passion, and by faith. Faith that if we have the courage to take the first step, the second will appear, and that if we take the second — never seeing where it will take us, having faith *moment by moment by moment*, being ridiculed and dismissed by the old world we are leaving behind — having faith that if we dare take it, the next will appear, and that step by step, rope by rope, we will lead the world to sanity and peace.

---

*In the sense of the word as Mary Daly uses it.

As pioneers we are destined to live always with profound ambiguity, incalculable uncertainty, with no one to praise us or reassure us or understand us but ourselves.

Faith is the pioneer's basic plan, but it's had bad press in the women's movement for being corrupted and reversed by patriarchal religion.

But when I say faith, I mean something quite different. Since women are the pioneers of the new world, what is required of us is the most prodigious and difficult, the most enduring faith ever required of any people: faith not in god (or goddess) but in ourselves, in our own voices, in our own judgment, our own abilities, right now, this minute, and despite everything! Faith in our own worldview, which is feminism. Faith in other women. Faith that we are here on this planet at just this time in history to midwife the human race through a rebirth of spirit and mind such as has never before been witnessed on earth. Faith in a miracle.

Part of the miracle will be to stop believing in what we *can* see and begin believing, passionately, in what we *can't*; begin believing in what can be only inferred or postulated, only felt, only undeniably affirmed by the spirit.

Lawrence Blair writes in *Rhythms of Vision*:

> When Magellan's expedition first landed at Tierra del Fuego, the Fuegans, who for centuries had been isolated with their canoe culture, were unable to *see* the ships which anchored in the bay. They were so far beyond their experience that, despite their bulk, the horizon continued unbroken: the ships were invisible.
>
> . . . The shaman first brought to the villagers' attention that the strangers had arrived *in* something, something which, although preposterous beyond belief, could actually be *seen* if one looked very carefully. We ask how could they *not* see the ships—they were so obvious, so "real."[8]

Yet we sense that we can't "see" things just as obviously real. During the whole of my twenty-year marriage, I had a running argument with my husband, Rick. As a statistician and evaluation expert, he believed absolutely that anything that exists, anything "real," can be measured; that although we don't always have the means to measure it, if it exists it is *measurable*. Feeling very naive and out of my depth, I nevertheless disagreed. "Based on what?" Rick would demand. "What evidence do you have?"

I was always humiliated to have to admit that something about that idea just didn't *feel* right. He found this unaccountably stupid of me and though I, too, was embarrassed at this sign of irrationality in myself, I would not give in. Neither of us understood that I was operating out of an entirely different culture and perspective. We were both puzzled by my clinging to the apparently unscientific, illogical, foolish faith in my hunch that most of what is "real" cannot be seen, let alone quantified. Our ideas of "real" coincided at painfully few points. Since the ships in the harbor were unthinkable to Rick, for him to look for them would have been the purest absurdity. But sometimes over the years, when I have blinked just right, or turned my head quickly at just the right moment, or, in the midst of activity, suddenly stood very, very still, I have surprised a ship with billowing sails bright against the sky.

So long as we think dugout canoes are the only possibility — all that is real or *can be* real — we will never see the ship, we will never feel the free wind blow. But with faith in our inner voices, refusing to pay attention to the nightmare men call "reality," we *will* see and understand. Best of all, we will feel ourselves to be amazing, miraculous. As we walk off the edge of the building, the rope will turn up in our hands. That's where we are right now in the history of our race — on the edge of a doomed building, needing to believe and feel certain that we can jump off now and save ourselves before it's too late, needing to believe in the ropes — that they are really there and will surely appear when we have the courage to leap out of the known world and reach for them.

We don't need to wait for someone to show us the ropes. We are the ones we've been waiting for. Deep inside us we know the feelings we need to guide us. Our task is to learn to honor our own inner knowing.

Being pioneers is lonely and scary. Believing in ourselves is hard, especially when what we are doing can't immediately be seen from the outside. Patriarchy has no real concept of revolution from the inside out — which is the only genuine revolution. It values appearances above everything. So it is difficult for us to believe that we are *doing* something, let alone actually taking the most radical action possible, as we rid ourselves of our deeply ingrained slave habits of heart and mind. Those with conventional, patriarchal minds laugh at us. We simply must not care.

None of us can be sure where the next rope will take the movement. How can we even say where her next rope will, or should, take any individual woman? We are all at different places in the trapeze act, and part of that act is trusting that each woman of us can and will manage it in her own time and in her own way.

Not long ago in evaluating my own progress, I realized that I would soon have to let go again or go backwards. The question was, what do I need to let go of this time? Everything that far in my experience as a feminist had led me to the knowledge that one piece of patriarchal balderdash I still hung on to was my distrust of the spirit as guide to truth, as superior intelligence. I decided that this time out I am going to begin to learn to use — despite patriarchy's scorn — the immense and various resources of my spirit and deep mind.

A dream helped me understand this. I dreamed one night that I was in a laboratory peering at a set of scales. One side was weighted heavily with books. The tray on the other side, almost all the way up, had in it only a few small gems. Though the stones were so dazzling I could hardly take my eyes off them, they could not begin to balance the books on the other side. When I awoke, I knew what it meant: I have been too faithful to patriarchal doctrine, disproportionately trusting and relying on "reason" and the second-hand knowledge of experts, not according the same attention and validity to my own heart and voice. In its underdeveloped state, my spirit, my feelings, my hunch-originator is often not a strong enough guide to lead that unruly machine called the brain; it cannot be heard often or clearly enough over the brain's clamor. The dream was a warning to me that my understanding of the role of feelings and my control of their immense power was inadequate for the tasks ahead, and that I needed to bring all aspects of myself into balance.

Heeding this admonition to myself, I began listening deeper. What I finally heard was that all power for basic change and genuine growth lies in present feelings, how we feel *at this very moment.*

I am beginning to believe that this simple fact has in it revolutionary potential far exceeding that of the split atom, and that if enough of us can quickly learn to live this way, nuclear weapons will have no chance against us.

Part of bringing all parts of myself into balance involves believing that powers other than those sanctioned by patriarchy abound within me — and within us all — that they are all intimately interconnected, and that discovering and learning to control and use them is the next frontier in human development. Since such metaphysical, such "outsider" powers have always been accorded womanly status — meaning they have been considered mysterious and mystic as well as barmy — they should be right up my alley. At one point in my life, I wanted to learn how to know across time and distance, ultimately across solar systems and universes, across centuries and ages. I wanted to be able to heal myself and others. I wanted to learn how the women raised the stones at Stonehenge. But now most of all I want to learn how to root the slave instincts out of the marrow of my bones, how to be fully and freely Sonia, how to feel the power of my woman's life all through my body and all through my consciousness, every moment of every day. From this, I am increasingly certain, everything necessary will follow. Perhaps these goals are the same goal.

Because our feelings about ourselves have been the major target of patriarchal attack for millennia, they are now our most serious vulnerabilities. We can sing bravely to the fathers: "You can forbid nearly everything, but you can't forbid me to feel," but unfortunately they can and do all the time. Because our feelings are so fecund and threatening, the patriarchs — forgetting that everyone everywhere acts entirely out of feelings every moment of every day — heap contempt upon feelings. Feelings, they assure us, are not "objective," and men adore the idea of objectivity, as if they or anyone else ever *is* objective, as if there is even such a thing as "objectivity" or should be. In patriarchy's muddled mind, feelings are invariably on the one-down, the female side of the intellect/emotions, or reason/feeling dichotomy, as if somehow feelings and reason and intellect are entirely different, separate, and distinct. This has never been women's experience. We have always known that this split was untenable, like all the other splits in the man-shattered world, but didn't believe ourselves when we told ourselves so, just as we didn't believe ourselves about all the other humbuggery of patriarchy. What a relief now to be able to look at it all and say, at last and just once because it's too boring to contemplate further: YUK!

Throughout the centuries, men have made very clear to women that we and our children would live longer and suffer less if we would forget our woman's desires and adopt theirs instead. They have forced us by violence and ridicule and incessant propaganda to relinquish our feelings of dignity and worth. Stripped of these, we have lived powerless in their nightmare of violence and death.

For men to maintain their dominance over us during all those long, long years of our exile from ourselves, it was essential that we cease to be able to remember, or to imagine, or, most important, to *feel* the possibility of any order other than male supremacy and domination over us. This is equally true today; they must prevent us from throwing off those feelings about ourselves that keep us powerless; they must at all costs prevent us from feeling what we need to feel to be free.

Patriarchy could not have survived for so painfully long if women had been able somehow, by whatever incredible underground effort, to remember the glory of our love for ourselves, and to live emotionally in the midst of the stunning power that is born of that love. I believe a few of us did—for a while. Until the European churchmen bound us alive to millions of trees and burned the glory and the hope and the life out of us.*

We are now several centuries removed from that great four-hundred-year bonfire of women's bodies, and our hearts are no longer cinders in our breasts. We are very much alive. We have grown stronger than even our captors suspect, though they in their suspicion have stepped up the "torture machine."† We long day and night to escape from our prison. We lust, we are wild with desire, for a new world order where human hearts can rest and love.

To have that world, we must be at rest now, must love now. There is no future apart from this moment. So there is no need to feel frantic about time, terrified that we haven't enough of it in which to change things. Panic about the shortness of time incapacitates us in our letting go, paralyzes us as does all fear. If we can feel hopeful and confident and full of life and vigor right now, we have made the future one of hope and power and life.

Going out of our minds means not being afraid to make mistakes. It means throwing off forever the fear of looking stupid, naive, fuzzy minded, unrealistic (whatever that means), irrelevant, and even crazy. Really, who cares? When we think

---

*From the 13th through the 16th centuries in Europe and England, at least 9 million women were burned as witches, and the power of their view of themselves, their feelings about being women, their mode of being, were lost to us. Their genetic stuff, their DNA, was lost to us as well, making us all less than we might have been, the heirs of compromised mothers, collaborators, beaten women.

†Mary Daly's informal term for patriarchy's subliminal manipulation.

about it we realize that, cosmically speaking, we look far more foolish hanging for safety on to the coattails of our hell-bent-for-destruction slave masters than we can ever look having the courage to let go and trust ourselves, trust that we can certainly do no worse than they, and are very likely to do infinitely better at finding the way out of our global dilemma.

Going out of our minds means making a genuine, permanent disengagement announcement and from that moment not taking men or patriarchy seriously ever again; not denying them, simply forgetting them. Patriarchy and men are both profoundly irrelevant. Going out of our minds means knowing that women are now the only relevant people on earth as far as change is concerned, women and the way we view the world, the way we live in it at our best. It means taking ourselves seriously for the first time in recorded history, the only act now possible that has in it the power to transform the world.

Our new minds, governed by new positive feelings, our awakening spirits, *are* the revolution — "the pulse of summer in the ice"[9] — changing everything around us. Much preliminary work has already been done. Women are now in global consciousness. We are now included, however tentatively, however weakly, in that image called "human" in the brain of the species. And the world will never be the same. It was the destiny of the women who went before us to move us into human consciousness. Our destiny is different from theirs. It is to crowd patriarchy off the stage of history with our own rich, vital reality; in the midst of the rubble of the androcentric, gynocidal world, to create within ourselves right now a post-patriarchal paradise. As we do this, that ugly sick old world — unsupported by slave emotions, unsupported by our belief and attention and energy — will collapse of the weight of its own misery and evil; already it begins to quake. The most essential and difficult part of our challenge is to rid *ourselves* of the evil, to get it out of our minds, to disengage our feelings from it, and to keep free of it forever.

Something is required of us living women that was never

347

required of any previous women. Something that will take more courage, more vision, more faith in ourselves and in one another, more love for ourselves and other women and all that is accounted "womanly"; more love and pity and forgiveness for all humankind, more unity among us, more connectedness, more loosening up and giving of ourselves to one another than has ever been asked of anyone.

Like many of us, I know from experience that we can bestow grace and power mightily upon one another. I've been one of the very lucky ones; when I stand before a group of women to speak, I am almost lifted off my feet by the flood of passionate energy and invincible spirit that pours forth from them. Though this can also be felt to some degree in the audience, I always wish every woman there could stand where I'm standing and get the full impact of it. None of them would ever lose heart again.

Recently, a woman told me an experience she had had when she heard me speak. She had been able to see auras for many years, but while I was speaking she saw something new: dozens of multi-colored, fiery comets arcing from the heads of the women in the audience up into my aura and back again from me to them. I told her that though I haven't seen that phenomenon, I know when it's happening, and it happens often. I also know we don't have to be in an audience, or in a group, or even with anyone else to help recharge one another's spiritual batteries in this most amazing way.

So many of us have had this experience that it can't be ignored or denied. What it tells us is that none of us needs to be stingy with our passion, saving it only for our few politically correct friends. We have now an unfailing fire, we women with our torches and our blazing looms. Like flame-winged doves escaped from our cages, all over the world we are mutinously, bravely burning.

The time for women-wrought miracles has finally come, the time for which women have waited and worked for over 5000 years. How lucky we are to be alive now in history's most fecund hour, to be who we are, to be unafraid and, especially, to be together. Delighting now moment by moment in our growing sense of power and joy, we make joy and power accessible to all women everywhere. Learning moment by moment to be free in our minds and hearts, we make freedom possible for everyone the world over. Thank goodness it is now up to the women because now it will get done.

Women have given the world a new power symbol: no longer the upraised fist, because we know that force is the antithesis of strength; instead, hands holding hands holding hands holding hands. . . .

Hand in hand now let us leap off this stinking rubbish heap men call "civilization," out of our limited, lightless, dying patriarchal minds, and reach for our lives—for *all* life—deep into the cosmos that is our own souls.

Notes

Preface

1. Ronald Bottrall, "Darkened Windows." *The Poetry Anthology,* 1912–1977, eds. Daryl Hine and Joseph Parisi. Houghton Mifflin Co.: Boston, 1978, p. 193.

Chapter 1: Suddenly She Realized . . .

1. That this epiphany burst upon me during a Mormon church meeting is deliciously ironic. Perhaps nowhere, except in Moslem society, is the daily sacrifice of women's lives more evident than in Mormondom. It has the naive beauty of fate that a Mormon elder giving a puerile anti-ERA presentation inadvertently loosed me from my cage and catapulted me into the greatest spiritual revolution in history.

2. It is no accident that the women's movement has become home for so many lapsed Catholics and Jews. Catholicism and Judaism are also accredited universities for the study of rampaging male supremacy.

3. Mary Daly, *Beyond God the Father.* Boston: Beacon Press, 1973, p. 19.

4. Marlene Mountain, *Pissed Off Poems and Cross Words.* Hampton, Tennessee, 1985, p. 9.

5. Nelle Morton, "The Goddess as Metaphoric Image," *The Journey Is Home.* Beacon Press: Boston, 1985, p. 155.

Chapter 2: Aerobic Politics

1. One of these men became so angry at us at one point during the morning that he smashed his fist through the glass door trying to hit us. He spent the rest of the day holding it out for us to see, all swathed and pitiful in accusing bandages.

2. Susan B. Anthony, *Diary*, 1873.

3. That vigil was held for nearly five years despite the government's repeated harassment and a two-year legal battle.

4. During my 1984 campaign for President of the United States, women from my office joined with women from the Community for Creative Non-Violence in front of the White House for an anti-Reagan protest the month before the election. Because my name was on the press release, the Secret Service was out in force behind the fence. They hadn't forgotten. Whereas the first time we got nearly to the door of the White House before we were caught, this time we couldn't have got to the fence to go over it even if we'd wanted to—which we didn't.

5. Speech given during antislavery tours in 1857 and 1858 and again during the winter of 1860-61. In a manuscript in the Anthony Collection at the Schlesinger Library at Radcliffe, titled "No Government" and inscribed "1857 about & 1858," p. 9.

6. Just recently I learned that Michigan NOW apparently did not send the letter out after all. Such evidence of faithlessness is disheartening even now, five years later.

7. When I use the word "radical," I do not intend the popular meaning— wild-eyed, extremist, out-of-control. Radical comes from the Latin *radicalis*, or *radix*, and means "at the root." Radical feminists view patriarchy as the root of the most fundamental evils of global society.

Chapter 3: Women Against Women

1. Mary Wollstonecraft, *A Vindication of the Rights of Women*, ed. Carol H. Poston. W. W. Norton: New York, 1975, p. 82.

2. C. S. Lewis, *The Last Battle*. Collier Books: New York, 1956, pp. 144–148.

3. Ibid., p. 149.

4. Liz Seaborn, Speech at fundraiser for my presidential campaign, Pittsfield, Massachusetts, February 1984.

Chapter 4: "They Need to Lose Weight Anyway!"

1. Sandy Hoefler, "ERA Fast Has Religious Meaning for its Participants," *Springfield Journal-Register*, May 30, 1982.

2. Though seven of the eight of us had abandoned religion by this time, we discovered that we were still stuck with its language — or what it calls "its" language. Religion has wrongfully appropriated all language belonging to the spiritual province.

3. Odd how one's perceptions can change. Early in the fast, humanity rapidly divided itself into two classes in our minds: eaters and non-eaters. We felt as if eaters could do anything. Certainly there was nothing *we* couldn't do if we were eaters. We found impossible to understand why any eater failed at anything. As long as one can eat, we agreed, all things are possible.

4. Rick, my ex-husband, cared for the children the last two weeks of the fast.

5. As far as I can remember, Mary Ann is the only one who was not tormented by hunger much of the time.

6. "Give up the ERA Fast," Opinion, *The Daily Journal*, Kankakee, Illinois, May 26, 1982.

7. Fletcher Farrar, "Starving ERA," May 27–June 2.

8. G. Robert Hillman, "Ryan Calls Hunger Strike 'Foolish,'" May 30, 1982.

9. "Fasting Concerns Both Sides," Associated Press, Springfield, Illinois, May 30, 1982.

10. Opinion, June 6, 1982.

11. "Seven Brave Women," Guestwork, *Illinois Times*, June 17–23.

12. "Fasting Is Unladylike," *Illinois Times*, May 20–26.

13. Larry Golden, "Seven Brave Women," Guestwork, *Illinois Times*, June 17–23.

Chapter 5: High Treason

1. Jan Raymond, "A Genealogy of Female Friendship," *Trivia: A Journal of Ideas*, Fall 1982, p. 12.

2. Andrea Dworkin, *Right-wing Women*. G. P. Putnam's Sons: New York, 1983, p. 220.

Chapter 6: The Think Tank

1. I am indebted to Sheila Feiger for framing most of these questions.

2. Nelle Morton, *The Journey Is Home*. Beacon Press: Boston, 1985, p. 29.

3. Even though there was rebellion against small-group Hearing into Being, by evening of the first day, everyone had begun to be able and willing to suspend reaction and to listen without interruption while we were in our large group. We learned how adept we had become at this, what second nature it was fast becoming, when a friend of our hostess dropped by and began telling us some of her ideas. Though few in the group agreed with her, none of us interrupted her, or evaluated what she had said when she finished. We all just listened quietly to the end, far longer than we would ever have listened without responding, especially to ideas we would ordinarily challenge. When we realized afterward what we had done, we laughed about it a lot.

Chapter 7: Experimenting with Our Large and Coherent Motion in Time

1. The following three examples of morphogenesis are taken from a speech by Marilyn Ferguson at the Human Unity Conference in Vancouver, B.C., in 1981.

2. Ken Keyes, *The Hundredth Monkey*. Vision Books: St. Mary, Kentucky, 1981, pp. 12–17.

3. From a song by the Washington, D.C.-based women's singing group, "Sweet Honey in the Rock."

4. Rupert Sheldrake, *A New Science of Life: The Hypothesis of Formative Causation*. J.P. Tarcher: Los Angeles; Houghton Mifflin: Boston, 1981.

Chapter 8: Drowning in the Mainstream

1. I borrowed this title from Lolette Kuby of Cleveland, Ohio. She mentioned in a telephone conversation during the winter of 1985 that she was writing an article by that title for a local women's newspaper.

2. Whatever we may feel about the ERA now, at the time of its defeat, most of us who had cared about it never mourned sufficiently. In fact, we had to pretend that somehow we'd really *won*, had to put a good face on it — like men do — and not let anyone see how devastated we were. We were not allowed to act like women, which means we were discouraged from responding appropriately. NOW provided the example of toughing it out, and women nationwide followed suit. When what we should have

done was to get together all over the country as sisters and weep about it in each others arms. Instead, we were saddled with oceans of left-over frustration and grief that we couldn't place correctly so we internalized it. And there it sits, fueling our anger—not toward the system that crushed us again, but against ourselves and one another.

3. Ellen Goodman, "Sisterhood May Be Losing Out to Equality," *Boston Globe*, syndicated column, 1985.

4. Elizabeth Oakes Smith, speech delivered at the Woman's Rights Convention, 1852, in *History of Woman Suffrage*, ed. by Elizabeth Cady Stanton, Susan B. Anthony, and Matilda Joslyn Gage. Fowler and Wells: New York. 1881, I, pp. 522–23.

5. Geraldine Ferraro played the same role in politics that liberals in all churches play in religion. They render tolerable that which should, because intolerable, force change or drive certain groups out of the organization. Liberals are indispensable to the system to gloss over contradictions as they arise and begin troubling people. Indulging in rationalization in this way, liberals stand as the enemies of real movement and change, acting instead as arbitrators or mediators between the powerful and the powerless when no arbitration, no mediation, no compromise is useful or appropriate. Liberals are Uncle Toms and Aunt Sallys. They buy privilege with collusion. Tokenism is the apex of this syndrome and a most venerable ploy in preserving the status quo.

6. Benjamin R. Barker, *Atlantic Monthly*, June 1984, pp. 45–55.

7. Liz Seaborn, Speech at fundraiser for campaign, February, 1984.

8. Ibid.

9. Sally Roesch Wagner, intro. to *Woman, Church and State*, by Matilda Joslyn Gage, Persephone Press: Watertown, Mass., 1980, p. xxii:

Gage made one exception to the rule of never supporting a political party. She not only supported one, she ran on the ticket. Belva Lockwood, the first woman lawyer to practice before the Supreme Court, and an NWSA member, ran for President in 1884 on an Equal Rights Party ticket, advocating equal rights for women, blacks, Indians, and immigrants. Although Anthony opposed the party, and Stanton would have nothing to do with it, Gage ran as one of the two Electors-at-Large, seeing it as yet another means to bring the issues of oppression before the public. The campaign caused quite a sensation, and the press widely ridiculed it, but Lockwood and the others gained a wider audience for their ideas because of the mud-slinging. Maintaining their dignity, they spoke to wide audiences wherever they lectured, and Lockwood received 4,149 votes in six states.

Chapter 9: "Now, If I Were President . . ."

1. But some realized it after the election. I received the following letter in December:

   Dear Sonia, this has been a difficult year for so many. . . . I recently lost my mother. I remember she was so proud and happy at the party for your campaign. A mother of daughters, it meant much to her that a woman — and, more importantly, a woman of your convictions — could run for president in her lifetime, which began in 1897. I am sorry that we didn't participate in the later stages of the campaign, but we were both convinced that Mondale and Ferraro were "good enough" as presidential contenders, and that in this instance we would be happy if these "lesser of two evils" prevailed. Of course they didn't — perhaps in part because they *were* "good enough," and of course I'm sorry, in retrospect, that I did not brazen it out with you, who showed such immense courage and intelligence and honesty throughout.

2. The struggle for equality goes on in them in much the same way as it goes on in the churches. The similarities are very striking . . . and amusing. Try telling the Socialists that what is happening within their party — their level of ethical development — is almost identical to what is happening in the Methodist church and to its level of ethical development. I didn't tell them. Nor did I tell them, as Hazel Henderson quipped one day, that the marriage of Marxism and feminism is Mrs. Marx.

3. As I understand it, there are around 3000 appointments the president could make. Appointing one tenth that number of the right women to key positions would change the world — positions on the Supreme Court, Secretary of Defense, Secretary of State, Attorney and Solicitor Generals, Director of EPA, etc.

4. Still, I was pleasantly surprised during the campaign at how receptive some of the most radical leftists were. The Peace and Freedom Party in California nominated me as their candidate, as did the Consumer Party of Pennsylvania. In addition, the Citizens Party at its August 1984 convention where I was nominated, adopted a Preamble to their platform that is the most radically feminist statement existing at this time in electoral politics. Something may be changing in some Leftist hearts.

5. Carol Gilligan, *In a Different Voice*. Harvard University Press: Cambridge, Mass., 1982.

6. Only the Democrats and Republicans have automatic access to ballots; since they monopolize state legislatures, they pass laws to keep the rest of us off and themselves in almost total control of the electoral process.

355

In this "greatest democracy in the world," only two parties out of at least a dozen can get their candidates on the ballot without expending incredible effort and spending a fortune. In many states, third party candidates have no access to the ballot in reality at all. I smile a little cynical smile to myself every time I hear the President righteously lambasting the Sandinistas for their lack of democracy!

7. This is a favorite phrase of our attorney for the case, John C. Armor.

8. I was foiled in this, however. My home state of Virginia has totally outrageous ballot-access requirements for third parties that are impossible to meet, and the law prohibits write-ins. Since I could not vote for the only candidate with integrity, I did not go to the polls.

Chapter 10: Telling the Truth

1. Mondale's calling women, in their push to get a female vice-presidential candidate, "a special interest group" (*New York Times*) is inexcusably boorish.

2. Hazel Henderson, *The Politics of the Solar Age: Alternatives to Economics*. Doubleday & Co.: New York, 1981, p. 325.

3. Jan Raymond, "A Genealogy of Female Friendship," *Trivia: A Journal of Ideas*, Fall 1982, p. 11.

4. Andrea Dworkin, *Right-wing Women*. Wideview/Perigee Books; G. P. Putnam's Sons: New York, 1983.

5. Virginia Woolf, *Three Guineas*. Harcourt, Brace & World, Inc.: New York, 1938, p. 142.

6. Daniel McQuire, "The Feminization of God and Ethics," *Christianity and Crisis*, March 15, 1982, p. 59.

7. I agree with Mary Daly that "no biophilic person need be determined to stay within the confines of necrophilic species," and that we can be — and really are — each a distinct species in ourselves. As I use it here, the word "species" can be viewed in any light one chooses. (Quote from *Pure Lust*. Beacon Press: Boston, 1984, p. 413.)

8. Mary Wollstonecraft. *A Vindication of the Rights of Women*, ed. Carol H. Poston. W. W. Norton: New York, 1975, p. 62.

9. It is no accident that as women rise in our own kind of power, men madly produce more and bigger evidences of their kind of power — bigger and more hideous weapons, missiles, warheads.

10. Diana Russell, *Sexual Exploitation*. Sage, 1984, p. 137.

11. Someone always complains when I speak that I am not dealing with male incest victims. I'm not. Incest is a female problem. Largely because women and children are always associated in men's minds — men want women to be children, powerless, hairless, immature, dependent — male children sometimes suffer the fallout. The overwhelming percentage of incest victims are female and the overwhelming percentage of incestors are male.

12. Lenore Walker, as quoted in *This Way Daybreak Comes: Women's Values and the Future*, ed. Annie Cheatham and Mary Clare Powell. New Society Publishers: Philadelphia, 1985, p. 182.

13. During the last few years, we have been watching women (and men) who should know better, some who once *did* know better, accepting — as if they were hypnotized — the incredibly transparent rationalizations of patriarchy about pornography. Witness the ACLU and the women associated with it having become the leading defenders of the pornographers.

    But we have also watched the most brilliant approach to this problem yet developed within the system come upon the scene in the form of the Minneapolis Pornography Ordinance, created by Katherine McKinnon and Andrea Dworkin. The ordinance is a law that for the first time would allow victims of pornography to bring civil lawsuits against pornographers on the basis that pornography subordinates women and perpetuates sex discrimination.

14. Genoveffa Corea, "Dominance and Control," *Agenda*, May/June 1984, p. 21 + .

15. Pornographers' speech, as Dworkin points out — which is our hurt and wounded bodies — is "protected" speech. Though pornographers cannot "speak" without hurting and degrading women, women cannot protest without being accused of un-American activities, of undermining the precious "freedom of speech" which obviously only men have. Our voices cannot even be heard in officialdom because our freedom of speech was never guaranteed by the Constitution, that greatest document of freedom *for men* in history.

    Women are not protected anywhere in the Constitution. That's what the 60-year struggle for the ERA has been all about. Susan B. Anthony and the feminists of her time knew this very well. They still remembered that at the Constitutional Convention the majority of the founders voted against the proposal that women and Negroes be guaranteed basic human rights in the instrument the rich white male leaders had met to frame.

16. There is pornography devoted to generating hatred and oppression of

other groups, but it exists on a very small scale in comparison with that which victimizes women. Even in our racist society, gender can be the only logical determinant of the huge majority of victims of pornography, because pornography is the educational arm of patriarchy's Enforcement Department, and patriarchy is a sex-based caste system.

17. FACT—Feminists Against Censorship Taskforce—are very concerned about men. In their amici brief against the Minneapolis Ordinance they write: "[The ordinance] delegitimates and makes socially invisible those men who experience themselves as gentle, respectful of women, or inhibited about expressing their sexuality," and "Further, the ordinance is wholly blind to the possibility that men could be hurt and degraded by images presenting them as violent or sadistic." But what about *women?*

18. Pauline Bart, Review of Phyllis Chesler's *Women and Madness*, in *Society*, Vol. 2, No. 2, January/February, 1979, p. 98.

19. Rosalie Bertell, Remarks at The Conference on Women's Alternatives for Negotiating Peace, in Halifax, Nova Scotia, June 5-9, 1985.

Chapter 11: Listen to Women for a Change

1. At this point in a speech one night in Madison, Wisconsin, a woman shouted from the audience, "He'll be sure to run for president!" "He *is* running for president," I shouted back over the laughter, "both of him."

2. Cheri Lesh,"Hunger and Thirst in the House of Distorted Mirrors," *Against Sadomasochism*, eds. Linden, Pagano, Russell, and Leigh Star. Frog in the Well: East Palo Alto, 1982, pp. 202-203.

3. Hazel Henderson, *The Politics of the Solar Age: Alternatives to Economics*. Doubleday: New York, 1981.

4. Mariette Nowak, *Eve's Rib: A Revolutionary New View of the Female*. St. Martin's Press: New York, 1980, pp. 27 and 28.

5. Marilyn Frye's discussion of this in her fine book, *The Politics of Reality: Essays in Feminist Theory* (The Crossing Press: Trumansburg, New York, 1983, "Oppression," pp. 1-16), is the best I have read. She gave me language for what I knew intuitively.

6. Song by Frankie Armstrong, London, 1983, for the Women's Peace Movement in England.

Chapter 13: Going Out of Our Minds

1. Virginia Woolf, *Three Guineas*. Harcourt, Brace & World: New York, 1938, p. 143.

2. Suzette Haden Elgin, "Lo, How an Oak E'er Blooming," *Fantasy and Science Fiction*, February 1986, p. 109.

3. I also firmly believe we must say no to alcohol and tobacco, no to tranquilizers, no to all the sacraments of the death cult. It is sobering to reflect that most decisions that profoundly affect our lives are made by people who are to one degree or another under the influence of these and other drugs.

4. Linda Barufaldi told me this story: "I heard [a female author] speak on her know-the-military-so-you-can-resist-the-arms-race book promotion tour. She ended by saying, 'our missiles' and 'our weapons.' I got up and said they weren't mine and that I didn't want fewer, I wanted a new approach to world problems. She called me a Pollyanna and naive. Then an ROTC guy got up and said the speaker's position wasn't a feminist position (as she had maintained) but rather a liberal Democrat position. I thought, 'What's going on? I agree with something an ROTC guy says!' "

5. Suzette Haden Elgin, *Native Tongue*. Daw Books: New York, 1984, p. 290.

6. Ibid.

7. Ibid.

8. Lawrence Blair, *Rhythms of Vision: The Changing Patterns of Belief*. Schocken Books: New York, 1975, p. 22.

9. Dylan Thomas, "I See the Boys of Summer," *The Poems of Dylan Thomas*, ed. Daniel Jones. New Directions: New York, 1971, p. 92.